Adapting to E-books

Electronic books are now having a major impact on library collections. This book provides models for acquisitions policies and reports on several surveys of faculty and librarian attitudes toward e-books. It discusses issues in acquiring cataloguing and collection development regarding this important new library resource.

Its subject matter deals with the different types of e-books, statistical data available for e-book usage, the development of e-book collections, learning environments, integrating e-books into local catalogues, acquisitions and usage monitoring of e-books.

This book will be of interest to librarians across all educational sectors, library science scholars and e-book publishers.

This book was originally published as a special issue of *The Acquisitions Librarian*.

William Miller is Dean of University Libraries at Florida Atlantic University. He formerly served as Head of Reference at Michigan State University, and as Associate Dean of Libraries at Bowling Green State University, Ohio. Presently, he also teaches courses in English Literature and Library Science.

Rita M. Pellen is the Associate Director of Libraries at Florida Atlantic University. Previously, she was Assistant Director of Public Services and Head of the Reference Department.

Adapting to E-books

Edited by William Miller and Rita M. Pellen

Routledge
Taylor & Francis Group

LONDON AND NEW YORK

First published 2009 by Routledge
2 Park Square, Milton Park, Abingdon, Oxon, OX14 4RN

Simultaneously published in the USA and Canada
by Routledge
270 Madison Avenue, New York, NY 10016

Routledge is an imprint of the Taylor & Francis Group, an informa business

© 2009 Edited by William Miller and Rita M. Pellen

Typeset in Times by Value Chain, India
Printed and bound in Great Britain by CPI Antony Rowe, Chippenham, Wiltshire

British Library Cataloguing in Publication Data
A catalogue record for this book is available from the British Library

ISBN10: 0-415-48377-8 (h/b)
ISBN10: 0-415-48378-6 (p/b)

ISBN13: 978-0-415-48377-3 (h/b)
ISBN13: 978-0-415-48378-0 (p/b)

CONTENTS

Introduction: Moving into the World of E-books

William Miller

While E-books have yet to make a big impact on the general public, they have become a major aspect of library collections in the past several years. E-books have been quietly taking their place beside more traditional materials, and many academic libraries now count hundreds of thousands of electronic books as part of their collections. E-books offer many advantages; they cannot be lost, stolen, or mutilated, and they are particularly valuable to distance-learning students, 24 hours a day. Depending upon what licensing arrangements are made, E-books can be available to multiple users at once. Libraries that have suffered major physical disasters such as fire or flood can continue to offer large parts of their collection online. E-books may also offer a level of searchability completely beyond what could be accomplished with more traditional printed text.

Conversely, E-books can be difficult to catalog and make accessible to users. Platforms vary, with some being extremely clunky and difficult for users to navigate. Some librarians are uneasy with the idea of renting rather than owning a major part of the collection and having to pay perpetually for continued access. Many users remain uncomfortable with the idea of E-books, and libraries need to promote this resource much more effectively than most have done heretofore. Despite such difficulties, one can easily foresee a tipping point in the near future, when the bulk of new monographic acquisitions are electronic rather than in print, as publishers decide to switch their predominant mode of publication. Like it or not, most libraries will be acquiring most of their books in electronic form, as is already the case with their serial publications.

Great Britain appears to be further along than the United States in the adoption of E-books. David Ball, Jill Beard, and Barbara Newland of Bournemouth University illustrate the degree to which group purchasing can help to shape E-book availability, requiring publishers to supply specific titles rather than omnibus, generalized, all-or-nothing collections. This idea of "bespoke" collections is a model for others to follow, and the authors point out the value of electronic resources in an era which will increasingly be marked by e-learning rather than by more traditional campus-based work. In a complementary piece, "E-books in the University of California Libraries," Jim Dooley, Martha Hruska, and Lorelei Tanji discuss the process of arriving at system-wide collection development principles for the acquisition and licensing of E-books.

In "Making Sense of E-book Usage Data," John Cox provides an overview of the types of statistical data available and discusses ways in which these data can be useful, especially as significant amounts of money are spent on E-book resources. The largest survey to date of user opinion regarding E-books, recently conducted by the ebrary company, is described here in detail by Marty Mullarkey, of ebrary, with analysis by librarian Allen McKiel. The ebrary "Global E-book Survey," completed by 580 librarians, and a companion "2007 Global Faculty E-book Survey," completed by 900 faculty members, give the most complete picture available right now regarding faculty and librarian opinions about various aspects of electronic book resources; this survey is referred to repeatedly by other authors in this volume.

Two other articles in this collection complement the massive ebrary surveys. Barb Losoff, in "Academic E-books: Supply Before Demand in the Life Sciences?" reports on a small survey she did of life science faculty members at the University of Colorado, Boulder, and Rickey D. Best, in "The University of Pittsburgh Study in an Electronic Environment: Have E-books Changed Usage Patterns of Monographs?" confirms that the 80/20 rule found by Trueswell and Kent when studying book usage patterns more than 30 years ago still holds true in the electronic environment.

Several "think" pieces in this collection take a broad perspective on the future of the E-book. Tony Horava, in "Mission Possible: E-books and the Humanities," discusses the E-book in the humanities field, concentrating on questions of faculty behavior, digital scholarship, and the development of our visual culture. He examines patterns of use at his institution of major resources such as EEBO, ECCO, and NetLibrary. In "Moving from Book to E-book," Reeta Sinha and Cory Tucker discuss various aspects of collection development and incorporation of E-books into a collection, as well as collection assessment. Aline Soules, in "New Types of E-books, E-book Issues, and Implications for the Future," discusses new notions of what a book could be, enabled by the existence of electronic text, and considers the role of librarians and libraries in this evolving medium.

Kavita Mundle, in "Integration of Electronic Books into Library Catalogs: the UIC Library Experience," provides a factual and thorough discussion of the issues surrounding integration of vendor-supplied records into a local catalog and suggests alternative ways to catalog electronic books. In "Managing Users' Expectations of E-books," Elizabeth Kline and Barbara Williams present the public service side of the equation and discuss how to deal with the users' unhappiness regarding the different formats and technical requirements that make accessibility difficult too often. Timothy Cherubini and Sandra Nyberg discuss the role of consortia in "Expanding Access and Defining Business Models: Consortia and E-books." In addition to providing access to large collections of E-books for their members, Cherubini and Nyberg see expanding roles for consortia in the areas of functionality, education, assessment, and preservation. The final article in the collection, James Gray's "From Print to "e": An Industry Perspective," as its name implies, offers a publisher's perspective on the creation of E-books and in particular discusses the MyiLibrary product.

We are still in the early stages of our integration of electronic book resources, symbolized by the inconsistency in how the various authors in this collection spell "e-book" (which we have regularized as "e-book" throughout this volume). Consistency will no doubt develop over time, as we learn to make electronic book resources a normal part of our collections, a state of affairs that will probably develop much more quickly than has seemed likely until quite recently. Technical issues must first be resolved, including accessibility and metadata problems, as well as attitudinal changes, but it is now inevitable that E-books will be taking their place as cornerstones of the average library's collection.

E-books and Virtual Learning Environments: Responses to a Transformational Technology

David Ball
Jill Beard
Barbara Newland

INTRODUCTION

The Digital Natives

In 2001, Marc Prensky pointed to a singularity—"an event which changes things so fundamentally that there is absolutely no going back"—in education. This singularity was the "arrival and rapid dissemination of digital technology in the last decades of the 20th century." Today's university students are the first generation to have grown up surrounded, and conditioned, by this universal digital technology.

Prensky'sevocativename for them is the Digital Natives. Those of us who grew up in the pre-digital age are the Digital Immigrants. The major problem identified by Prensky is that Digital Natives and Digital Immigrants speak different languages.

The differences as regards education have been elaborated by Jukes and Dosaj (2006: 37) and are expressed in the following Table 1.

TABLE 1. Characteristics of Digital Natives and Digital Immigrants

Digital Natives	Digital Immigrants
Parallel process & multi-task	Singular process and single or limited task
Prefer picture, video and sound to text	Prefer text to picture, video and sound
Random access to interactive media	Linear, logical sequential access
Interact/network simultaneously to many	Interact/network simultaneously to few
Comfortable in virtual and real spaces	Comfortable in real spaces
Prefer interactive/network approach to work	Prefer students to work independently
Prefer multiple multimedia information sources accessed rapidly	Prefer slow controlled information release limited sources

This assessment is borne out by the recent market research study by Ipsos MORI study (2007) for the United Kingdom's Joint Information Systems Committee (JISC) of student expectations. The study found that information and communication technology (ICT) had for the vast majority of prospective students faded into the foreground: these young people regarded complex systems and applications as a natural part of their learning environments, not as manifestations of ICT. The same is true in their social sphere: only 5% claimed never to have used social networking sites; 65% used them regularly, and 62% used Wikis, Blogs, or online networks. Other interesting results from the study are that young people are generally discerning in their use of technology: They embrace it when it is perceived to add value but not for its own sake. They also are wary of universities encroaching on their social space and very aware of boundaries between learning and social activity.

The discontinuity identified by Prensky is here to stay—the expectations and experience of the Digital Natives are very different from those of the Digital Immigrants—and differences will only intensify over time. Our challenge therefore is to provide an environment and resources that satisfy both the expectations and sensitivities of the Natives and the needs of the curriculum. Bournemouth University's pathfinder project, Innovative E-Learning with E-Resources (eRes), is a step toward meeting that challenge.

Student Use of Electronic Resources

The overwhelming popularity of e-resources has long been recognized. Tenopir's digest and analysis of surveys and research studies (2003: 45) document two intuitively quite obvious facts. First, convenience "remains the single most important factor for information use. Desktop access, speed of access and the ability to download, print and send articles are top advantages of electronic journals" for all groups of users surveyed. Second, younger users, the Digital Natives, are more enthusiastic adopters and rely on electronic resources more heavily.

These trends are evident in statistics from Bournemouth University Library (see Figure 1). Downloads of full-text articles from e-journals and, latterly, from e-books have increased from 280,000 in 2002–2003 to 690,000 in 2006–2007. This represents a rise of 146% in 4 years. Over the same period, issues of hard-copy books have dropped from a peak of 349,000 in 2003–2004 to 272,000 in 2006–2007. This represents a decline of 28% in 3 years. However the aggregate of hard-copy loans and

FIGURE 1. Hard-Copy and Electronic Usage

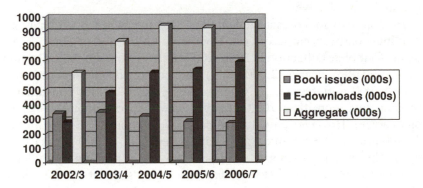

electronic downloads has risen from 620,000 in 2002–2003 to 962,000 in 2006–2007—a rise of 55%. This suggests that students and staff are reading more, or at least accessing a wider range of materials. Of course no statistics are available for free resources from Web sites, which must add significantly to the figures for electronic resources.

There is research evidence to show that this increase in the volume of reading is repeated elsewhere. Liu's survey (2005: 704–706) of staff and graduate students at San Jose University shows that 67% of respondents spend more time on reading in the digital age, while 32% have experienced no change. This is partly due to the fact that each document of the Web has on average nine links to other documents. The survey also showed big increases in browsing or scanning, reading selectively, and non-linear reading. These findings and our experience indicate that students and staff are reading more documents but are increasingly selective in what they read within a document.

Returning to our own statistics, one interesting factor is that Bournemouth has traditionally been a teaching rather than a research university. In the 5 years 2002–2003 to 2006–2007 we have therefore seen an explosion in the use by undergraduates of journal articles, traditionally the preserve of the researcher, because of the factors documented by Tenopir: convenience of availability and the preference of a younger generation for the electronic form. This is borne out by Hernon's study of e-book use by undergraduates (2007: 7), which found that, despite both forms being electronic, respondents preferred e-journal articles to e-books because they were shorter and more packaged. Respondents also tended to read very selectively. Use by undergraduates (Digital Natives) is not intensive, as it is by researchers; however, it is widespread and increasing and tends to be granular and selective.

Hernon also found that students are selective when downloading or printing—partly because of cost. Bournemouth's usage of ebrary's Academic Complete collection in 2006–2007 bears this out. Of the collection's ca. 40,000 titles, nearly 12,000 (30%) were consulted at least once in more than 55,000 user sessions, giving an average of 4.7 titles consulted per session. Just more than 700,000 pages were viewed (about 60 per title on average). However only 17,000 pages were copied (1.5 per title) and 21,000 printed (1.8 per title), giving an aggregate of 38,000 pages (3.3 per title). This does not represent wholesale copying or printing by students.

Another interesting factor is that this high usage of e-books in the ebrary collection occurred before catalogue records appeared in the OPAC, although there were links from reading lists, a good publicity campaign and prominent links to ebrary on the Library's e-resources Web page. Many studies (including ebrary's own) suggest that really high usage is achieved through the traditional OPAC route. This may be the case where titles appear on reading lists (and there is no link from reading list to e-book). However, our statistics seem to represent a different kind of usage, where the collection is searched and exploited as a database rather than a collection of 40,000 discrete entities.

The view of e-books as databases, rather than aggregations of individual titles, is also evident in two recent studies. The experience of Staffordshire University, also an ebrary subscriber, is similar to Bournemouth's. Parkes (2007: 259–260) notes the value of the database approach, searching across 30,000 titles, and characterizes students as hunters, seeking the most useful extracts rather than browsing. This is of course a reflection of the trend towards fostering the independent learner rather than one spoon-fed on a limited range of textbooks. Belanger (2007: 208) also notes that many libraries treat other large collections of e-books, such as Early English Books Online and Eighteenth Century Collections Online, as databases, not cataloguing individual titles.

In summary we see clear trends emerging in usage of e-resources by Digital Natives: They seek granularity in the retrieval of information, are selective in what they read, copy and print, but are accessing more and more materials. Our practice in supporting and providing resources for these independent learners through VLEs must respond to these trends.

The Virtual Learning Environment

One can define a virtual learning environment (VLE) as "the components in which learners and tutors participate in 'online' interactions of various kinds, including online learning." The principal functions of the VLE are as follows:

- Controlled access to curriculum that has been mapped to elements (or "chunks") that can be separately assessed and recorded;
- Tracking student activity and achievement against these elements using simple processes for course administration and student tracking that make it possible for tutors to define and set up a course with accompanying materials and activities to direct, guide, and monitor learner progress;
- Support of on-line learning, including access to learning resources, assessment and guidance. The learning resources may be self-developed

or professionally authored and purchased materials that can be imported and made available for use by learners;
- Communication between the learner, the tutor, and other learning
  support specialists to provide direct support and feedback for learners,
  as well as peer-group communications that build a sense of group
  identity and community of interest; and
- Links to other administrative systems, both in-house and externally.
  (Everett, 2002)

The introduction of VLEs has seen a steady and consistent growth in
the United Kingdom (Browne, Jenkins, and Walker, 2005). Their implementation and development within universities have already enabled some
changes in teaching practices, and they are becoming a transformational
technology, changing fundamentally how students and their universities
interact. Evaluations undertaken at the University of Durham (Newland,
2003) showed that both staff and students had the opinion that the VLE is
promoting more effective learning. In 2001, 81% of staff rated the effectiveness of the VLE as a learning resource as either excellent or very good,
and this increased to 93% in 2002. In both years, 18% of staff felt that their
basic approach to teaching had changed in part because of the VLE, and
69% (2001) and 78% (2002) stated that even if their basic approach had
not changed, they could now do certain things better by using it.

One of the main reasons that many staff use a VLE is to enhance their
teaching (Newland et al., 2004). The most frequently cited factor affecting
the further development of VLE use is time (Browne and Jenkins, 2003).
The result of staff having difficulties in finding the time, among other
competing demands, reinforces small-scale developments to supplement
face-to-face delivery in an evolutionary approach.

Wider institutional adoption of eLearning requires redevelopment and
redesign of existing courses and represents a significant time investment.
New course developments, therefore, provide the most accessible opportunities for significant change, with existing provision continuing to adapt
through evolutionary change. (Newland, Jenkins, and Ringan, 2006)

Conclusion

Universities and their libraries are therefore subject to a number of
significant forces: the expectations of the new generation of Digital Natives;
wide availability of electronic resources, both free and paid for; and a
transformational technology in the form of the VLE. Together these forces

will bring about a profound change in how we as librarians acquire, make available, and exploit resources.

THE CURRENT E-BOOK MARKET

In the longer term, there are encouraging signs in the e-book market. The study undertaken by EPS for the British Library (Powell, 2004) on publishing output in 2020 predicts that parallel publishing will grow: Only 12.5% of U.K. academic monographs will be uniquely print by 2020. However, growth may be slow: Only 10% of new titles will be uniquely electronic by 2014; this proportion is set to rise to 40% by 2020. By 2014, the proportion of academic monographs available in electronic form (uniquely electronic or in hybrid form) will rise to nearly two-thirds.

There are reports that Apple's next iPod will have a much larger screen and a book-reading mode. Apple is also reported to be acquiring rights to the content of at least one publisher (Block, 2006). If this is true, and if Apple has the functionality right, the next 5 years could see a transformation of book buying on a par with the current transformation of the recorded music market, where music downloads overtook sales of traditional singles in 2005.

However, in the short term there are a number of impediments. The complexity of the business models and licences for e-books is documented by Wicht (2006); this makes it very difficult for librarians to make purchasing decisions, particularly within tight budgets. Only a small proportion of titles is available electronically: Just (2007) estimates that there are currently about 135,000 English-language e-books available to the US market, only about 11% of the print offering. Bennett and Landoni (2005) have also noted the reluctance of publishers to make titles, particularly textbooks, available because of fears of lost revenue.

These impediments are echoed in a study undertaken by CHEMS Consulting for the JISC (quoted in Woodward, 2007), which found:

- Ignorance in the higher education (HE) sector of what e-books are available;
- Low awareness within higher education institutions (HEIs) of the value and relevance of e-books;
- Poor understanding by library staff and publishers of each others' needs;
- Complexity of access routes to aggregators' or publishers' platforms;

- Too few e-books available;
- Available e-books not up to date or relevant to U.K. users;
- Pricing models not appropriate; and
- Publishers not making the right textbooks electronically available on the right terms.

This combination of the overwhelming preference of students for electronic materials and of e-learning permeating universities is creating the expectation among students that all materials should be available electronically. Students are starting to ignore hard copy, even when it is the only medium for some recommended reading, in favor of electronic alternatives from whatever source. Given the shrinkage of the textbook market, publishers need to be aware of this factor and make more books available in the end-user's preferred medium. The challenge for academic libraries is to provide appropriate resources in electronic form and through interfaces meeting the expectations of the Digital Natives. Bournemouth University and other organisations in the United Kingdom are responding to this challenge in a number of ways.

THE PROCUREMENT OF E-BOOKS

The SUPC Tender for E-books

The first response to the challenge was the Southern Universities Purchasing Consortium's (SUPC) innovative tender for e-books. (A more detailed analysis of this particular tender process can be found in Ball, 2005a, and of the procurement cycle in general in Ball, 2005b). The main aims of the tender were to provide members with agreements that:

- Were innovative in terms of business models giving, value for money;
- Were flexible, offering those with differing requirements appropriate options;
- Exploited the electronic medium in terms of granularity and multi-user access;
- Focused on users' needs rather than libraries' requirements; and
- Encouraged the addition of library-defined content.

The agreement resulting from this tender was also to be made available to all higher education institutions in the United Kingdom and to members of the U.K. higher education regional purchasing consortia.

Two distinct requirements were identified in the tender:

1. **Requirement A:** a hosted e-book service from which institutions can purchase or subscribe to individual titles, and
2. **Requirement B:** a hosted e-book service of content that is specified by the institutions. It was anticipated that this service could be subject based and subdivided by subject area.

From eight initial tenders, four suppliers were selected for detailed consideration, the selection being based on criteria such as the academic nature of the content, satisfactory authentication arrangements, demonstrable benefits for the consortium, and customer service. Three were general aggregators; the fourth offered a subject approach.

The three general aggregators offered pricing models based on the e-book list price. The e-book prices for 1,190 titles common to the three bidders covering four publishers were compared, and it was clear that for many titles there was no common e-book price. This comparative exercise demonstrated that the average e-book price for these four publishers ranged from $99.90 to $102.20, a spread of 2.3%.

The most depressing aspect of the tender was that two of the three general aggregators tended to mimic hard-copy business models very closely, allowing only single concurrent user access, or a fixed number of accesses each year. The electronic medium is ignored, and many of its benefits lost under such restrictive models, which do not match the requirements of the modern university student for flexibility and immediacy of access. There is no reason why such models should be carried over from the printed to the electronic medium, and this lack of innovation influenced the outcome of the tender.

Comparing the prices of the different aggregators proved a complex matter, given the different elements, such as platform fees and costs per full-time equivalent student, to be included. The comparison was, however, well worth while, since it demonstrated some very wide variations. With the outright purchase models, the cheapest, calculated on 1,500 titles, was 63% of the price of the costliest. With the subscription models, the cheapest on offer was only 20% of the most expensive.

These differentials are quite startling. However, it must be borne in mind that, given the variations in coverage of the different aggregators, one is not comparing the price of exactly the same content. Rather one is comparing the purchasing models, based on the average list prices referred to above. In my view, it is the models that are important: Over time, as more publishers provide their titles in e-book form and as the size of the available general collections grows, the aggregators will be offering very similar content.

This tender was an opportunity to send an unmistakeable message to the e-book marketplace: that vendors have to provide flexible and cost-effective business models reflecting the needs of users and exploiting the potential of the medium.

Following a long and painstaking tender process, ebrary and ProQuest were chosen under Requirement A and ebrary under Requirement B. These two suppliers were felt to offer most to SUPC members in terms of innovative business models giving value for money; of flexibility, offering those with differing requirements appropriate options; and of exploiting the electronic medium for granularity and multi-user access.

It is worth examining the progress of Requirement B in more detail, since it seeks to address the question of textbooks and recommended reading, which is an inhibiting factor in the e-book market of particular relevance to the transformational technology of the VLE. Despite generally offering business models derived from the hard-copy world, e-book aggregators do not fulfill one basic requirement of any hard-copy aggregator, namely to supply any book from any publisher. To overcome the restricted nature of the e-book content on offer, Requirement B of the tender addressed bespoken collections. Before the SUPC tender, work had been under way by a group of universities (Anglia Ruskin, Bournemouth, Glasgow Caledonian, and West of England) and the Royal College of Nursing (RCN) to define a core collection of nursing texts for use in higher education, based on the Libraries for Nursing/RCN core collection for nurses (the Nursing Core Content Initiative, or NCCI). The object was to negotiate with aggregators to make this collection available in electronic form, in order to overcome some of the problems experienced by nurses in U.K. higher education, who work and study in different locations under great time pressure.

This nursing collection was seen as the first in a series of bespoke subject collections to be defined by higher education. There would obviously be potential benefits both to students, who would have access to prescribed and recommended reading material in electronic form, and to the aggregators, who would be assured of take-up by the higher education community. One problem that arose was the well known issue of core textbooks that sell in relatively high volumes (see, for instance, Armstrong, Edwards, and Lonsdale, 2002). Publishers may be unwilling to make these available to libraries at economic prices because they fear the loss of substantial revenue from sales to individual students.

Since the award of the tender under Requirement B, work has continued on the NCCI. Core lists of 200 and 600 titles have been identified, with the large majority of titles coming from 12 publishers. Our aggregator has agreements on the principle of providing content with 11 of these 12 publishers. However, recommended reading, as well as the high sales-volume textbooks, remains a problem, with publishers unwilling to release them under the present business model. Progress in developing appropriate business models and making these texts available has been slow but is now gathering pace with ebrary taking a strong lead.

The JISC National E-books Observatory Project

A further development is the JISC national e-books observatory project, which continues the focus on business models and subject collections of textbooks and recommended reading (http://www.jiscebooksproject.org/). It "will assess the impacts, observe behaviours and develop new models to stimulate the e-books market, and do all this in a managed environment." The core original aims were as follows:

- License a collection of online core reading materials that are highly relevant to U.K. higher education–taught course students in four discipline areas;
- Achieve a high level of participation in the project by making the e-books available on the bidder's own platform (where appropriate) and on a variety of e-book aggregator platforms. Higher education institutions will thus have the option to access the e-books on platforms they already use and which are familiar to their users;
- Evaluate the use of the e-books through deep log analysis and to asses the impact of the 'free at the point of use' e-books upon publishers, aggregators and libraries; and
- Transfer knowledge acquired in the project to publishers, aggregators and libraries to help stimulate an e-books market that has appropriate business and licensing models.

To this end, 36 titles in four subject areas (business, engineering, media, and medicine) have been licensed, following consultations with libraries, for a period of 2 years. They will be freely available to higher-education libraries in the United Kingdom, together with catalogue records, for integration into collections and VLEs. During all of 2008, a deep-log analysis will be undertaken to provide quantitative information about users in the four subject areas, their behaviours and patterns of use.

The advantages and benefits are seen to be as follows (Woodward, 2007):

- Provide an in-depth understanding of how e-books that support U.K. higher education–taught course students are actually used in teaching and learning;
- Enable publishers, libraries, and aggregators to assess the demand for core reading list e-books;
- Enable all parties to measure the effect of free at the point of use e-books on the buying behaviours of students;
- Enable libraries to measure the benefits and potential costs of providing core reading list e-books to students;
- Inform the creation of appropriate business and licensing models;
- Inform the promotion of e-books within an institution;
- Raise awareness generally of e-books throughout the academic community; and
- Stimulate the e-books market in a managed environment.

This is an innovative approach that should yield interesting results. Some concerns have, however, been expressed about the small number of e-books to be made available and the consequent validity of evidence derived from the deep-log analysis. Such validity and applicability of the results are particularly important since it is hoped that the evidence will affect publishers' decisions on making business models for core reading list books available. The fact that each title is available on only one aggregator's platform (Ovid for medicine, MyiLibrary for the rest), and not, as originally intended, on the library's platform of choice, may affect usage and the generic application of its analysis: Usage may, for instance, not reflect the database approach discussed above because of the very small number of titles available compared with ebrary's collection of 40,000. These problems may be overcome if the results can be validated by comparison with usage through libraries' preferred platforms; the Taylor & Francis titles on media studies, for instance, have also been available through other platforms for some time: Comparisons may be possible between libraries.

Together it is to be hoped that these initiatives will give rise to business models satisfying publishers, libraries, and students, enabling the integration of more content into the e-learning environment. Publishers must realize that, if their content is not available electronically, it will not be used, much less bought, by students; if it is not used by students, it will not be bought by libraries either.

INTEGRATION OF RESOURCES INTO THE
BOURNEMOUTH VLE

There is currently some debate about the virtues of linking to e-books through the library catalogue and through library Web pages (e.g., Busby, 2007; Dinkelman and Stacy-Bates, 2007). While linking from traditional catalogue records in an OPAC does seem, as already noted, to drive some usage, this approach ignores the granularity of searching that electronic resources provide and the opportunities for integrating library resources into other systems used heavily by the student population.

Work to integrate library resources into the Bournemouth VLE (known as myBU) has been concentrated in four areas: reading lists, e-reserves, exam papers, and a dedicated Library tab (a fuller description is given by Beard et al., 2007). Federated searching has also been introduced (available from the VLE Library tab among other locations) to enhance access at the granular level.

At a very basic level, myBU has offered a great boost to the humble reading list. Forty-four course clusters now have more than 1,500 reading lists available in myBU, one click away from the individual course units. Fully interactive, they link directly to the electronic resource or to the Library catalogue and are immediately accessible and visible. This availability has provided that long-sought catalyst to encourage academic staff to keep the lists up to date and to include more electronic resources. The lists for our e-business course are now exclusively populated by e-resources.

The eReserves area of myBU has provided an opportunity to address another challenge, that of managing the Short Loan Collection (i.e., printed items in high demand). This has always been a labor-intensive and inefficient process. eReserves obviously functions as a host to born-digital e-resources. Perhaps more importantly, it can also provide access to scanned items and copyright-protected documents, which need to be managed or controlled. Using the Copyright Licensing Agency's (CLA) Scanning Licence, a program of work has scanned course-related material in the Short Loan Collection. These items now total more than 280 and include book chapters, all of which are made available to targeted student audiences at appropriate points in their courses. Overall, the printed Collection has more than halved in the last year to around 1,000 items. Only 50 hard-copy journal articles remain, which fall outside the scope of the scanning licence. The replacement of books in this high-demand Collection is more problematic. However, it is encouraging that Bournemouth's next wave of e-book availability, from a different aggregator, should enable another 100 titles to move from print to electronic form and so be available for integration into the VLE.

Past exam papers have traditionally been stored in printed format within the Short Loan Collection. The system was cumbersome and time consuming to maintain and also open to abuse through theft and vandalism. Electronic versions of exam papers for the past 4 years are now available through the VLE. Academic staff can then link them to relevant units within myBU. There is also a link to the exam papers on the Library Web page. Students are therefore provided with unlimited electronic access to a heavily used resource from various entry points.

In addition to the resources available through the individual course units, there is a Library tab on myBU. Although in its first iteration it simply linked to the Library Web page, it now links to a cluster of modules designed to enable fast access to both resources and help. Students use this to access the databases, e-books, and e-journals not included in their reading lists and all the other advice and content usually made available. The log-on to myBU now enables a customized view of help and advice, which includes pod casts and Blogs and the potential for the introduction of Wikis and the SCHOLAR social bookmarking tool.

Perhaps the greatest enhancement has been the integration of a federated search engine into the Library tab. From its first launch in September 2007, it had the capacity to trawl over 60 resources with Athens authentication as well as giving the user choice about whether to include not only full-text content but also the Library Catalogue and Google Scholar. This has the potential to simplify students' access to resources by searching across databases, whether internal or external. As well as the VLE itself, an obvious internal target is the institutional repository of Bournemouth's research output, which will become more and more significant for students with the increasing focus on research-led teaching.

HIGHER EDUCATION ACADEMY PATHFINDER PROJECT

Bournemouth's innovative approach has been recognized by the award of pathfinder funding by the United Kingdom's Higher Education Academy for a project entitled Innovative E-Learning with E-Resources (eRes). eRes, which began in May 2007, seeks to develop active approaches to learning in an online environment through the exploitation and integration of e-resources. It will adopt an action research methodology that will encourage reflection and change for the individual and the organisation.

The first and most important focus is the development of innovative pedagogic frameworks in the form of case studies that bring together learning activities and academically led quality e-resources within the unit of study. Each will start with an exploration of the alignment of intended learning outcomes and teaching strategies and the identification of appropriate e-resources. The case studies of different approaches will include:

- Collaborative learning through group work made possible by the provision of multiple simultaneous users of e-resource with online discussions or Blogs;
- Reflecting on current events through Web 2.0 technologies;
- Understanding concepts through the social construction of knowledge in a Wiki;
- Individual learning from feedback from quizzes relating to e-resources;
- Developing critical thinking skills by comparing and contrasting e-resources; and
- Problem-based learning, with students finding and analysing statistical data to solve problems.

The second focus is the e-reading strategy, which will help redefine the traditional concept of reading for a degree and build on previous studies of enabling access to e-resources. The current scope of e-resources will be identified and an assessment made of strategies needed to exploit them to their fullest. This scope has radically changed this year, through the CLA scanning licence allowing us economically to deploy and target to the relevant students 10% of content digitized from any U.K.-published work held in BU's print collection. If this is exploited to its logical conclusion, students will be able to work in groups accessing key information from a number of sources in a way that would never have been possible through traditional hard-copy library lending. Although the development of e-content by publishers as course cartridges or the availability of digitised texts under the HERON scheme (http://www.heron.ingenta.com/) can offer bespoke content, there are significant cost implications for such deployment. By exploiting readily accessible e-resources, including CLA scanned items and social bookmarking, this project will drive practical and affordable innovations in pedagogy and working practices.

THE FUTURE

This article has pointed up some of the innovative responses by one academic library to the challenge of meeting the expectations of the Digital Natives. There are many other initiatives that will also shape library provision in the future, and most academic libraries are embracing the new technologies and exploiting their potential to support learning. However, the frustrations noted by Woodward (2007) still apply. Many of them, such as lack of appropriate content and unsustainable business models, arise from a mismatch between the attitudes and practices of academic publishers and the requirements and expectations of libraries and their end-users.

Publishers must respond quickly to these requirements. Davy (2007) notes that, although publishers of textbooks have been competing strongly by incorporating more and more online features, over the past three years the market has been static in value terms; given annual price increases of 5%, this translates into a significant decline in sales volumes. He attributes this decline to two factors: the move to independent learning, and Digital Natives' expectations of digital, packaged, just-in-time resources. His vision for the future is not books on screens but digital learning objects: related content at a granular level (articles, chapters, case studies, the open Web, databases) clustered round learning objectives and delivered through VLEs. Publishers need to learn from community (such as MySpace) and music sites (such as iTunes) how content is packaged, accessed, mixed, and shared by the Digital Natives. A similar point is also made by Wheatcroft (2006): Content will need to be viewed as a set of assets to be developed, used, re-used, recombined, updated, traded, and transmuted into a range of clearly differentiated products.

Academic libraries and publishers stand at a critical junction. The arrival of the Digital Natives in universities, coinciding with the adoption of a transformational technology, the VLE, requires a fundamental shift in the creation and provision of learning resources.

REFERENCES

Armstrong, C., Edwards, L.& Lonsdale, R. (2002). Virtually there?: e-books in UK academic libraries. *Program, 36*, 216–227.

Ball, D. (2005a). A new model for procuring e-books. In: *Internet Librarian International 2005: Transcending boundaries: Information technologies & strategies for the 21ˢᵗ Century* (pp. 154–162). Compiled by Carol Nixon and Jennifer Burmood. Medford: Information Today.

Ball, D. (2005b). *Managing suppliers and partners for the academic library*. London: Facet.

Beard, J. et al. (2007). Integrating e-resources within a university VLE. *Library and Information Update, 6*(4) 35–37.

Belanger, J. (2007). Cataloguing e-books in UK higher education libraries: Report of a survey. *Program, 41*(3), 203–216.

Bennett, L., & Landoni, M. (2005). E-books in academic libraries. *Electronic Library, 23*(1):9–16.

Block, R. (2006). Apple to do ebooks? [online], Engadget. Retrieved August 8, 2006, from <http://www.engadget.com/2006/07/22/apple-to-do-ebooks>

Browne, T., & Jenkins, M. (2003). VLE surveys: A longitudinal perspective between March 2001 and March 2003 for higher education in the United Kingdom. Retrieved November 1, 2007, from <http://www.ucisa.ac.uk/ groups/tlig/vle/index_html>.

Browne, T., Jenkins, M., & Walker, R. (2005). VLE surveys: A longitudinal perspective between March 2001, March 2003 and March 2005 for higher education in the United Kingdom. Retrieved November 1, 2007, from <http://www.ucisa.ac.uk/groups/tlig/vle/index_html>.

Busby, L. (2007). Turning pages: Reflections on e-book acquisitions and access challenges. *Against the Grain*, April, 28–32.

Davy, T. (2007). E-textbooks: Opportunities, innovations, distractions and dilemmas. *Serials, 20*(2), 98–102.

Dinkelman, A., & Stacy-Bates, K. (2007). Accessing e-books through academic library web sites. *College & Research Libraries, 68*(1), 45–58.

Everett, R. 2002. MLEs and VLEs explained. London: JISC. Retrieved November 1, 2007, from <http://www.jisc.ac.uk/index.cfm?name=mle_briefings_1>.

Hernon, P., et al. (2007). E-book use by students: Undergraduates in economics, literature and nursing. *Journal of Academic Librarianship, 33*(1), 3–13.

Ipsos MORI (2007). Student expectations study: Key findings from online research and discussion evenings held in June 2007 for the Joint Information Systems Committee. London: JISC. Retrieved November 1, 2007, from <http://www.jisc.ac.uk/publications/publications/studentexpectations.aspx#downloads>.

Jukes, I., & Dosaj, A. (2006). *Understanding digital kids (DKs): Teaching and learning in the new digital landscape*. N.p.: The InfoSavvy Group. Retrieved November 1, 2007, from <http://www.ldcsb.on.ca/schools/cfe/internet_safety/documents/understanding%20digital%20kids.pdf>.

Just, P. (2007). Electronic books in the USA: Their numbers and development and a comparison to Germany. *Library Hi Tech, 25*(1), 157–164.

Liu, Z. (2005). Reading behaviour in the digital environment: Changes in reading behaviour over the past ten years. *Journal of Documentation, 61*(6), 700–712.

Newland, B. (2003). Evaluating the impact of a VLE on learning and teaching. In *EDMEDIA World Conference on Educational Multimedia, Hypermedia and Telecommunications*. Honolulu: EDMEDIA.

Newland, B., et al. (2004). *VLE longitudinal report, duo (Durham University Online) 2001–2003*. Bournemouth: Bournemouth University.

Newland, B., Jenkins, M., & Ringan, N. (2006). Academic experiences of using VLEs: Overarching lessons for preparing and supporting staff. In J. O'Donoghue (Ed.), *Technology supported learning and teaching: A staff perspective*. London: Information Science Publishing.

Parkes, D. (2007). E-books from ebrary at Staffordshire University: A case study. *Program, 41*(3), 253–261.

Powell, D. J. (2004). *Publishing output to 2020*. London: The British Library. Retrieved November 1, 2007, from <http://www.bl.uk/about/articles/epsintro.html>.

Prensky, M. (2001). Digital natives, digital immigrants. *On the Horizon, 9*(5), 1–6.

Tenopir, C. (2003). *Use and users of electronic library resources: An overview and analysis of recent research studies*. Washington: Council on Library and Information Resources. Retrieved November 1, 2007, from <http://www.clir.org/pubs/reports/pub120/pub120.pdf>.

Wheatcroft, A. (2006). 20/20 vision?: E-books in practice and theory. *Serials, 19*(1), 10–14.

Wicht, H. (2006). Buying ebooks. *Netconnect*, Spring, 15–17.

Woodward, H. (2007). *The National E-Books Observatory Project & the UK academic vision for e-books*. London: JISC National E-Books Observatory Project. Retrieved November 1, 2007, from <http://www.jiscebooksproject.org/archives/62>.

E-books in the University of California Libraries

Jim Dooley
Martha Hruska
Lorelei Tanji

INTRODUCTION

Individual University of California libraries have been acquiring various e-book packages and individual titles for several years, both through subscription and purchase. As a result, many UC librarians began to ask whether it were time to investigate a system-wide license for one or more aggregator packages. In response, the UC Libraries' Collection Development Committee (CDC) determined that there was a need to develop principles to integrate e-books into existing collection development activities and to try to influence the emerging marketplace of e-books. In June, 2007, the CDC charged a task force to develop "a set of guiding principles for collecting books in electronic format, in the broader context of system-wide monographic collection development, shared print goals, mass digitization projects and preservation." The final report of the task force is available on the CDC Web site <http://libraries.universityofcalifornia.edu/cdc/>. The authors of this article are the chair and two members of the task force.

On the basis of the work of the task force to date, this article will discuss the current state of e-book implementation on the University of California campuses as well as the draft "Principles for Acquiring and Licensing E-book Packages and Services" developed by the task force. It will also discuss recommendations for integrating e-books into current UC consortial decision making.

RECENT HISTORY

In 2001, the California Digital Library's Joint Steering Committee on Shared Collections (JSC) charged a task force to "evaluate academic experiences with electronic books." The task force report is available at <http://www.cdlib.org/inside/groups/jsc/ebooks/#reports>. This report shows the considerable advances made in the e-book marketplace over the last six years while at the same time pointing to several unresolved issues.

The report was written at a time when there was considerable uncertainty surrounding the future development of e-books and when the e-book market was still very immature. As Karen Coyle said, "The e-book hype of the 1990s, promising huge libraries of electronic books, available to everyone, everywhere, all the time, burst along with the rest of the dot-com bubble" (Coyle, 2003). This uncertainty is captured by the use of the word "experiments" twice in the task force charge. Overall, the task force "concluded that all the elements that would make the e-book market viable are not yet in place." This echoes a report on an e-book conference in 2000 called E-Book World that stated, "It was clear that the new technology has captured the attention of the book publishing community, but it was equally clear that no one has a good idea on how e-books will eventually be integrated in the larger industry" (Hilts, 2000).

Though e-books may no longer be "experiments," the 2001 task force report does highlight several issues that have not been fully resolved:

- The continued lack of a device that would allow reading an e-book with anything approaching the resolution of a printed book;
- The use of proprietary software systems;
- Limitations on use imposed by licensing requirements and digital rights management systems, particularly in regard to interlibrary loan; and
- Standards and methods for archiving perpetual access titles.

Clearly there have been significant improvements over the last several years. Though widespread acceptance of e-books may have progressed more slowly than some envisioned, it would not be accurate to describe the current situation as a "muddle," as Walt Crawford wrote in 2000 (Crawford, 2000). There have been significant advances during this period in usability, MARC record availability, integration with print vendor systems, licensing, and business models. At the same time, however, it must be recognized that e-book sales are still a tiny proportion of total trade publishing revenue. In 2002, e-book sales were $3.3 million of total trade revenues of $26 billion (Coyle, 2003). By 2005, e-book revenues had grown to $12 million, with the total U.S. book publishing market between $25.1 and $31.6 billion (Crawford, 2006). So even with nearly 400% growth in revenues in three years, e-books still accounted for less than $1/20^{th}$ of 1% of total sales. By 2006, e-book revenue was 6% of total book revenue for one major publisher (Strauch, 2007). While the trend in e-book revenues is clearly upward, e-books still have a long way to go to achieve significant market share.

A survey conducted in spring 2007 by the e-book vendor ebrary highlights many of the barriers still remaining to the widespread adoption of e-books. This Global eBook Survey was completed by 552 libraries, 77% of which are academic, and is available through the ebrary Web site at <http://www.ebrary.com> (and see elsewhere in this volume). Major barriers to usage were identified as lack of awareness, difficulty in reading and using e-books, lack of training, price, and restrictive access models. Though at first glance it may appear that little has changed since 2001, the UC CDC believes that e-books are here to stay and that the e-book market has developed to the point where it is worthwhile to charge a new task force.

UC COLLECTION DEVELOPMENT PROCESS

Before proceeding with an examination of the task force's work to date, it will be helpful to describe the collection development process for centrally licensed electronic resources in the University of California Libraries. Though the libraries are constituents of a single system and have a long history of cooperation, they act in many ways as a consortium of separate libraries in matters of joint collection development. There are 10 campus libraries plus the California Digital Library. Though the CDL provides many tools and services, its primary responsibility in the collection development process is to provide licensing services, acquisitions, and cataloging for what are called Tier 1 resources—those resources centrally acquired and available to all campuses.

Recommendations for the acquisition of new system-wide electronic resources primarily come from the bibliographer groups. Currently there are 30 bibliographer groups, each of which is composed of at least one subject specialist from each campus. These groups meet regularly either virtually or in person to discuss issues and to surface recommendations for new resources.

Annually, usually during the summer, a CDL body, the Joint Steering Committee on Shared Collections (JSC) sends a survey to the bibliographer groups to collect their recommendations. It is the responsibility of the JSC to prioritize the requests based on a review of the budget and to prepare the annual licensing work plan that lists those resources that the CDL proposes to attempt to license on behalf of the campus libraries. The work plan is then submitted to the CDC, which is composed of the collection development officers of each of the campus libraries. After approval by the CDC, the work plan is used to guide CDL staff in negotiations with individual vendors.

The results of the negotiations are then presented for a go–no-go decision. If the decision is favorable, a final proposal, including proposed campus co-investment scenarios, is submitted to the CDC. It is important to note that the large bulk of funds to acquire system-wide electronic resources come from the individual campus library budgets and not from the CDL, thus the necessity for CDC approval of licensing proposals. After approval, the proposal is forwarded to CDL Acquisitions, and the Shared Cataloging Program, which distributes catalog records for Tier 1 resources, is notified.

This system works quite well for those resources that are relatively discipline-specific and so can be championed by an individual bibliographer group. Acquisition of multi-disciplinary resources is correspondingly harder to coordinate. As regards e-books, it is easier to surface a proposal for a discipline-specific collection or a collection of electronic reference works than to find sponsors for a broad multi-disciplinary package from, for example, ebrary, EBL, MyiLibrary, or NetLibrary. For this reason, the current task force has been charged to examine mechanisms by which the libraries can make decisions regarding such packages. These mechanisms include assigning the task to an existing bibliographer group, creating a new bibliographer group, appointing an ad-hoc group, or some combination of these methods. After reviewing the options, the task force recommended that an ad-hoc group be appointed. The CDC has accepted this recommendation and is in the process of appointing the group.

ENVIRONMENTAL SCAN OF CURRENT UC E-BOOK ACTIVITIES

One of the first things the task force did was conduct an environmental scan of the e-book activities at each UC campus via a survey. The survey focused on products licensed independently by each campus library. It identified resources that were uniquely held at a single campus and resources held at more than one campus, which could be potential opportunities for system-wide licensing.

Broad ranges of e-book products were covered, and the responses included subject-specific e-books and reference works (e.g., Die Deutsche Lyrik in Reclams Universal-Bibliothek, Grzimek's Animal Life Encyclopedia), general reference works (Gale Virtual Reference Library), and aggregator e-book packages (e.g., NetLibrary, ebrary, EBL, MyiLibrary, and the like). In some cases, libraries had licensed these on their own, because there was no consortial advantage available (Thesaurus Linguae Graecae) or because it was of specialized interest to only a few campuses (e.g., Old English Corpus, Apabi Chinese e-books).

The survey also asked whether campuses had formed local e-book task forces. It was clear that there was still interest in investigating e-books as five of the 10 campuses had e-book task forces (UCB, UCI, UCLA, UCR, UCSD) to assess and address the local needs of the campus libraries and to monitor e-book publishing and technology developments.

The survey also requested feedback about products campuses were investigating locally and suggestions for areas to target at the system-wide level. Some campuses expressed interest in the following:

- Online reference titles purchased on a title-by-title basis;
- E-books for course reserves;
- Multi-subject and subject-specific packages;
- Health and life sciences e-books and selected encyclopedias;
- E-books published in Japan, Korea, Taiwan, or Hong Kong;
- E-books for IT professionals; and
- Selecting e-books via monograph vendor's interface.

The following were some of the issues and concerns mentioned by campuses:

- Unhappiness with access models;
- Inability to easily purchase single titles;
- Untimely provision of MARC records;
- Challenges in acquiring accurate usage statistics;
- Developing better assessment methods;
- Monitoring non-vended content (government documents, grey literature, small press items, other one-offs); and
- Impact of mass digitization projects vis-à-vis licensed e-book resources.

Many of these issues and concerns pointed to the need to develop principles for acquiring and licensing e-book packages and services.

PRINCIPLES FOR ACQUIRING AND LICENSING E-BOOKS

The task force reviewed the original "University of California Principles for Acquiring and Licensing Information in Digital Formats" <http://libraries.universityofcalifornia.edu/cdc/principlesforacquiring.html> with the aim of broadening these to include e-book packages and services. Many of the same basic principles apply as well to e-books. However, e-books introduce the need for clear statements on additional business and access models, licensing terms, and content and management requirements. The task force, therefore, will recommend a revision to the UC Principles that can include e-books as an important part of the carefully coordinated and collaboratively managed variety of UC library collections.

The e-book revisions to the Principles are intended to apply to two types of e-books: the digitized versions of printed books and those that are born digital. Increasingly, the commercially available packages contain books that are available only electronically. At the same time, digitization initiatives are ramping up, greatly increasing the volume of digitized versions of print books. In either case, it is important that e-book acquisition and access options may be exercised flexibly and as needed and appropriate to meet changing demands for instructional support. Decisions on retention of e-book titles need to be considered at the time of acquisition as these help inform a preferred access option.

The following e-book principles highlight those that the task force will recommend be added to the original document to guide the University at both campus and university-wide levels in setting the terms of business relationships with providers of e-book packages.

Content-Collection Development

- E-books that replicate print should be true to the print original, including graphics, color, and original page display including numbering;
- In cases where e-books duplicate printed books, including those that result from mass digitization projects, a Shared Print monograph strategy should be considered and planned;
- For effective management and evaluation of e-book packages, title-by-title usage statistics, by campus, are needed; and
- In evaluating e-books that are only in digital form, it is important to have provisions for the archiving of content in a trusted digital repository.

Costs and Pricing

Given the potential for dynamic updating of e-book content, the choice of business terms will vary depending on the need to retain content. Therefore, vendors that offer a range of reasonably priced access options—lease, own, user-driven, and the like—will be preferred.

If there is a differential price for single vs. multiple user access, multi-user access should preferably cost no more than one-and-a-half times single user access and in no event more than two times single user access.

Because the University of California has a coordinated and collaboratively managed variety of library collections and services in which the collections of the individual campuses are enriched by capabilities to access the resources of all the others, "cross-access" should be a contractual option. Cross-access business terms should be based on actual or realistic estimates of UC audience, account for the fact that the university is a single system, and acknowledge efficiencies in conducting business with one rather than multiple (campus) parties.

Transformative Strategies

The libraries make principled investments in publishing business models that produce high-quality scholarly content and have the potential for transforming scholarly communication. In addition to transformative models that reduce access barriers (e.g., open access models) or that provide a sustainable alternative to expensive for-profit efforts, e-book publishing models, such as those emerging with WordPress, can build on the success of collaborative social networking to further transform scholarly communications. E-books offer the potential of truly integrating commentary and updating ongoing, developing research.

University presses that are redefining their monograph publishing strategies offer opportunities for libraries to collaborate in support of new means of scholarly communications, especially in providing innovative forms of quality or peer review processes. Strategies for the access and use of mass-digitized books can also aid in development of transformative models for libraries.

Licensing

E-book service packages should allow fair use such as classroom use and interlibrary loan. Users should not be required to establish an individual account in order to view titles; such an account may be required for added value features such as bookmarking or highlighting. "Click-through" licenses should not be required.

Functionality and Interoperability

E-book package titles should be integrated in common acquisition vendor tools. E-book services should be interoperable and not be dependent on proprietary vendor hardware.

E-book software should easily support printing, downloading, e-mail, and copying. E-book software should add value through advanced searching, browsability, highlighting, and marking text, citation tools, interoperability, and linking with outside references, cited sources, dictionaries and media, and the like.

E-book vendors that can supply standard MARC records are preferred. E-book software should support access to all types of content, including graphics and sound. E-book software should protect the privacy of users. Access to e-book packages should be solely by IP range without any additional login or password requirements.

CONCLUSION

This article presents some preliminary findings and recommendations of a University of California Libraries' task force examining the current state of the e-book marketplace. One goal of the task force is to influence this emerging marketplace. Hopefully, the final report of the task force will achieve this objective.

REFERENCES

Coyle, K. (2003). E-Books: It's about evolution, not revolution. *Library Journal Net Connect* (Fall), 8–12.

Crawford, W. (2000). Nine models, one name: Untangling the E-book muddle. *American Libraries, 31*(8), 56–59.

Crawford, W. (2006). Why aren't Ebooks more successful? *EContent, 29*(8), 44.

Hilts, P. (2000). Looking at the E-Book market. *Publishers Weekly, 247*(47), 35–36.

Strauch, K. (2007). ATG interviews James R. Gray. *Against the Grain, 19*(4), 41–42.

Making Sense of E-book Usage Data

John Cox

INTRODUCTION

The range of e-books available for purchase or subscription has expanded significantly in recent times and, though uptake continues to lag e-journals, they now form an important element in libraries' e-resource collections. The very fact that uptake is variable according to discipline and other circumstances creates a strong imperative for libraries to study usage data carefully. There are many unanswered questions regarding the impact of e-books and, as for other e-resources, librarians need to understand patterns of usage in order to monitor value for money and to guide collection development decisions. Ideally they would enjoy easy access to a comprehensive array of usage data consistently collected by different vendors. Unfortunately, this is not currently the case, and librarians need to be prepared for some frustration and the investment of an amount of extra effort in establishing the effectiveness of their e-book collections.

Despite the fact that e-books have been around for some time, they remain less established than e-journals, particularly in terms of subscription models that vary widely but also with regard to usage analysis. For e-journals, there is consensus that the full-text article provides a consistent unit of measurement (Shepherd, 2006). E-book products are more diverse, and possible metrics include whole book titles or individual chapters, sections, and entries. In addition to the diversity of offerings from vendors, there are different data collection practices, while delivery of usage data is also complicated by digital rights management issues. Efforts at standardization are very welcome but face many challenges. This article examines what is currently possible in the area of e-book usage analysis and describes some encouraging initiatives. It argues throughout, however, the need to inform the deployment of vendor-supplied usage statistics with a keen awareness of possible limitations and the value of supplementary approaches such as surveys in understanding the actual usage and impact of e-books.

E-BOOK USAGE STATISTICS

What types of usage data can we expect from e-book vendors? (A list of e-book vendors is provided in the Appendix). As already mentioned, there are many variations between vendors, but Table 1 outlines the more common metrics, and Figures 1 and 2 show sample reports. These metrics are not universally reported by vendors. Early English Books Online (EEBO) and Oxford Reference Online are examples of services that do not show usage by title, whereas session duration is not included in NetLibrary or Eighteenth Century Collections Online (ECCO) reports. Additional reports may include usage by subject (NetLibrary, ebrary), unsubscribed books browsed (Safari, Ebook Library [EBL]), details of pages accessed within a book (EBL) or copied/pasted from a book (informaworld [Taylor & Francis]), activity by IP subnet (ebrary), and number of unique users (EBL). Commonly available facilities include limiting reports by time period and output of data to spreadsheet software for further manipulation. However, not all services provide a self-service administration module, and it may be necessary to request reports from vendors.

TABLE 1. Common E-book Usage Metrics

Metric	Explanation	Notes
Sections viewed, printed or downloaded	The number of full-text content units viewed, printed or downloaded by users.	Content units may be whole books, chapters, vendor-defined sections or, for reference works, individual entries.
Usage by title	The number of times a title was accessed.	May be the total use of constituent parts, e.g., chapters or sections, which are counted separately.
Number of sessions	The number of user sessions (i.e., period from opening to closure of access).	Sessions can also be counted as ended at timeout following a specified period of inactivity.
Duration of sessions	The total length of time for all sessions.	Average session length may be given separately or can be calculated.
Number of turnaways	Frequency with which users are denied access.	Usually because the maximum number of permitted concurrent sessions is in use.
Searches	The number of searches conducted by users.	Supplementary data may include details of search terms used or the number of searches returning zero hits.

Applications for E-book Usage Statistics

Library staff employ e-book usage data for a number of purposes, primarily in the contexts of monitoring levels of use and making collection development decisions.

Monitoring Use

Usage statistics enable varying levels of e-book uptake measurement. Raw numbers can at least show patterns of use for any given product although, as discussed later, comparison between products is more difficult. Thus, Dillon and Langston provide examples of the analysis of title and subject data for early NetLibrary subscriptions at the University of

Adapting to E-books

FIGURE 1. *NetLibrary* Usage by Title (http://www.oclc.org/netlibrary/)

Accesses	Title	Subject	LCC	Dewey	Authors	Publisher	ISBN	Year	eContent ID	Content Type
163	Monitoring for Health Hazards At Work	Medicine	RA1229.A64 1999ab	615.9 /02	Ashton, Indira.; Gill, F. S.	Blackwell Science.	9780632050413	2000	51411	eBook
148	Politics in the Republic of Ireland 4Th Ed.	Political Science	JN1415.P65 2005ab	320.9417	Coakley, John.; Gallagher, Michael	Routledge in association with PSAI Press	9780203411810	2005	116438	eBook
113	Environmental Hazards : Assessing Risk and Reducing Disaster	Social Sciences: General	GE5014.S6 2004eb	363.34	Smith, Keith.	Routledge	9780203354315	2004	94678	eBook
109	International Law 5Th Ed.	Law	KZ3275.S53 2003ab	341	Shaw, Malcolm N.	Cambridge University Press	9780521824736	2003	125137	eBook
63	Public Administration and Public Policy in Ireland : Theory and Methods	Political Science	JN1435.P83 2003ab	320 /.6 /09417	Adshead, Maura.; Millar, Michelle	Routledge	9780203411551	2003	96997	eBook
54	Political Ideologies : An Introduction	Political Science	JA71.H49 2003eb	320.5	Heywood, Andrew.	Palgrave Macmillan	9780333961773	2003	101548	eBook
51	The Evolution of EU Law	Law	KJE947.E99 1999eb	341.242 /2	Craig, P. P.	Oxford University Press.	9780198264811	1999	18319	eBook

Texas at Austin (Dillon, 2001a) and California State University (Langston, 2003), respectively. Safley reports data for a wider range of e-book services and genres at the University of Texas at Dallas, with significant increases between 2004 and 2005 (Safley, 2006). Cox noted the role of data in identifying peaks and troughs in uptake of the Safari service at National University of Ireland, Galway (Cox, 2004b), while Christianson and Aucoin examined trends in monthly use of NetLibrary titles at Louisiana State University for a 13-month period (Christianson and Aucoin, 2005).

The latter study is one of a number employing usage data to compare the use of e-books with their printed equivalents. Littman and Connaway studied activity for 7,880 titles in print and via NetLibrary at the Duke University Libraries over the period from February 2001 to August 2002 (Littman and Connaway, 2004). They noted a key deficit of earlier studies that compared the number of times an e-book was accessed with the number

FIGURE 2. *EEBO* Usage Summary Report (http://eebo.chadwyck.com/) (Image published with permission of Pro uest. Further reproduction is prohibited without permission)

Date	Web Sessions	Searches	Citation Views	Illustration ToC Views	Document/Page Image Views	PDF Downloads	Full Text (ASCII) Views	Searches Returning No Hits	Turnaways
May 2007	75	212	37	5	164	21	61	93	0
Apr 2007	277	1091	146	15	747	156	295	567	0
Mar 2007	285	880	106	59	1848	252	179	429	0
Feb 2007	133	361	62	40	896	202	119	146	0
Jan 2007	398	333	84	10	588	163	124	111	0

of circulations for its printed equivalent. This tended to operate in favor of e-books that might attract multiple accesses over a short period of time, while a single circulation tended to take up a relatively long period. Furthermore, in-library use of printed books did not feature. Their study therefore compared *whether* the books had been accessed or borrowed rather than the frequency of transactions. They found that the e-books involved received 11% more use than their printed counterparts in the study period and had the potential to deliver good value. There were also some interesting patterns of overlap and format preference, with 39% of titles being used in both formats, 34% as e-books only and 27% used only in print. Christianson and Aucoin focused on 2,852 titles available in both formats at Louisiana State University and found some differences, with higher use of printed books but greater concentration of e-book usage in fewer titles (2005).

The analysis by Safley (2006) at the University of Texas at Dallas, already mentioned, found that print circulations had decreased from 67,465 in 2004 to 50,993 in the first 11 months of 2005, a period during which usage of a variety of e-book services had increased significantly. This indicates a gain for e-book uptake at the expense of printed books. Bailey (2006) reported the same trend at Auburn University at Montgomery Library where printed book usage declined by almost a third from 2000 to 2004, and use of NetLibrary titles increased considerably, reaching almost 23% of the level of printed book usage.

Uptake according to discipline was a common focus of all these studies and others besides. Littman and Connaway (2004) found that e-books were used more than their printed equivalents in education, medicine, psychology and computing, whereas Safley observed strong uptake overall, notably in computer science and engineering but also in history (Safley, 2006). Relative to its representation in the collection of NetLibrary titles at California State University, Langston (2003) reported strong use in computer science and technology and engineering. Among the subjects more fully represented, economics and business, medicine, sociology, and psychology received the greatest number of accesses. Business and computing, along with literature and medicine, feature prominently in Bailey's figures for e-book usage at Auburn University itself but also in his table of comparative use at a number of universities based on raw numbers of accesses (2006). The similarity in subject profile among a number of institutions suggests that e-books are best suited to certain subjects.

Collection Development and Management

Data on uptake by discipline and the impact of e-books on the use of printed titles inform collection development decisions (e.g., influencing the balance between print and online book purchase in certain subjects or identifying titles where online access may satisfy demand better than multiple printed copies). A survey of librarians by ebrary Inc. [Ed. Note: the survey appears elsewhere in this volume] asked respondents to indicate decisions influenced by e-book usage statistics (ebrary Inc., 2007). Collection development issues accounted for three of the four choices offered and ranked highest, with renewal and budget allocation both at 59% and title acquisition not far behind at 53%.

Value for money is a key factor, and usage data can provide some insight in this respect. Wilkins describes the deployment of usage statistics to assist in renewal decisions at the University of Derby and the use of spreadsheets to record how much each title has cost over a number of years (Wilkins, 2007). Taylor-Roe and Spencer (2005) highlight the reporting of investment in, and usage of, e-textbooks acquired for a newly established distance learning course at Newcastle University. Safari offers a book-swapping facility, and Cox notes the benefit of dropping two low-use titles in favor of two new titles on Java, one of which established itself as the most used book in the subscription at National University of Ireland, Galway (Cox, 2004b). Where provided (e.g., EBL, NetLibrary, Safari [Fig. 3]), details of attempted access to, or previews of, unsubscribed titles can help to identify priorities for acquisition. Data regarding turnaways can also help to monitor the adequacy of concurrent user license provision, as highlighted by Cox and Dillon (Cox, 2004b; Dillon, 2001a).

E-book usage data offer the opportunity to check the effectiveness of content selection procedures. Thus, Safley compared usage of a

FIGURE 3. *Safari* Previews Report (http://www.safaribooksonline.com/)

Hit Type	Total Hits (Views)	Title
Preview	155.00	Knowledge Management Toolkit, The
Preview	82.00	RESTful Web Services
Preview	70.00	A First Look at SQL Server 2005 for Developers
Preview	51.00	UML for Mere Mortals®
Preview	46.00	How Personal & Internet Security Work
Preview	44.00	Sams Teach Yourself Java™ 2 in 21 Days, Third Edition
Preview	43.00	Python Programming on Win32
Preview	41.00	Refactoring: Improving the Design of Existing Code

librarian-selected e-book collection (NetLibrary) with that of a vendor-supplied collection (ebrary) and discovered almost identical usage by subject, raising some questions about the impact of selection activity (2006). Williams and Best found that favorable *Choice* reviews had little impact on the likelihood on e-book circulation which was actually higher for non-*Choice* titles, although the sample at Auburn University at Montgomery was very small (2006). The effectiveness of cataloging is another possible focus, exemplified by Dillon's reporting of the impact of cataloging of e-book titles on patterns of uptake at the University of Texas at Austin (Dillon, 2001b). Encouragingly, the addition of catalog records appeared to have a positive immediate effect and resulted in a significant increase in use with changes in uptake by subject, too. Less positively, an earlier analysis by Dillon found that many high-use titles had previously been acquired in print but were now missing (Dillon, 2001a).

Other Uses

While collection development issues dominated the ebrary survey mentioned earlier, a third of the respondents also made use of e-book usage statistics to plan training and promotion (ebrary Inc., 2007). Data on usage can be used to influence focusing of information literacy initiatives for a given e-book service or to plan training according to discipline. Allied to this, it may be possible, depending on the level of reporting offered, to get some insight into how e-books are being used. Data on most frequently accessed titles or sections may show a high concentration on a small number of readings, suggesting a focus on recommended texts; conversely, a wider distribution of titles might indicate supplementary reading by students. The number of pages viewed and the volume of printing may offer some indication of levels of onscreen reading or of a tendency to use an e-book service simply as a delivery mechanism for hardcopy access. Equally, session duration may suggest different levels of use from casual browsing to intensive research or simply quick reference. Safley reported session length and activity data for ebrary, Safari, EEBO, *Oxford English Dictionary* and Oxford Reference Online (Safley, 2006), while Cox adduced some possible learner behaviors from *Safari* statistics (Cox, 2004a).

In reality, raw usage data can offer only limited assistance with understanding e-book user behavior and tend to support speculation rather than authoritative comment. As outlined later in this article, there is wide recognition of the need to supplement usage statistics with deeper studies of actual use. It is perhaps telling that 14% of the respondents to the ebrary survey indicated that usage statistics had no influence on decisions, possibly reflecting some of the deficits in data provision discussed next.

Difficulties with E-book Usage Statistics

Some of the difficulties with e-book usage data are common to e-journals, and others are specific to e-books, or at least far more pronounced than for e-journals. This is certainly true of one of the major issues, the lack of consistency between vendors in the data they deliver. Safley is by no means alone in noting that "each publisher provides different variables to approximate the intensity of the use. Comparing statistics between companies is a problem because of the lack of standards" (Safley, 2006).

Reference has already been made to variations in data collection practices, and some examples of data provided by one vendor but not another were given. This has immediate implications for attempts to compare use between services or to get an overall picture of e-book uptake as a whole across the range of subscriptions, which is typical for the majority of libraries. For example, it is unlikely that a library could generate an average session duration for all e-book use because this metric is not supplied by all vendors. Some vendors present the entire book as a single downloaded file whereas others count chapters or entries as separately downloaded sections (Shepherd, 2006). Exactly what constitutes a section is another variable. For Oxford Reference Online "full-content units requested" correspond to the number of discrete entries viewed in its constituent reference works, but five print pages viewed online is the measure for Oxford Scholarship Online. Safari sections typically correspond to three pages of the printed book, though there is no differentiation by section in NetLibrary which simply counts "accesses" to a title.

At the heart of these inconsistencies is the range of different access models offered by e-book vendors and, in particular, restrictions on use generated by digital rights management (DRM) policies. DRM is more complex for e-books than e-journals owing to publishers' concerns about possible loss of print revenue for academic textbooks especially. Rice provides an overview of e-book licensing models (Rice, 2006) and Ferguson (C. Ferguson, 2006, 2007) summarizes practice with regard to user-permitted printing, downloading, and copy-paste activity. Restrictions such as allowing only the printing of one page at a time (e.g., NetLibrary), not supporting downloading (e.g., ACLS Humanities E-books), or disallowing copying and pasting (e.g., informaworld) inevitably impact on user behavior. Usage reporting, as well as being subject to variation according to the access model used by different vendors, only reflects the extent of actual permitted use rather than full potential activity. DRM significantly affects opportunities for comparing usage across e-book platforms.

Sessions and searches represent further areas of frustration, although the issues here are not exclusive to e-book services. Vendors may set different timeout periods, effectively resulting in different definitions of a session. Blecic, Fiscella, and Wiberley (2007), in a study of e-resources, generally found variations of from five to 30 minutes among six e-resource vendors questioned. Such variations will affect the numbers of sessions and turnaways counted by different vendors. The same study also noted the tendency for federated searching to inflate the number of sessions counted, resulting in a lowering of the search-per-session ratio. This may be a greater issue for databases but is worth bearing in mind for e-books, too, as is another variable among vendors with regard to the counting or non-counting of zero-hit searches, which was also noted in this study. Reporting of zero-hit searches and the terms used can help in understanding user experience but is rare. Frustratingly, Safari no longer offers this facility whereas EEBO reports the number of such searches but does not indicate which search terms were used.

Returning to search sessions, it is worth remembering that one session may represent many users. The notes on EEBO's usage statistics point out that a session begins when a new user starts to use EEBO and ends when the browser they are using is closed. It is possible, for example, that a public-use workstation could support a number of users in the same session. Furthermore, all sessions, consecutive or otherwise, on such a workstation might only be counted as a single access by some vendors. Duy and Vaughan noted ProQuest's practice of only counting visits from unique IP addresses (2003). Their study excluded e-books but noted variations between local and vendor counting of sessions, as did Ferguson and Chan (A. Ferguson and Chan, 2005), whereas Blecic et al. reported significant differences in session and search counts between vendor-specific and COUNTER-compliant statistics for the same e-resources at the same time periods (2007). The work of Project COUNTER is described later, but the clear message is that interpretation of e-book and other e-resource usage statistics needs to be done with caution and a clear understanding of how usage is measured by the vendor. A further consideration, and one that COUNTER has striven to address, is the possibility of double-counting when a title is available through an aggregator service such as MyiLibrary but its publisher also reports usage.

FIGURE 4. *Safari* Reports List (Partial) (http://www.safaribooksonline.com/)

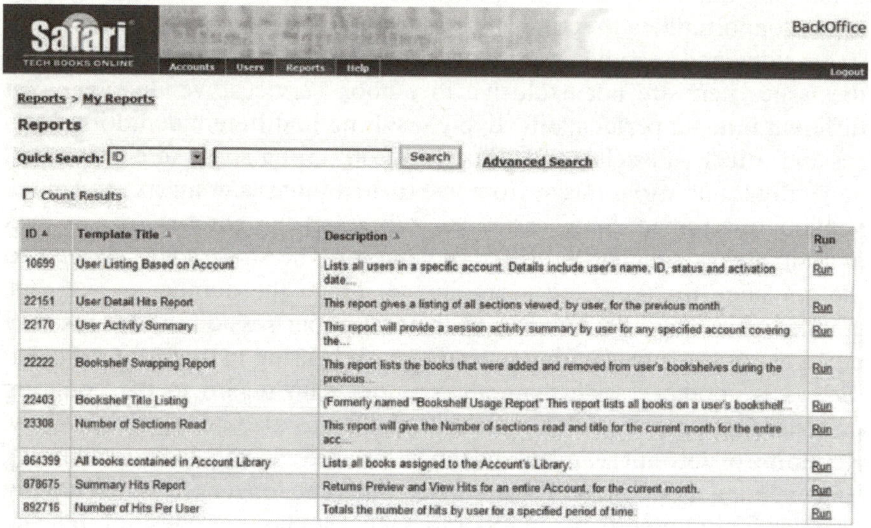

ID	Template Title	Description	Run
10699	User Listing Based on Account	Lists all users in a specific account. Details include user's name, ID, status and activation date...	Run
22151	User Detail Hits Report	This report gives a listing of all sections viewed, by user, for the previous month	Run
22170	User Activity Summary	This report will provide a session activity summary by user for any specified account covering the...	Run
22222	Bookshelf Swapping Report	This report lists the books that were added and removed from user's bookshelves during the previous...	Run
22403	Bookshelf Title Listing	(Formerly named "Bookshelf Usage Report" This report lists all books on a user's bookshelf...	Run
23308	Number of Sections Read	This report will give the Number of sections read and title for the current month for the entire acc...	Run
864399	All books contained in Account Library	Lists all books assigned to the Account's Library.	Run
878675	Summary Hits Report	Returns Preview and View Hits for an entire Account, for the current month.	Run
892716	Number of Hits Per User	Totals the number of hits by user for a specified period of time.	Run

Collecting and analyzing e-book usage data is hard work. McLuckie observes that some usage statistics for e-books are sent by e-mail, others have to be downloaded from a vendor Web site, and some may need to be requested by the subscriber (McLuckie, 2005). For vendors who provide a Web site for usage data report generation, there is a need to schedule visits at appropriate intervals and to know a range of usernames, passwords, and URLs. Choosing the right report can be a challenge, as in the case of Safari (Fig. 4), but at least the element of choice is welcome. In other instances, there is only a predefined standard report available and subscribers have very little flexibility. EEBO and Oxford Reference Online are examples, and neither service offers data for individual titles within it, greatly limiting possibilities for analysis.

Downloading to third-party software for further manipulation may be necessary, and Wilkins describes the supplementary use of spreadsheets to keep track of annual cost per e-book title, to remove data for earlier but now lapsed titles, and to analyze accesses on a per-title basis (2007). Spreadsheets may assist with the generation of graphical output, which emerged as one of a number of common deficits in a *Charleston Report* informal survey of more than 100 librarians on electronic usage statistics in 2007 (The Charleston Report, 2007). There is a need to assign the right staffing resources, both in terms of time and skills, to gathering and interpreting usage data. The survey just mentioned found that the electronic resources librarian or serials librarian usually collects usage statistics and that few respondents allow student employees to undertake this function. Kidd (2005) notes the absorption of significant senior library assistant time in collecting e-resource data at Glasgow University, but Taylor-Roe and Spencer (2005) report dialogue with other libraries that do not have a staff member specifically designated to this role.

A further consumer of time is the need for liaison with vendor company personnel to clarify the specification employed for usage data and to seek improvements. Cox (2004b) reports extensive discussion with ProQuest regarding the usage data provided for Safari, while Duy and Vaughan (2003) observe that it can be difficult to locate a vendor company representative who can advise authoritatively on data interpretation. Identifying the right vendor contact may be a particular issue for e-books, as Milloy also noted a need to consult several departments when seeking project bids from e-book publishers (Milloy, 2007).

Librarians need continually to ask questions of the figures presented to them. A single book or maybe a small number of titles could account for much of the usage of an e-book service. Thus, five titles from a subscription of 64 e-books generated half (2,011 of 4,026 hits) of Safari usage at National University of Ireland, Galway between September 1 2003 and February 8 2004 (Cox, 2004a). A significant proportion of titles had no use or very limited uptake, a factor to be considered in assessing the overall success of the subscription. Langston (2003) notes that the apparently strong uptake of e-books in anatomy and physiology at California State University was almost entirely the result of intensive use of a single title that accounted for 121 of 143 uses in that subject between March and December, 2001. He also advises against the over-reliance on reports by subject in NetLibrary, noting the very general headings used and the assignment of a heavily-used computer software manual to the business and economics category rather than to computer science. Another point to make sure of is that accesses to unsubscribed content in a service are not included in its overall hit counts or can at least be easily separated from the total. Remember also that not all e-books are equal. Different patterns of use can be expected between historic works, such as those included in EEBO, reference titles in Oxford Reference Online, and textbooks in NetLibrary, all reported in Safley's study (2006).

E-book usage data leave many questions unanswered. The number of turnaways is of interest but, with the exception of Safari, there is often no further information regarding the time of day when they occurred or the number of users locked out at the same time. Information about on- or off-campus use would be welcome, but ebrary is an exception in providing details of calling IP address. As noted at the end of the previous section, the biggest frustration lies in trying to employ usage statistics to understand meaningfully the actual user experience or satisfaction with e-books. How many sessions, hits, or downloads represent success from the viewpoint of the user or indeed the subscribing library? The point is neatly summarized in the summary of responses to the e-resources usage statistics survey in *The Charleston Report* already mentioned: "The stats are purely quantitative. They don't tell you whether the users got the information they were looking for, whether it was enough, too much, etc." (The Charleston Report, 2007). It is necessary to use other methods to get a deeper understanding of e-book usage and users.

BEYOND USAGE STATISTICS

Surveys of e-book users represent the most common way of supplementing the numerical picture provided by usage data. They can provide deeper insights into user demographics, levels of satisfaction, and actual nature of use. California State University, as reported by Langston (2003) encountered limitations with usage statistics and also conducted a voluntary online survey when evaluating NetLibrary during 2001. This survey gleaned information on user profile, location of use, routes to e-book discovery, and satisfaction levels. A generally positive view of e-books emerged. Levine-Clark (2007) used a general survey of awareness and usage of e-books at the University of Denver in 2005 to establish usage patterns specific to the arts and humanities, exploring issues such as discovery, frequency of use, reasons for use, e-book collections used, and format preference between print and online. There was an overall preference for print from this survey population, along with a focus on content rather than software features. The Irish university libraries surveyed users, mainly in IT subjects, of the Safari service in 2004 to assess user satisfaction and reasons for use but with a focus on support for learning activities (Cox, 2004b). Respondents reported high satisfaction with coverage, varying knowledge of software functions, and differences in purpose of use between students and academics. The learning support section of the survey revealed consultation of a wider range of books in Safari than in the library, along with definite views that Safari had improved respondents' work and saved time.

A more recent survey of more than 1,800 faculty at the University of London (Rowlands, Nicholas, Jamali, and Huntington, 2007) forms part of the SuperBook project conducted by the Centre for Information Behaviour and the Evaluation of Research (CIBER) team and featuring more than 3,000 e-books contributed by Oxford University Press, Wiley Interscience, and Taylor & Francis. The survey examined patterns of current e-book use according to age group, gender, and academic status along with format preference, purpose of reading, discovery routes, and awareness of library e-book provision. One of the interesting findings in this particular survey was considerably higher uptake of e-books by males. Conflicting messages emerged regarding format preference, however. In one section of the survey users claimed a strong preference for reading from screen rather than paper but later reported a definite preference for hard copy in terms of ease of use. As noted by the authors, this highlights a weakness in surveys in that they deliver data on reported rather than actual behavior.

CIBER has been at the forefront of research into actual user behavior through its use of deep log analysis, initially for e-journals but now e-books, too. For e-books, Connaway and Snyder (2005) offered a precursor to this work by publishing the results of a transaction log analysis of NetLibrary usage. They studied raw transaction logs from NetLibrary on a given date, February 26, in 2002, 2003, and 2004 and were able to obtain information often unavailable from vendor-supplied e-book usage statistics. This included number of unique users, peak times of day, length of time on the site and within an e-book, and the number of unique pages viewed per session. Extraction of the data proved to be a large and time-consuming effort, and it is not surprising that log analysis has been undertaken by research teams rather than by individuals or by library staff.

The deep log analysis technique developed by CIBER was able to go a step farther by correlating usage data and demographic user data in a study of the Blackwell Synergy e-journals service (Nicholas, Huntington, and Watkinson, 2005). This service required user login, enabling the characterization of users according to academic status, geographical location, and institutional affiliation. The deep log analysis employed in this study examined "site penetration," including types of item viewed, referral link used, and subject of journal searched, along with repeat visitor identification and activity.

Advantages claimed for this technique include its inclusion of all users, as opposed to the tendency in surveys to limit to a sample or self-selected population, and the focus on actual behavior rather than self-reported activity, which may be influenced by a range of factors including questionnaire design. It is limited, however, in terms of explaining behavior but is effective in identifying issues for further examination through surveys or other methods.

Deep log analysis is now being applied to studies of e-book usage, including the SuperBook project already mentioned, where it has delivered a number of insights into the usage of Oxford Scholarship Online at University College London, as reported for the period January–March 2007 (Nicholas et al., 2007). Compared with e-journals, findings in this particular study included more intensive use and greater consultation of older titles. Cataloged titles were found to be much more likely to be used, while examination of use according to sub-networks enabled some analysis by subject and according to on- or off-campus location.

Another application for deep log analysis and other forms of user study will be in the Joint Information Systems Committee (JISC) national e-books observatory project in the United Kingdom (JISC Collections, 2007). This project commenced in mid-2007 and aims to study e-book usage at U.K. higher education institutions in depth, focusing on a collection of 36 titles, including some of the most popular texts in business studies and management, medicine, engineering and media studies, accessible via the MyiLibrary and Books@Ovid platforms. The project will include a deep log analysis study by CIBER as part of the overall effort to understand e-book user needs and behavior and the impact of e-books on teaching and learning practices and on library print circulation data, as well as to inform promotional activity, pricing, and licensing. There will be student and academic focus groups, interviews with librarians, and a final user questionnaire, making for a multifaceted approach to delivering insights into e-book usage and information-seeking behavior by users.

A further technique to note is direct observation of users. Hernon and others report a study of e-book use by undergraduates in nursing, literature, and economics at Simmons College in Boston (Hernon, Hopper, Leach, Saunders, and Zhang, 2007). This study involved direct observation and interviewing of 15 students who were undertaking an assignment in each of the three disciplines. Participants used a think-aloud protocol to describe what they were doing and why; notes were taken to document their actions, and the interviews provided some further insight. The study encompassed a range of e-book services and probed awareness, reasons for use, services used, and activity such as browsing, printing, downloading, and annotation. Improvements in the layout of e-books by publishers in order to facilitate online reading and in the presentation of resource discovery facilities by libraries emerged as areas for further action.

COUNTER AND SUSHI: A BETTER FUTURE?

Two standardization initiatives promise valuable progress in addressing some of the current difficulties with e-book usage statistics. The first of these is Project COUNTER (COUNTER, 2007). COUNTER initially focused its efforts on e-journals. It built on earlier work by the International Coalition of Library Consortia (ICOLC) which originally published its *Guidelines for Statistical Measures of Web-Based Information Resources* in 1998, with further revisions in 2001 and 2006 (International Coalition of Library Consortia, 2006). ICOLC identified five key data elements to be included in usage reports, namely numbers of sessions, searches, menu selections, full-content units accessed, and turnaways. It also defined delivery parameters, including Web-based access within 15 days of the end of the preceding month. Oxford University Press is an example of an ICOLC-compliant e-book publisher. Unfortunately, the ICOLC guidelines were not mandatory, and vendors chose to interpret them in a variety of ways. In 2003, COUNTER published the first release of its *Code of Practice for Journals and Databases*, followed by Release 2 in April 2006. COUNTER is a collaborative venture between publishers, intermediaries, and libraries. This approach has enabled it to secure agreement on definitions for formerly vaguely used terminology and to get buy-in from vendors for the generation of standard user reports. Vendors are keen to advertise COUNTER compliance, and 100 have met the requirements of the code for journals and databases.

The success of COUNTER with e-journals provided an excellent springboard for an expansion of its work to e-books, leading to the publication of the *COUNTER Code of Practice for Books and Reference Works* in March 2006. As described by Shepherd, the same collaborative approach used for e-journals guided this initiative (Shepherd, 2006). The task was less straightforward than for e-journals owing to the more diverse range of publishing and access models for e-books. As a result, the code has had to take account of situations where only a whole book could be downloaded or where content might be presented in smaller units such as chapters or entries such as dictionary definitions (all grouped by COUNTER under the term *section*).

Its first two reports, therefore, provide separately for the number of title and section requests by month and title, with the remaining reports focusing on the number of turnaways and total searches and sections. For each report there are tight definitions of the terminology used and specific requirements to be met in generating the usage reports, including protocols applicable when aggregators and gateways are involved. An impressive feature is the requirement for third-party auditing of reports to ensure continuing compliance, reinforcing user confidence in these reports. The 38-page code, supplemented by appendices, also specifies formats for report delivery, access via a password-controlled Web site with e-mail alerts when updates occur, monthly reporting at least, and updates within 4 weeks of the end of the reporting period.

COUNTER at least offers the prospect of comparable usage statistics from a range of vendors. It has to be noted that the approach is to achieve a fairly basic standard that most vendors can meet rather than to push for a fuller range of possibilities that might be delivered only by a smaller range of vendors (Borghuis, 2005). A standard level of comparability is the aim, and its achievement will be valued by librarians. Initial progress has been frustratingly slow, however, with only 11 publishers listed on the COUNTER Web site as compliant with the e-book code more than two years after its publication. Walker, executive vice-president at Credo Reference, one of these publishers, advocates compliance, and urges publishers to "just do it" (Walker, 2007). There are reports of increased interest in the code, and it must be hoped that many more vendors will follow this lead.

The second development of note is closely linked with COUNTER. The Standardized Usage Statistics Harvesting Initiative (SUSHI) promises to reduce significantly the labor involved in retrieving and analyzing usage data (National Information Standards Organization [NISO], 2007). This is a NISO initiative that aims to automate the delivery of COUNTER-formatted statistics. SUSHI, still a draft standard at the time of writing, is a retrieval protocol that should save the need for visiting lots of Web sites and manually downloading usage data on a vendor-by-vendor basis. It is a simple object access portal (SOAP) request-response Web services "wrapper" for the XML version of COUNTER reports. It will work best with an electronic resource management (ERM) system acting as the client, thus facilitating the downloading of usage data into a system already populated with bibliographic, financial, and licensing data. This offers the possibility of automatic analysis of subject, cost, and cost-per-use data, with the potential for more detailed and extensive calculations than heretofore (Hendricks, 2007). The prospects are certainly exciting, but these are early days, and there is a need for further development in terms of support for SUSHI among a critical mass of publishers and also of ERM capability and adoption.

CONCLUSION

Making sense of e-book usage data is a complex process and demands persistence and flexibility on the part of librarians. Assembling the data available from vendors involves considerable effort, but the real work begins only with trying to analyze the data. There is a distinct lack of consistency between vendors in the data supplied, a trend further complicated by the wide range of access and licensing models on offer. DRM practices designed to protect print revenues, especially for textbooks, are a significant influence. Some vendors offer a variety of reports, whereas others deliver a single summary report with little scope for customization. Elements of data provided by one vendor are often not supplied by another, making comparison of e-book usage across a number of services difficult or impossible. Even when data appear to be comparable, it is important to establish how each vendor collects information, to ascertain what is and is not counted, and to clarify definitions for terms such as *sessions* and *downloads*. There remain many unanswered questions in terms of demographics, actual user experience, and levels of satisfaction, and it is not surprising that many libraries have used surveys to supplement usage data, while researchers have developed deep log analysis. Keeping up to date with user studies and projects is an important part of understanding the uptake and impact of e-books.

Despite their limitations, e-book usage data are essential for libraries and play a vital role in monitoring uptake and in a range of collection development and management decisions, often involving significant sums of money in the case of subscriptions or of labor as regards cataloging or promotion and training. Standardization and automation of e-book data collection, as promised by COUNTER and SUSHI, respectively, are prizes well worth fighting for, and librarians need to use their influence to accelerate progress in these domains. It is not enough to bemoan current inconsistencies and inadequacies, and there is a vital lobbying role for librarians to play in seeking improvements and supporting industry-wide initiatives. There are definitely opportunities to exert more influence with vendors by bringing usage reporting requirements to the fore in negotiating subscriptions and renewals. As e-books grow in popularity, it is clear that the importance of consistent, comprehensive and accurate usage data will also increase. Though frustrations will endure in the immediate term, improvements are certainly attainable.

REFERENCES

Bailey, T. P. (2006). Electronic book usage at a Master's Level I university: A longitudinal study. *The Journal of Academic Librarianship, 32*(1), 52–59.

Blecic, D. D., Fiscella, J. B., & Wiberley, S. E. (2007). Measurement of use in electronic resources: advances in use statistics and innovations in resource functionality. *College & Research Libraries, 68*(1), 26–44.

Borghuis, M. (2005). How COUNTER continues to help librarians and vendors make sense of usage reports [Electronic version]. *Library Connect, 7,* 8–9. Retrieved from <http://libraryconnect.elsevier.com/lcp/0701/lcp070112.html>.

Christianson, M., & Aucoin, M. (2005). Electronic or print books: Which are used? *Library Collections, Acquisitions, and Technical Services, 29*(1), 71–81.

Connaway, L. S., & Snyder, C. (2005). Transaction log analyses of electronic book (E-book) usage. *Against the Grain, 17*(1), 85–93.

COUNTER (2007). COUNTER: Counting Online Usage of NeTworked Electronic Resources. Retrieved October 26, 2007, from <http://www.projectcounter.org>.

Cox, J. (2004a). *E-books in support of a new learner environment.* Paper presented at the IUISC 2004: Irish Universities Information Services Colloquium. Retrieved October 26, 2007, from <http://www.iuisc.ie/2004/presentations/Thursday/John%20Cox.pdf>.

Cox, J. (2004b). E-books: Challenges and opportunities [Electronic version]. *D-Lib Magazine, 10.* Retrieved October 26, 2007, from <http://www.dlib.org/dlib/october04/cox/10cox.html>.

Dillon, D. (2001a). E-books: The University of Texas experience, part 1. *Library Hi Tech, 19*(2), 113–124.

Dillon, D. (2001b). E-books: The University of Texas experience, part 2. *Library Hi Tech, 19*(4), 350–362.

Duy, J., & Vaughan, L. (2003). Usage data for electronic resources: A comparison between locally collected and vendor-provided statistics. *Journal of Academic Librarianship, 29*(1), 16–22.

ebrary Inc. (2007). *ebrary's global eBook survey.* Retrieved October 26, 2007, from <http://www.ebrary.com/>.

Ferguson, A., & Chan, G. R. Y. C. (2005). Usage statistics at Hong Kong University: From fun to fundamental in just a few years [Electronic version]. *Library Connect, 7,* 4–5. Retrieved October 26, 2007, from <http://libraryconnect.elsevier.com/lcp/0701/lcp070104.html>.

Ferguson, C. (2006). Technology left behind—eBook rollout. *Against the Grain, 18*(5), insert.

Ferguson, C. (2007). Technology left behind: The second eBook rollout [Electronic version]. *Against the Grain, 19.* Retrieved October 26, 2007, from <http://www.against-the-grain.com/_old/ebookrollout/>.

Hendricks, A. (2007). SUSHI, not just a tasty lunch anymore: The development of the NISO Committee SU's SUSHI standard. *Library Hi Tech, 25*(3), 422–429.

Hernon, P., Hopper, R., Leach, M. R., Saunders, L. L., & Zhang, J. (2007). E-book use by students: Undergraduates in economics, literature, and nursing. *The Journal of Academic Librarianship, 33*(1), 3–13.

International Coalition of Library Consortia. (2006). Revised guidelines for statistical measures of usage of web-based information resources, October 4, 2006. Retrieved October 26, 2007, from <http://www.library.yale.edu/consortia/webstats06.htm>.

JISC Collections. (2007). JISC national e-books observatory project. Retrieved May 12, 2008, from <http://www.jiscebooksproject.org>.

Kidd, T. (2005). Usage statistics and how we're using them: The example of Glasgow University [Electronic version]. *Library Connect, 7*, 3. Retrieved October 26, 2007, from <http://libraryconnect.elsevier.com/lcp/0701/lcp070102.html>.

Langston, M. (2003). The California State University E-book Pilot Project: Implications for cooperative collection development. *Library Collections, Acquisitions, and Technical Services, 27*(1), 19–32.

Levine-Clark, M. (2007). Electronic books and the humanities: A survey at the University of Denver. *Collection Building, 26*(1), 7–14.

Littman, J., & Connaway, L. S. (2004). A circulation analysis of print books and e-books in an academic research library. *Library Resources and Technical Services, 48*(4), 256–262.

McLuckie, A. (2005). E-books in an academic library: Implementation at the ETH Library, Zurich. *Electronic Library, 23*(1), 92–102.

Milloy, C. (2007). E-books: Setting up the national observatory project. *Library and Information Update, 6*(11), 32–33.

National Information Standards Organization. (2007). NISO Standardized Usage Statistics Harvesting Initiative (SUSHI). Retrieved October 26, 2007, from <http://www.niso.org/committees/SUSHI/SUSHI_comm.html>.

Nicholas, D., Huntington, P., & Rowlands, I. (2007). E-books: How are users responding? *Library and Information Update, 6*(11), 29–31.

Nicholas, D., Huntington, P., & Watkinson, A. (2005). Scholarly journal usage: the results of deep log analysis. *Journal of Documentation, 61*(2), 248–280.

Rice, S. (2006). Own or rent? A survey of eBook licensing models. *Against the Grain, 18*(3), 28–29.

Rowlands, I., Nicholas, D., Jamali, H. R., & Huntington, P. (2007). What do faculty and students really think about e-books? *Aslib Proceedings, 59*(6), 489–511.

Safley, E. (2006). Demand for e-books in an academic library. *Journal of Library Administration, 45*(3–4), 445–457.

Shepherd, P. T. (2006). The COUNTER Code of Practice for books and reference works. *Serials, 19*(1), 23–27.

Taylor-Roe, J., & Spencer, C. (2005). A librarian's view of usage metrics: Through a glass darkly? *Serials, 18*(2), 124–131.

The Charleston Report. (2007). TCR electronic surveys: electronic resource usage statistics. *The Charleston Report, 11*(5), 3.

Walker, J. (2007). COUNTER: Getting the measure of ebooks [Electronic version]. *eLucidate, 4*, 3–7. Retrieved October 26, 2007, from <http://www.ukeig.org.uk/>.

Wilkins, V. (2007). Managing e-books at the University of Derby: A case study. *Program: Electronic Library and Information Systems, 41*(3), 238–251.

Williams, K. C., & Best, R. (2006). E-Book usage and the Choice outstanding academic book list: Is there a correlation? *Journal of Academic Librarianship, 32*(5), 474–478.

Appendix. E-book Services Cited

Title	URL
ACLS Humanities E-Books	http://www.humanitiesebook.org
Books@Ovid	http://www.ovid.com/site/products/books_landing.jsp
Early English Books Online	http://eebo.chadwyck.com/
Ebook Library	http://www.eblib.com/
Ebrary	http://www.ebrary.com/
Eighteenth Century Collections Online	http://gale.cengage.com/EighteenthCentury/
informaworld	http://www.informaworld.com/
MyiLibrary	http://www.myilibrary.com/
NetLibrary	http://www.oclc.org/netlibrary/
Oxford English Dictionary	http://www.oed.com/
Oxford Reference Online	http://www.oxfordreference.com/
Oxford Scholarship Online	http://www.oxfordscholarship.com/
Safari	http://www.safaribooksonline.com/

ebrary and Two International E-book Surveys

Marty Mullarkey

ebrary is one of the first players in the e-book market, serving the library and publishing communities since 1999. The company continues to expand its product line, and as of November, 2007, has more than 1,200 library customers representing more than 12 million end-users throughout the world.

To better understand the needs of the library community with regard to e-books and electronic resources, ebrary conducted two informal surveys in 2007. The first, *Global E-book Survey*, conducted in Spring, 2007, was completed by 580 librarians throughout the world. The second, *2007 Global Faculty E-book Survey*, designed by more than 200 librarians and announced in Fall, 2007, was completed by more than 900 faculty members. ebrary intends to conduct similar surveys on an annual or biannual basis.

This article provides a brief history of ebrary and examines the results of both international e-book surveys.

- Section 1: A brief history of ebrary
- Section 2: ebrary's *Global E-book Survey*
- Section 3: Analysis of the *Global E-book Survey* results by Allen McKiel, then Director of Libraries, Northeastern State University
- Section 4: ebrary's *2007 Global Faculty E-book Survey*
- Section 5: Analysis of the *2007 Global Faculty E-book Survey* results by Allen McKiel, then Director of Libraries, Northeastern State University

A BRIEF HISTORY OF EBRARY

The idea for ebrary was spawned in 1990, when Christopher Warnock, ebrary's CEO, wanted to build a recumbent bicycle while studying at the University of Utah. Mr. Warnock went to the university's Marriott Library to research his project, but had a challenging time finding the information he needed. At the time, half of the titles were in the printed card catalogue and half were in the library's newly released OPAC system. Furthermore, engineering books were stored in the basement, books about bikes in general were on the third floor, and periodicals were on the fourth floor in microfiche.

"The only information I could find, easily, was information that I already knew about," said Mr. Warnock. "The titles were either not where the OPAC system said they were, or not what I had hoped they would be about."

"Finally, I found a book on gear ratios. I remember thinking that the information I needed was somewhere in the book, but that I would have to change my major from Philosophy to Engineering, just to understand what it was that I needed to know," said Mr. Warnock. "I thought: at some point, all of this information would be accessible from the computer. I also realized that since the majority of publishers use PDF during the print production process, this would be the most cost-effective format for searching, sharing and archiving electronic content."

Nine years later, that idea evolved into ebrary. Based in Palo Alto, CA, ebrary was founded in 1999 by Christopher Warnock, Kevin Sayar, President, and Mohamad Al-Baghdadi, Vice President, International Sales. ebrary first developed its platform, which turns industry-standard PDF files into highly interactive databases of content with features geared toward conducting research. The company then simultaneously began forming partnerships with leading publishers and aggregating e-books and other authoritative content.

In 2001, the company launched its first product, which was a database of approximately 300 business and economics e-books available under a pay-per-use model, where patrons paid to either copy or print text. There was a revenue share component between the library, ebrary, and the publisher. Over the course of the year, ebrary received feedback from the market that its pay-per-use model was not ideal, as the libraries were not capable of receiving money, nor did they wish to charge their patrons directly. ebrary's business model evolved to enable libraries to subsidize payments on behalf of their patrons, but the libraries had issues with budgeting for use.

"We heard loud and clear from the market that a pay-per-use model, at that time, was not suitable primarily due to challenges associated with budget allocation," said Mr. Sayar. "It was difficult for libraries to plan ahead, especially for something as brand new and 'experimental' as e-books." On the basis of feedback from the market, in 2002 ebrary began offering e-book database subscriptions under a simultaneous, multi-user access model—very different from the traditional, single-user download model available at the time. The company continued to increase its product line over the next several years, with a primary focus on the academic market. As of November 2007, there are more than 150,000 e-books and other titles in the ebrary system, available from more than 285 leading publishers and content aggregators.

In 2006, owing to further market feedback and demand, ebrary developed a perpetual access offering, where libraries can purchase and own individual titles. Unlike other perpetual access offerings, the company offers single-user access as well as simultaneous, multi-user access. In addition to licensing and selling content, ebrary licenses its e-content platform to companies that need to market and distribute their own content online, such as the McGraw-Hill Companies, Blackwell Book Services, Stanford University, Cyberlibris, Gibson Library Connections, and Duke University Press.

"Today, libraries and other organizations have a choice of subscribing to or purchasing ebrary's content and distributing their own content using a single platform that is seamless to the end-user," said Mr. Sayar. Future developments at ebrary include a Java-based Reader (in beta as of November 2007), a redesigned interface that is more intuitive and useful, and a licensed version of its platform that the organizations own and maintain behind their own firewall. These and other ebrary initiatives were validated by feedback generated from the company's *Global E-book Survey*.

(Additional information about ebrary is available at www.ebrary.com.)

EBRARY'S GLOBAL E-BOOK SURVEY

In Spring 2007, ebrary developed its *Global E-book Survey* to better understand the needs of the library community with regard to e-books and electronic resources. It was an informal survey, and ebrary never intended to make it publicly available. The survey questions were developed by ebrary's marketing team and created using the online tool Survey Monkey.

ebrary distributed the survey by posting a link on the home page and via email to its newsletter distribution list, which reaches approximately 7,000 librarians and information professionals in the United States, and 6,000 in the rest of the world, representing approximately 2,600 institutions. Within a month, 583 librarians and information professionals completed the survey.

"We were genuinely surprised by the response and felt that it would be doing the library and publishing communities a disservice if we did not share the results with the public," said Mr. Sayar. Hence, the results are included in this volume.

Survey ebrary Results

OVERVIEW OF SURVEY RESPONDENTS

Total number of respondents: 583
Total number of individual libraries: 552

Types of institutions

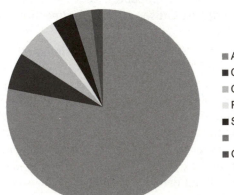

- Academic(77)
- Corporate(6)
- Government(5)
- Public(4)
- Special(3)
- -12(3)
- Other(2)

Role in the library

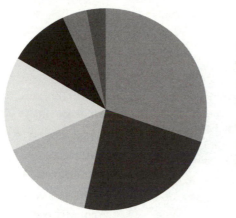

- Librarian(30)
- Director(23)
- ElectronicResour ces(15)
- Other(15)
- CollectionDevelopm ent(10)
- Acquisitions(4)
- TechnicalSer vices(3)

Total number of participating countries: 67

US   **52%**
Non-US   **48%**

Respondents by Region

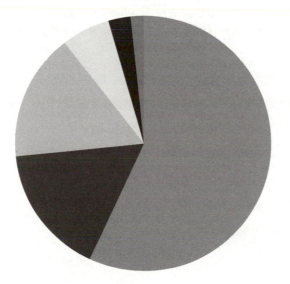

- NorthAmerica(56)
- Europe(17)
- Asia(16)
- Africa(6)
- MiddleEast(3)
- LatinAmerica(2)

USAGE OF EBOOKS

1. How many eBooks do libraries subscribe to or own?

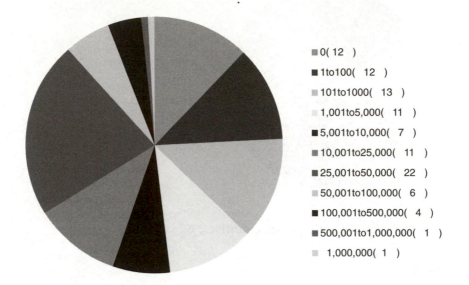

- 0(12)
- 1to100(12)
- 101to1000(13)
- 1,001to5,000(11)
- 5,001to10,000(7)
- 10,001to25,000(11)
- 25,001to50,000(22)
- 50,001to100,000(6)
- 100,001to500,000(4)
- 500,001to1,000,000(1)
- 1,000,000(1)

2. How do patrons find eBooks?

Respondents rated each item on a scale of 1 to 5, where 1 = most common and 5 = least common. The above chart indicates the average response for each item.

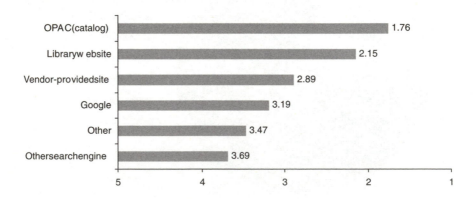

OPAC(catalog)	1.76
Libraryw ebsite	2.15
Vendor-providedsite	2.89
Google	3.19
Other	3.47
Othersearchengine	3.69

3. How is eBook usage overall?

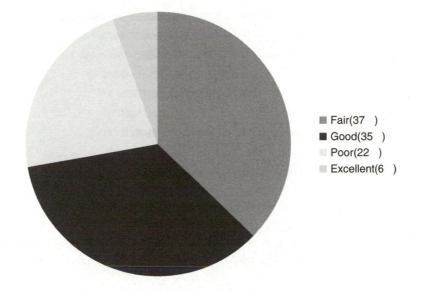

■ Fair(37)
■ Good(35)
  Poor(22)
  Excellent(6)

4. What drives eBook usage?

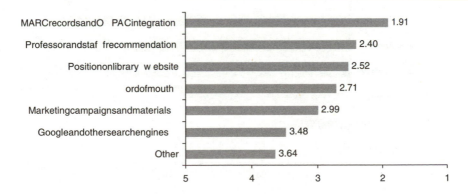

Respondents rated each item on a scale of 1 to 5, where 1 = most prevalent and 5 = least prevalent. The above chart indicates the average response for each item.

5. What inhibits eBook usage?

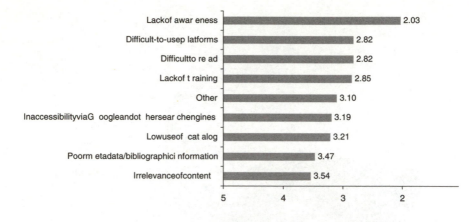

*Respondents rated each item on a scale of 1 to 5, where 1= most prevalent
and 5 = least prevalent. The above chart indicates the average response
for each item.*

6. What decisions do usage statistics influence?

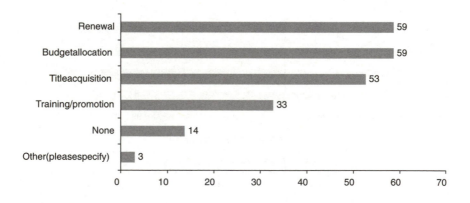

*Respondents indicated all of the items that apply. The above chart illus-
trates the percentage of respondents who selected each item.*

"Other" responses included the following:

Need for cataloging
Number of licenses
Facilities and equipment
Library hours

INTEGRATION

7. How important is the ability to integrate eBooks with other library resources and information on the web?

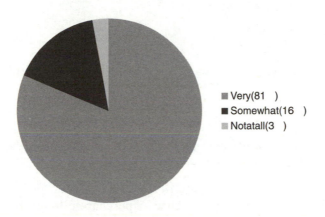

- Very(81)
- Somewhat(16)
- Notatall(3)

8. How are libraries currently integrating their electronic resources?

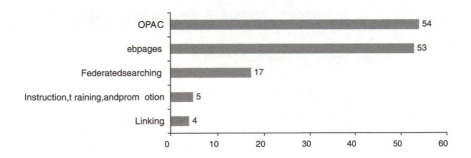

Respondents indicated all of the items that apply. The above chart illustrates the percentage of respondents who selected each item.

PURCHASE DRIVERS AND INHIBITORS

9. From which vendors do libraries purchase or subscribe to eBooks?

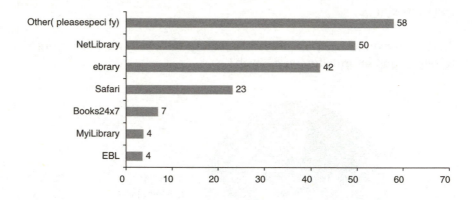

Respondents selected all items that apply. The above chart illustrates the percentage of respondents who selected each item.

10. In what cases does it make sense to purchase eBooks directly from publishers?

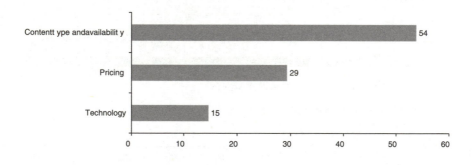

The above chart shows the percentage of respondents who indicated items in each category.

11. Do libraries intentionally duplicate print and electronic titles?

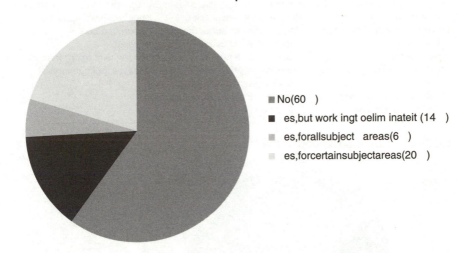

■ No(60)
■ es,but work ingt oelim inateit (14   )
■ es,forallsubject   areas(6)
  es,forcertainsubjectareas(20   )

Respondents were asked to describe which subject areas are most appropriate for duplicating print and electronic, and the responses varied significantly. No single subject area stood out. Some respondents did note duplication occurred for certain programs, out of student and faculty requests, and when usage is high.

12. Under which business models do libraries prefer to acquire eBooks?

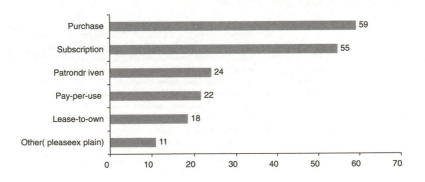

Respondents selected all items that apply. The above chart illustrates the percentage of respondents who selected each item.

"Other" responses included the following:

Depends on the specific title, collection or subject area	Purchase for high-use titles	Pay up front then pay a small ongoing maintenance fee depending on the number of titles
Depends on the platform or hosting fee for purchased titles	Purchase for newer titles	
	Pay-per-view or subscription for titles used over a defined time period	
Subscribe for big collections		Purchase with minor fees for updates if necessary
Free	Depends on price and convenience	
Purchase for recommended and requested titles	Combination of subscription and pay-per-use	

13. Are eBook models confusing?   .

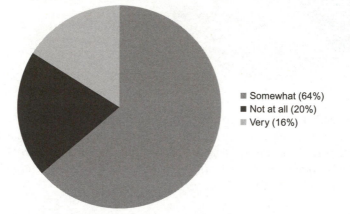

■ Somewhat (64%)
■ Not at all (20%)
■ Very (16%)

14. What are the most important things libraries look for when SUB-SCRIBING to an electronic database?

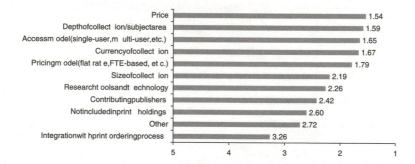

Respondents rated each item on a scale of 1 to 5, where 1 = most important and 5 = least important. The above chart indicates the average response for each item.

Other responses included the following:

Ease-of-use Functionality of interface	Recommendations Choosing specific
Relevance to user needs/programs	titles Bibliographies Content updates
Consortia agreement	
Overlap/uniqueness	

15. What are the most important things libraries look for when PUR-CHASING electronic titles?

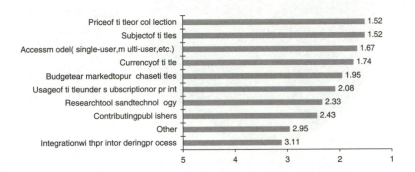

Respondents rated each item on a scale of 1 to 5, where 1 = most important and 5 = least important. The above chart indicates the average response for each item.

16. How important is interlibrary loan for eBooks?

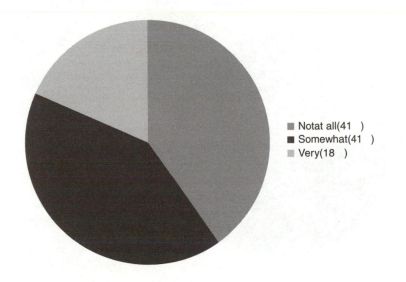

17. How important is Linux to the library community?

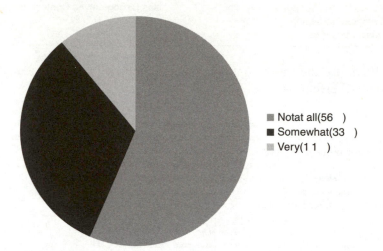

- Notat all(56)
- Somewhat(33)
- Very(1 1)

DIGITIZATION AND DELIVERY OF LIBRARIES' OWN ECONTENT

18. Are libraries digitizing their own content?

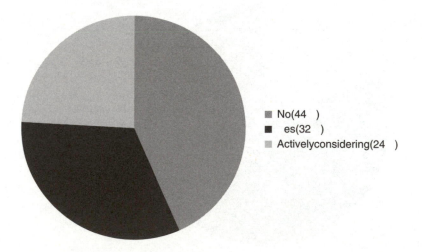

- No(44)
- es(32)
- Activelyconsidering(24)

19. What types of content are libraries digitizing?

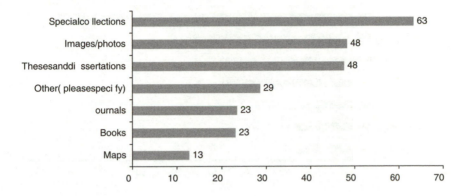

Respondents selected all items that apply. The above chart illustrates the percentage of respondents who selected each item.

"Other" responses included the following:

Internal documents (faculty correspondence, bulletins, etc)	Video
	Articles
Institutional publications	Technical manuals and reports
Audio	Government documents
Archives	Reports and research papers
Campus newspapers	Books and book chapters
Other newspapers	

20. How are libraries planning to digitize content?

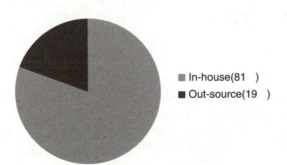

- In-house(81)
- Out-source(19)

21. What output option(s) are libraries using for their digitized content?

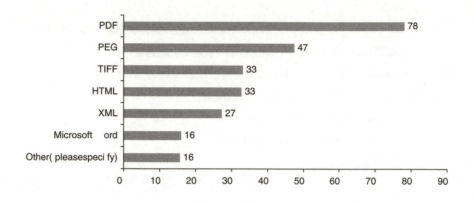

Respondents selected all items that apply. The above chart illustrates the percentage of respondents who selected each item.

22. What platform(s) are libraries using or considering to host and deliver content?

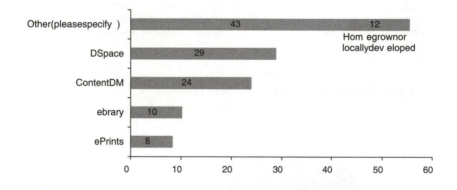

Respondents selected all items that apply. The above chart illustrates the percentage of respondents who selected each item.
*The majority of "other" responses were a variety of individual vendors. Just two vendors were written in more than once: Greenstone (nine write-ins) and ProQuest (five write-ins).

23. What metadata standards do libraries plan to support for their digitization efforts?

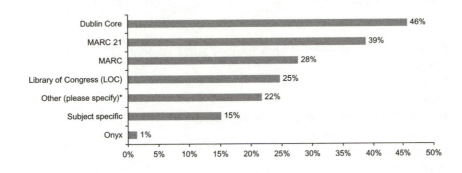

Respondents selected all items that apply. The above chart illustrates the percentage of respondents who selected each item.
*MODS and METS were indicated most frequently in the "other" category with five write-ins each.

24. What do librarians need from a delivery platform?

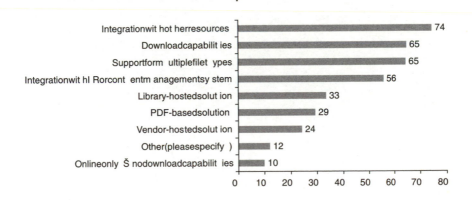

Respondents selected all items that apply. The above chart illustrates the percentage of respondents who selected each item.

"Other" responses included the following:

Appropriate search and retrieval
Good interface/functionality
Export metadata
Access levels
ADA-compliant
Coop with other aboriginal libraries to digitize content
DRM
Excellent Reader
Music compatible
Reasonable exit strategy if data is uploaded
Easy to use and maintain
Local control
Affordable price

Survey Analysis: ebrary User Survey

Allen McKiel

INTRODUCTION

This article reviews and analyzes the informal survey that ebrary conducted in March 2007 about e-content and includes a librarian's perspective on the responses from the survey. At the time that this survey was conducted, I was the Director of Libraries for Northeastern State University in Oklahoma and have been a member of ebrary's Technical Advisory Board since its inception.

ebrary did not anticipate the level of response from the survey. It was designed informally with a lot of open-ended questions that provided a massive amount of individual responses. After helping to sort through the data, they asked me if I would be willing to share my perspectives in an article.

OVERVIEW OF SURVEY RESPONDENTS

(See Overview of Survey Respondents in the survey results)

Librarians from 552 institutions responded to the survey of 2,600 institutions invited, an institutional participation rate of 21%. The sampling of opinion and thought is roughly representative of the variety of responses available among librarians on the topics. The patterns in the responses provide some indication of the likely majority perspectives. More important, however, they are generally instructive for better understanding the phenomenon because they provide a variety of perspectives. An effort to make sense out of the data advances understanding.

Academic librarians comprised the overwhelming majority of the respondents (77%). Data on the percentages of library types invited to participate are not available; consequently neither is the relative interest that the response rates from the types of institutions would provide. However, it would be expected that academic libraries would be more interested in the survey because of the obvious suitability of an indexed collection for research. Public libraries (4% of the responses) fulfill research needs for their patrons, but they serve a much higher proportion of their patrons with content that is read cover to cover, much of it fiction. The primary mission of an academic library is the provision of content for research and teaching. Corporate (6%), government (5%), and special libraries (3%) are all counted as special libraries. Taken together, they provided 14% of the responses. They also have research concerns for which an indexed collection of e-books could be useful.

However, they have more focused research needs than the broad usefulness of e-books to an academic community. The higher percentage of academic responses necessitates that this report will be biased toward the academic library perspective.

USAGE OF E-BOOKS

Acquisition

(Question 1. How many eBooks do libraries subscribe to or own?)

Of the respondents surveyed, 88% answered that they own or subscribe to e-books, and nearly half of the respondents (45%) have access to more than 10,000 e-books. Because of the variety of marketing models, it is not easy to understand what this means in dollars spent. If the books were purchased in print, it represents approximately $420,000 of access given $42 as an average cost for an academic title—Northeastern State University

(NSU) purchased 2,373 books in 2005/6 at a cost of $98,486, an average of $41.50 per book.

Patron Access

(Question 2. How do patrons find eBooks?)

The respondents confirmed that most librarians know about access to e-books. The primary path to e-books for students and faculty is the OPAC. For librarians who are troubled by the misuse of Google and the subsequent erosion of reliance on the wealth of more curriculum-relevant resources provided by the library, this is a comforting fact. The catalog for this purpose is still the center of the information universe. For those who appreciate the power of the new search tools provided by aggregator interfaces to e-books, this finding indicates possible underutilization of a powerful tool.

Overall Usage

(Question 3. What drives eBook usage?)

If you interpret fair as good, then 78% of the respondents described e-book usage at their libraries as good to excellent, which is good. If you interpret fair as not so good, 59% of respondents found e-book usage only fair to poor. Many librarians are aware that e-book usage is not what it should be. My conversations with students concerning difficulties with e-books and a 4% discrepancy in their usage at NSU indicate to me that there is a problem. Print books are preferred by a 4% margin over electronic books by patrons. Print is used 89% of the time even though it comprises 85% of the collection. At 15% of the collection, e-books are used about 11% of the time. There are two related issues that account for most of the negative experiences and the underutilization.

The first issue is a lack of understanding of the strength of the research nature of the e-book collection. Students are judging e-books as inferior to finding and using regular books—a process that they understand well and find easy to do. They also judge e-books inferior to books because of the portability and ease of use for reading print books. It is a process they also understand well and favor over reading an e-book. The e-book collection is not primarily purchased as a collection of books that would be read cover to cover. Student attitudes concerning e-books will likely improve as they come to understand that the e-book collection at this juncture is primarily a research collection that comes with a new set of research tools. Until e-book reading devices are preferred to printed books and are commonly available, the e-book collection will not be seen as preferable when the intent is to read an entire work.

The second issue is related to the first. It concerns difficulties with the interface to the collection. Students are often just deposited into the interface without warning. The catalog is their entry point. They were likely looking for print books. When they attempt to use e-books, they expect them to be as easy as print books to access. The interfaces to e-books are fairly robust and complicated tools not easily tamed by intuitive visuals. They are also works in progress. For example, use of e-books is further complicated by the frustration many students have in dealing with the different print and copy procedures that accompany the three types of file formats available in some databases.

This situation calls for comprehensive instruction. Aggregated e-books are new and powerful tools that are not well understood by a majority of students and faculty. If they knew better how to use them, they would be more likely to respond in a manner similar to the 6% who felt e-book usage overall was excellent.

Usage Drivers

(Question 4. What drives eBook usage?)

This is a reiteration of the earlier question concerning patron access. The question can be understood as asking how students become aware of e-books. The OPAC is the primary access point to and the primary driver of e-book usage. Recommendations from professors and staff and the library Web site show up as secondary drivers in the responses. Instruction was not one of the choices; however, some of those answering "professor and staff recommendation" may have been thinking of instruction. There are other factors that may compel a patron to use e-books that were not available in the response selection and a write-in was not available to collect open-ended answers. A percentage of the respondents would likely have commented that the power of the vendor interfaces as research tools and the 24/7 availability of the collections were drivers for experienced e-book collection users.

Usage Inhibitors

(Question 5. What inhibits eBook usage?)

A fairly clear set of perceptions emerges for the choices presented. For most of the respondents, "Lack of awareness" is the primary inhibitor of e-book usage. Second place is nearly shared by "Difficult to read," "Difficult-to-use platforms," and "Lack of training." Instruction is the remedy for all of the primary and secondary inhibitors except "Difficult to read." This likely represents the preference for reading a print book, particularly if reading the entire work. The remedy is a universally available reading device that competes favorably with the printed book for portability and readability.

ebrary's analysis team noticed that although the catalog was identified in an earlier question as the main way that patrons find e-books, "Low use of the catalog" was not seen by most as a significant inhibitor. This demonstrates an underlying awareness among librarians that the catalog is at present the primary way that students find e-books. It is doing a better job promoting e-books than anything else. However, the OPAC is not the best interface for e-books. E-books need to be integrated into the catalog, but students need to know about the research nature of the e-book collection and they need to know how to use the e-book aggregator interfaces.

Usage Statistics

(Question 6. What decisions do usage statistics influence?)

The primary purpose of usage statistics for librarians has traditionally been as an aid to acquisition decisions—that is, renewal (59%), budget allocation (59%), title acquisition (53%). These were the top three responses in the survey to the question asking what decisions were influenced by usage statistics. Training (33%) took last place in the options provided. A minority of respondents acknowledged a connection between usage and training. Low usage may indicate a need for training or promotion. As instruction in the use of the expanding information sphere grows in importance in academe, and as it becomes comprehensively and systematically integrated into the curriculum, usage statistics will also likely become more important as a measure of the effectiveness of instruction. The proliferation of library-procured databases with diverse interfaces to data requires enlisting usage statistics to assess the viability of the purchase but also as an indicator for instruction. In cases where usage is low, instruction rather than cancellation might be the remedy.

Integration

(Question 7. How important is the ability to integrate eBooks with other library resources and information on the Web? Question 8. How are libraries currently integrating their electronic resources?)

At 81%, the overwhelming response to the importance of integration of e-books with other library resources and information on the Web was that it was "very" important. With respect to how libraries are currently integrating e-books into their electronic resources, the open-ended responses have been summarized into five categories and arranged in order of percentage of responders in each—OPAC (54%), Web pages (53%), Federated searching (17%), Instruction (5%), and Linking (4%). The OPAC, the library Web site, and federated searching are the most commonly understood integration points. The OPAC integrates e-books into the traditional book collection through a method already well understood by librarians and patrons. Placement on the library Web site provides direct access to the vendor e-book interface. (Some of the comments refer to the location of the link on the library Web site—that is, A-Z listings of databases, subject lists of databases.) Integration into federated searching is conceptually attractive, but the weak third position betrays a lack of faith in its efficacy. Federated search engines have a ways to go before they deliver the promise latent in the concept, particularly when mixing formats (i.e., e-journal articles and e-books).

The fourth category, instruction, with only 5% of the responses, is a fairly small showing. However, the question focuses attention on the Web-based search tools—"How does your library currently integrate its electronic resources?" Most academic library training at this point is not on the Web. It is not viewed by many as an electronic resource. Nevertheless, the small number of librarians who saw instruction as an essential integration concern, like the previous question on the application of usage statistics, demonstrates that it is a new kid on the block of library concerns.

Finally, a number of the responses seem to refer to ways in which individual e-books could be accessed through durable links (i.e. in Black-Board, course reserves, and reading lists). Linking rather than copying is becoming more common.

PURCHASE DRIVERS AND INHIBITORS

Purchasing from Publishers

Question 10. In what cases does it make sense to purchase eBooks directly from publishers?)

This was another completely open-ended question. When asked to comment on when it makes sense to purchase e-books directly from publishers, content (54% of responders) and pricing (29% of responders) compete as the underlying drivers for purchasing decisions between publishers and aggregators. Librarians purchase or subscribe from publishers or aggregators via consortia or individually with an eye on cost. However, content is the primary concern. Librarians are mandated to purchase materials that are relevant to the needs of faculty and students. The expenditure of funds is optimized through balancing cost and perceived effectiveness at addressing curricular needs. When librarians provide a one-word response, price, it does not mean that it is divorced from the content concerns.

A third driver is the effectiveness of the technology (15% of responses). The best content at the lowest price is worth having only to the extent that the technology of delivery makes it usable for faculty and students. It is less prominent in this question probably because the distribution technologies among providers of content are not perceived as critically different. The responses probably assume that purchasing directly from the publisher will meet competency expectations for e-book delivery technology and that a significantly better delivery technology would be a reason to purchase directly assuming content and cost concerns were met.

Duplicating Print and Electronic Titles

(Question 11. Do libraries intentionally duplicate print and electronic titles?)

A strong majority, 74% of the respondents, indicated that they prefer not to duplicate the purchase of print and electronic titles, and 20% indicated that they purchase both electronic and print titles for certain subject areas. The focus on subject areas in the open-ended part of the question sidetracked the issue. It hinders open-ended responses for reasons that are

independent of subject. Respondents provided a very diverse set of subjects. No obvious subject areas emerged from the data as front runners. The
wide array of subjects in the responses indicates that decisions to purchase
both electronic and print titles are not driven primarily by subject.

Three other reasons surfaced in the open-ended responses that are probably closer to the actual motivations for duplicating. First, certain programs
require print (e.g., core reading). Some programs require electronic (e.g.,
distance courses). Second, some faculty and students request a particular
format (e.g., a history professor might want students to read a complete
work). And third, some librarians responded that they purchase duplicates
when usage is high.

Preferred Acquisition Model

*(Question 12. Under which business models do libraries prefer to acquire
eBooks?)*

The top two acquisition model preferences were the purchase model
(59%) and subscription (55%). It is interesting to note that both the purchase
and subscribe options received more than 50% of the selection. Librarians
were asked to select all that applied, so some of the librarians selected both
purchase and subscription models as preferred models. However, nearly
half of the respondents selected one or the other and made an exclusive
choice. Patterns that emerged from the 60 responses in the "other" selection
provide insight into the motives for model selection and reinforce the
theme that appeared in earlier questions. Content and price interplay as
co-motivators with content as the primary driver.

The 60 responses were sorted into 12 categories (see list associated
with Question 12 in the survey results). They all refer to content and
price, or both. The preference for either the subscription model or the
purchase model depends primarily on the content needs of the institutions. It is reasonable to associate control of access to and specific selection of content as motivations associated with respondents who prefer
the purchase model. Quantity and breath of content are likely motiva-
tors associated with the subscription model. Institutions that are heavily
research-centered have a stronger need for specificity than those focused
more on teaching and general education. In either case, content concerns
are primary, with price determining the model for optimizing access to
quantity.

The lower number of responses for the patron-driven model (24%), pay-per-use (22%), and lease-to-own (18%) have to do mostly with a lack of familiarity with the models as options in the content/price optimization calculation. In general, librarians are very familiar with both purchasing and subscriptions procurement. The written responses included nine additional suggestions for models, further evidence of a desire to optimize the content/price purchasing factors through whatever method is most effective for an institution's content needs.

Are E-book Models Confusing?

(Question 13. Are eBook models confusing?)

Many of the 80% that find e-book acquisition strategies at least somewhat confusing are likely referring to the options that are available or being discussed beyond those associated with purchasing print books or subscribing to journals. Most librarians are very familiar with the purchasing and subscription models that are associated with print. They are less familiar with the new models associated with e-books (e.g., patron driven, one person viewing at a time, lease-to-own, and pay-per-view).

There are additional reasons for confusion. Librarians may understand the conditions of the models well enough. However, access to and preservation of e-content are not settled issues. The ramifications under the increased variety of acquisition models may not be well understood. Local institutional access vulnerabilities increase for vendor supplied e-content because it is subject to the vagaries of budgets. The sense of permanence and control of access provided by physical collections is not apparent in electronic access. If purchasing of print slowed or stopped for a period of time, the physical collection still remained intact and accessible. A cessation of funding under a fully e-content library would discontinue subscription access. Some see a possible advantage in this. It makes it harder for the library funding to be cut because of how painfully obvious the loss becomes. However, there is no institutional track record for this scenario. The uncertainty adds to the feeling of confusion concerning e-content acquisition. It is difficult to assess how much options that hedge against budget cuts might be worth. Even if the short-term vulnerability were addressed, the long term viability of marketplace e-content provides another level of ambiguity. Certitude with respect to access in perpetuity waits for the implementation of cooperative preservation across aggregators, publishers, libraries, governmental agencies, and private interests.

Subscription Model Concerns

(Question 14. What are the most important things libraries look for when SUBSCRIBING to an electronic database?)

Respondents ranked price and content first and second, respectively, as factors important to subscription decisions. The single-user concern was ranked third. This is both a technology issue and a pricing/content issue because it uses technology to artificially restrict access, which is counter-intuitive to the purpose of using technology to increase access at lower costs. Currency of the collection is fourth. It is another content issue. And fifth is another pricing concern, the type of pricing model. The point spread among these top five response averages is only .25 (1.54 to 1.79, with 1 being most important in a scale of 1 to 5).

Sixteen percent of the respondents, 89 of 535, contributed a comment in the "other" category. Since content and price issues were addressed as options in the question, the volunteered responses provided nuances that the respondents felt were not addressed in the question options (i.e. "relevance to user needs/programs," "consortia agreement," "overlap/uniqueness," "recommendations," "choosing specific titles," "bibliographies," "content updates"). Sixteen comments reiterated that content must be relevant to user needs and programs. Most of the "other" comments dealt with greater specificity of choice, a concern that may be related to its being the weakness of the subscription model. Seven responses addressed lower prices in the consortial agreements. Taken together, the content and price concerns indicate that librarians want greater selection to address student and faculty need at lower prices—major surprise.

The primary technology issues, accounting for 16 of the "other" comments, concerned ease of use and functionality of the interface. One specified concerns for ease of use with respect to format (i.e., PDF, HTML, plain text) and printing. This is notable because the file formats require different nuances of the print and copy commands and can be a source of frustration for patrons. Remote access garnered six votes, with one noting that 60% of their usage is off campus. Reiterating comments from earlier questions, some were concerned with integrating e-books into the OPAC, federated searching, and link resolvers (i.e., MARC, Open URL compliance, SFX). Another concern for standards that two mentioned was COUNTER-compliant usage statistics.

Purchasing Model Concerns

(Question 15. What are the most important things libraries look for when PURCHASING electronic titles?)

Price and content are again joined at the hip when librarians are asked to rank issues relevant to the purchasing model for e-books. The price of the collection and the subject of the titles are tied as the primary concerns with an average rank of 1.52 on the scale of 1 to 5 where 1 is most important. The primary directive for librarians is to optimize the availability of curriculum-relevant materials. The single-user issue again ranks third, and title currency is fourth. The subject area concern is slightly higher in the purchase model ("title selection" from the purchasing model—1.52 vs. "depth of collection" from the subscription model—1.59). The number of respondents commenting using the "other" factor dropped nearly in half, 43 of 537. Nothing significantly different from the "Subscription Model" is apparent in the open-ended responses.

Some staff at ebrary commented about the low relevance score for publisher—2.43. Perhaps value of the publisher's reputation in providing quality content is associated with the peer review process. The relative positioning of publishers because of reputation is less significant than subject area relevance. Publishers may provide status to individual faculty when they publish because of the publisher's reputation; however, the volume of publication and the number of citations to a work occurring in peer-reviewed publications is probably of more value to tenure and promotion. Faculty opinion is also important in the acquisition process. Librarians will purchase whatever titles members of the faculty indicate are relevant to the curriculum regardless of the publisher reputation. Publishers may be considered significant to purchasing to the degree that they exercise dominance in a subject area (e.g., Elsevier and science). The dominance is not generally considered library-friendly—a monopoly by any other name.

Interlibrary Loan

(Question 16. How important is interlibrary loan for eBooks?)

A majority of the respondents (59%) are somewhat to very concerned about interlibrary loan in the context of e-books. This does not necessarily mean that the respondents believe that libraries should have the ability to pass on their access rights to another library. It likely means that some librarians are concerned about access to "everything" for researchers. This after all is the primary mandate for librarians—providing access to the information resource needs of students and faculty. Interlibrary loan has been the mechanism by which librarians could reach beyond the limited resources of their institutions to support research. Librarians striving to fulfill this need are concerned that the e-book distribution models may not provide a parallel mechanism. Pay-per-view models may eventually fill this need. Theoretically "everything" could become available. Libraries would pay for the access determined by students and faculty use. A mixture of models could coexist. Optimal institutional access to some collections might best be served through purchase, others through subscription, and some through pay-per-view. Students and faculty might have information resource allowances from their institutions for resources for which purchase or subscription models were not optimal for the whole of the institution.

Linux

(Question 17. How important is Linux to the library community?)

A significant percentage of the librarians (44%) are somewhat to very concerned about Linux as a platform in the context of e-content. The relationship between e-content and Linux is probably a concern for managing their own content management systems. If their institution runs Linux, they would want their CMS software to run on Linux.

Digitization and Delivery of Libraries' own E-content

(Question 18. Are libraries digitizing their own content?)
(Question 19. What types of content are libraries digitizing?)
(Question 20. How are libraries planning to digitize content?)
(Question 21. What output option(s) are libraries using for their digitized content?)
(Question 22. What platform(s) are libraries using or considering to host and deliver content?)

(Question 23. What metadata standards do libraries plan to support for their digitization efforts?)
(Question 24. What do librarians need from a delivery platform?)

A modest majority (56%) of the respondents are either currently digitizing their own content or actively considering it. Content management will become increasingly important for librarianship, particularly if libraries assume more of the publishing role for their communities. As the peer review processes evolve in the context of the Internet, the functions of publishing may be disassembled and absorbed by other entities (i.e. libraries, aggregators, faculties, editors, and formatters). The role of libraries may be associated with configuring and maintaining content management systems for the facilitation of peer review processes and controlling the metadata used for access. This is very speculative territory; however, the tension between the academic community and the current peer review-publishing model has a significant group of academics looking for alternatives. The responses indicate that libraries are cutting their teeth on a publishing role for their institutions even though the content at this juncture tends to be mostly special collections or materials for limited or internal distribution.

Of the respondents who signified that they were digitizing content, 63% indicated that they were digitizing their special collections. Nearly half of the respondents (48%) indicated that they were digitizing images and photos as well as theses and dissertations. Journals and books were indicated by 23% of the respondents and maps received 13%. The "other" responses (29%) included audio-visual materials, institutional publications, and archives.

A large majority of the respondents (81%) indicated a preference for digitizing their content in-house. The vendors listed by the 19% who indicated that they preferred outsourcing were all single entries except one vendor with two entries and "local vendor" which had six entries.

The following listing indicates the percentage of respondents who selected the formats as among those they use: PDF, 78%; JPEG, 47%; TIFF, 33%; HTML, 33%; XML, 27%; Word, 16%; and Other, 16% (i.e. MP3, WAV, DjVu).

Of the platforms provided for selection, Dspace received 29% of the responses, ContentDM, 24%, ebrary, 10%, and ePrints, 8%. The "other" selection was the top vote-getter in the content management system question with 43% of the responses. The top of the list in the "other" selection was "locally developed" with 32 write-ins (12% of all of the responses).

The platform list included 43 offerings with 31 receiving only 1 write-in. Greenstone had 9 write-ins, and ProQuest received 5.

Of the metadata standards available as a selection, 46% of the respondents indicated that they planned to use Dublin Core; MARC 21, 39%; MARC, 28%; Library of Congress, 25%; Subject Specific, 15%; and Onyx, 1%. Of the 36 responses in the "other" selection that provided a write-in, most were single entries. MODS and METS were the top entries; each had 5 write-ins.

Librarians were provided with eight factors related to content delivery platforms and asked to select all that were important. A majority of librarians selected integration with other resources (74%), download capabilities (65%), support for multiple file types (65%), and integration with institutional repository (56%). A minority selected library hosted solution (33%), PDF-based solutions (29%), vendor-hosted solution (24%), and online only—no download capabilities (10%). The "other" selection garnered 12% of the responses. All but two of the write-ins (good interface/functionality, 2, and appropriate search and retrieval, 2) were single entries. The only grouping appeared to be that all addressed some aspect of functionality or compatibility except one, which was concerned with affordability.

CONCLUSION

Three broad issues emerge from the survey. First, librarians make their decisions with an eye to optimizing access to content that is relevant to the curricula of their particular institutions. On the surface, this appears obvious and simple; however, complexities emerge from the diverse content needs of institutions. It necessitates the evolution of variety in the acquisition models. And the fluidity of marketing options that e-distribution permits promises increased complexity. For librarians, this means constantly assessing the evolving options for their institutions. For aggregators and publishers, it means that their success will be determined in good measure on the creativity and flexibility with which they respond to librarians trying to optimize access for their particular institutions. The intertwined relationship between print and electronic marketing strategies combined with the growing complexity of e-marketing models exacerbates an already tense relationship between librarians and publishers. Trust is a valuable asset for success in an arena of uncertainty. Publishers and aggregators will increase their continued viability in the e-content marketplace if they are also clear and candid in their presentation of options.

Second, the survey provides indications that e-book collections and the research tools that they provide are not well understood by a significant percentage of faculty and students. To me this is another of many indicators that librarians have an increasing responsibility to help their faculty and students better understand the growing complexities of the information sphere and the increasing diversity of research tools available. Knowing when and how to use the e-book collections through their vendor interfaces is as important as knowing how to use the OPAC. It is an example of the need for instruction in information literacy comprehensively and systematically across the curriculum.

Third, a growing percentage of libraries are participating in the distribution of e-content. While the efforts are fairly rudimentary, it is likely that academic libraries will play an increasing role in e-publication for their institutions. As the administration of content management systems becomes less technical and more focused on facilitating peer review and research processes, the skill sets and propensities of librarians become more germane to the task.

Faculty Experiences with Electronic Resources

Allen McKiel

INTRODUCTION

This article reviews the responses from the survey that ebrary concluded in late October of 2007 concerning faculty experience with electronic information resources. The questions evolved from an initial survey of approximately 200 academic librarians that ebrary conducted to gather thoughts on what the survey should cover. Very broadly, the survey examines faculty usage of electronic and print resources for research and instruction, their attitudes about information resources, perceived strengths and weaknesses of various resources, and experiences and preferences for information literacy instruction.

OVERVIEW OF SURVEY RESPONDENTS

The survey includes responses from 906 members of the faculty of higher education institutions from 38 countries. Tables in the results section provide a Carnegie Classification breakdown for U.S. institutions, a breakdown of participants by broad subject discipline, self-reporting of online course experience, years of experience in higher education, self-reporting of computer skills, and self-reporting of information literacy skills. Owing to the timeframe for publication of this review, no attempt has been made to analyze the responses by the categories of respondents. The respondent demographics were collected in questions 1 through 10. The questions concerning the focus of the survey begin with question 11.

The survey was promoted primarily through the ebrary Web site and its newsletter distribution list, which at the time included approximately 19,000 librarians in higher education, representing approximately 7,000 individual institutions. Approximately half of these institutions are located in North America, the other half in the rest of the world. The survey was created using the online tool Survey Monkey and was available for approximately 1 month. A total of 906 respondents completed the survey, representing nearly 300 individual higher-education institutions, from approximately 38 countries.

"We are very excited to have received such enthusiasm and support from the library community with regards to this faculty e-book survey," said Mr. Warnock. "This survey was developed almost entirely by librarians, and librarians took the initiative and facilitated participation among their faculty members. We extend an enormous thank you to everyone who contributed to this survey, and we look forward to our continuing collaboration with libraries in the future."

SURVEY RESULTS

Demographics/Overview

1. Dates of survey

The survey started on September 12, 2007, and ended on October 10, 2007.

2. Total number of respondents

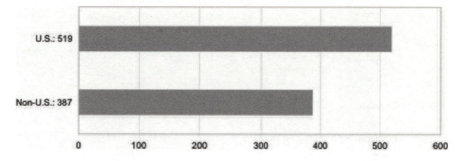

Number of respondents: 906.

3. Participating countries

Number of respondents: 906.

4. Basic Carnegie classification for U.S. institutions

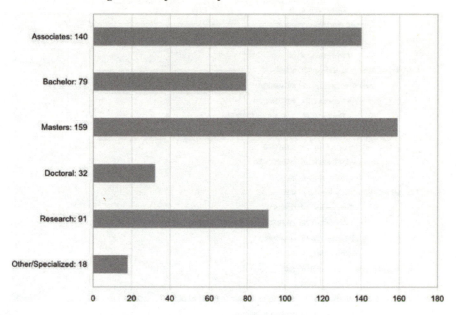

Number of respondents: 519.

5. Primary program

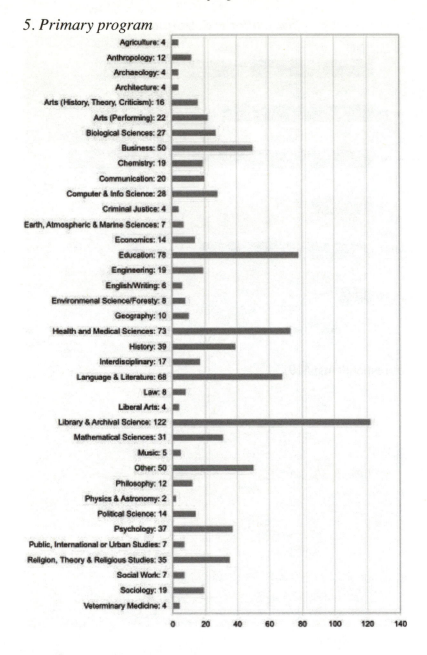

Number of respondents: 906.

6. *Respondent's primary program by category*

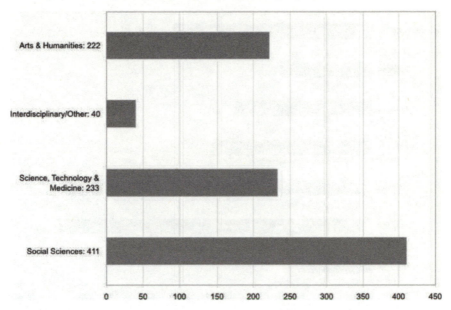

Number of respondents: 906.

7. *Do you offer or have you offered a course with an online component?*

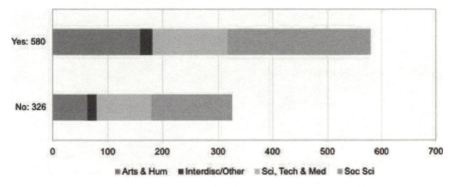

Number of respondents: 906.

8. Number of years as a faculty member in higher education?

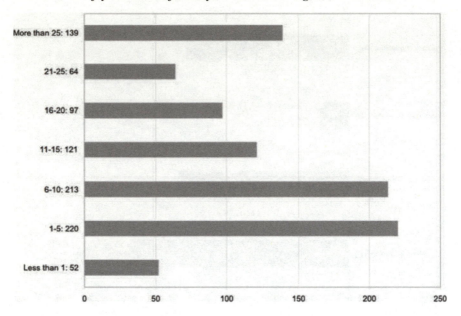

Number of respondents: 906.

9. *How would you describe your level of computer literacy?*

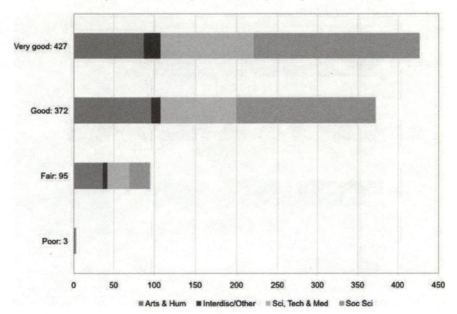

Number of respondents: 897.

10. How would you describe your level of awareness of electronic resources at your library?

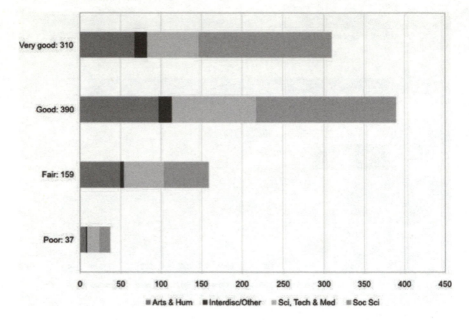

Number of respondents: 896.

11. What types of electronic resources and tools do you currently use for your research, class preparation, or instruction?

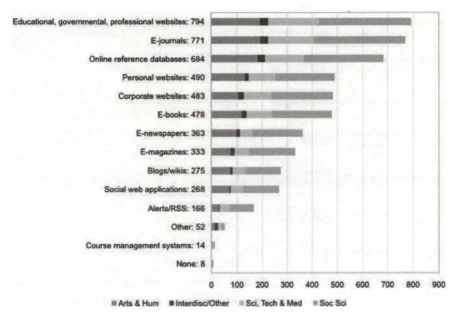

Number of respondents: 895.
Respondents selected all items that apply.

12. How do you currently integrate the use of e-journals into your courses?

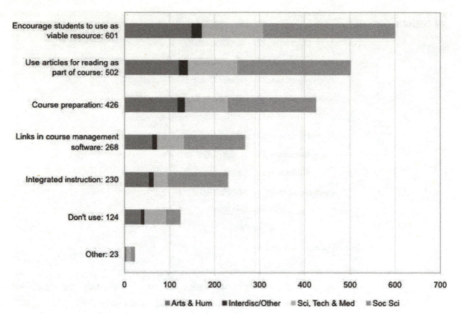

Number of respondents: 881.

Respondents selected all items that apply.

Reasons why respondents indicated they do not integrate the use of e-journals into their courses include the following:

> Difficult to read online
> Students don't read material online
> Difficult to use
> Not aware of resources and how to find them
> Use for research, but not teaching
> Not relevant to the subjects taught
> Undergrads not capable of reading journals

13. How do you currently integrate the use of e-books into your courses?

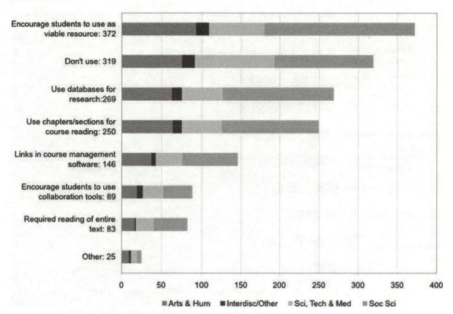

Number of respondents: 876.

Respondents selected all items that apply.

Reasons why respondents indicated they do not integrate the use of e-books into their courses include the following:

Do not know if they're available
Do not know how to find them
Not relevant to subjects taught
Difficult to read
Difficult to use
Students don't have easy access to computers

14. How do you find out about electronic resources available through your library?

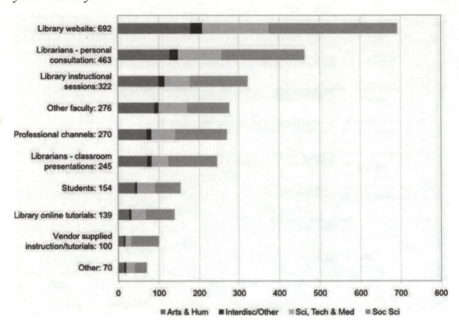

Number of respondents: 846
Respondents selected all items that apply.

"Other" responses indluce the following:

Email alerts from library
Publisher nitificatin and websites
Web searches

15. How would you characterize electronic access to journals as compared to print?

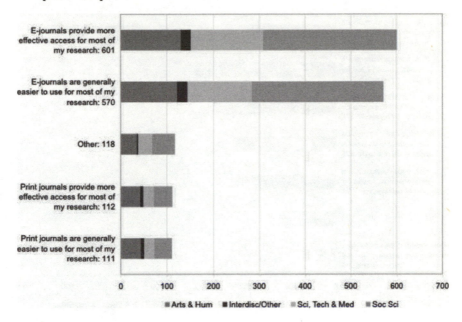

Number of respondents: 836.
Respondents selected all items that apply.

"Other" responses include the following:

- Both are valuable and equally important
- It depends on the subject
- Many e-journals do not include tables and graphs in the original text
- Older works are not available online
- E-journals are not as current
- Not all journals are available online, few e-journals in my subject area
- Print journals are easier to browse and read
- E-journals are easier to find and use
- E-journals are faster
- E-journals provide greater access to more students
- E-journals are not as stable. Publishers pull content
- E-journals are only useful if you can download and print article
- E-journals would be more useful if you could highlight text

16. How would you characterize electronic access to books as compared to print?

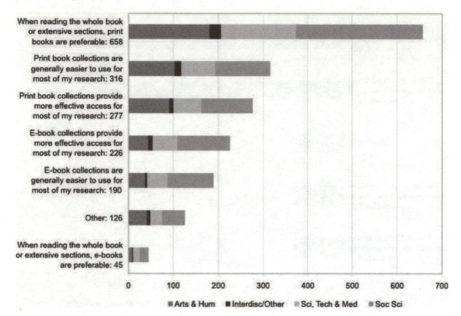

Number of respondents: 829.

Respondents selected all items that apply.

"Other" responses include the following:

- Both are valuable
- It depends on the subject
- E-books are better for research and quick reference, print books better for cover-to-cover reading
- E-books are a good way to find and search books available in print
- E-book collections don't have the breadth or depth of printed collections
- E-books are easier to search
- Print books are easier to read
- It depends on the e-book functionality and interface
- E-books can be accessed remotely
- Print is more portable

- Printed books are better for complex materials with statistics and graphics
- There are too many technical restrictions on e-books (printing, number of users, etc.)

17. How would you characterize the value of search engines like Google when you are doing research or preparing instruction?

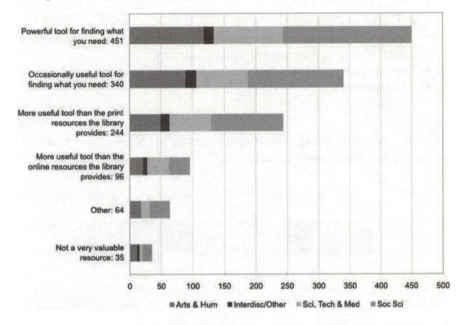

Number of respondents: 847.
Respondents selected all items that apply.
   "Other" responses include the following:

- They are useful tools when used in conjunction with print and online resources the library provides
- It depends on your ability and knowledge of how to search effectively
- Usefulness depends on the type of research
- They are good for pop culture and social networking, not as useful for peer reviewed resources
- Google is not scholarly enough yet
- Google is the easiest starting point for research

- Results are not always authoritative
- Google Scholar is not as comprehensive as the library's database
- Google Scholar is quick and easy for authors and citations but cannot lead to the library's journal subscriptions
- It's not the format or tool that's important, it's the information
- Information is more accessible, but not necessarily more reliable or better
- They are powerful tools as long as you know what you're looking for and can weed through the "junk"
- They are powerful tools for searching and teaching (finding syllabi, others' research, government agency resources, etc.)
- They are powerful tools, but don't always find what you need
- Results are often too broad and general

18. Do you prefer using online resources or print for your research, class preparation, and instruction?

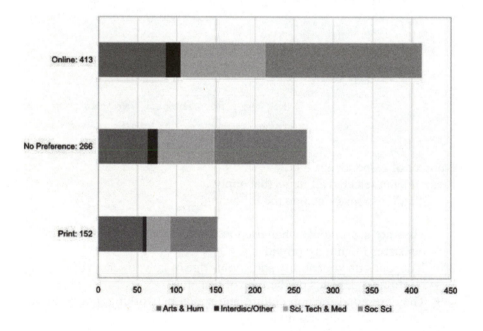

Number of respondents: 831.

Reasons why respondents indicated their preferences included the following:

Online	No preference	Print
• Accessibility	• Use both	• Easier to read and digest
• Availability	• Use both, depending on	• Easier to use
• Ability to access remotely	the task	• Better portability.
• More current information	• Print for research, online	• Ability to annotate and
• Online resources preferred	for teaching	highlight
by students	• Online for journals, print	• Easier to nd
• Searchability	for books	• Can have multiple
• Convenient/fast and easy	• Online for current data,	resources open and
• Scope and depth is more	print for older works not	visible at once
thorough	available electronically	• Do not know how to use
• Reduces costs to students	• Depends on availability	e-resources
• Saves on print-	and accessibility	• Unsure of validity of
ing/photocopying charges	• Depends on the length.	e-resources
• Better for distance	Print is better for longer	• Easier to le , track and
learners	materials.	manage
• Easier to use for	• Depends on the source.	• Ensures that materials
instruction	Some are easier to use	are peer reviewed
• Easy storage of source	electronically, others	• E-resources too slow to
information	in print.	use at home
• Ability to integrate with	• Depends on the subject	• Greater stabilityunlik ely
course management	taught. Some have more	to disappear
system	available electronic	• Index easier to search
• Better functionality	resources than others.	than keyword searching
• Can just print what you	• Depends on the subject,	• Less plagiarism issues
need, not the entire	available resources, and	• Many required materials
publication	search interface	only available in print
• Can use electronic images	• Electronic resources are	• More cost effective than
• Easier collation and	convenient, but browsing	e-books
comparison	through print materials	• Research process is
• Durable links	often renders information	more personal
• Ease of quotation	not found online.	• No fees or membership
• Gives students the ability	• It s the information that	required
to expand their inquiries	matters, not the format.	• Print out e-materials
• Prefer online, but need the	• Online is faster, but the	anyway
ability to download and	best sources are in print.	• Students make better
print	• Print is easier to read, but	sense of printed
• Saves trees	online is accessible to	materials: They read
• Linking capabilities	more students.	them more closely and
• Abstracts provided	• Some print resources are	take more notes.
• Necessary for visually	unavailable online, and	
impaired	vice versa.	
	• Prefer to start with	
	electronic, then use print	

*19. Please estimate the percentage of information resources for re-
search, class preparation, and instruction that you access electronically as compared to print*

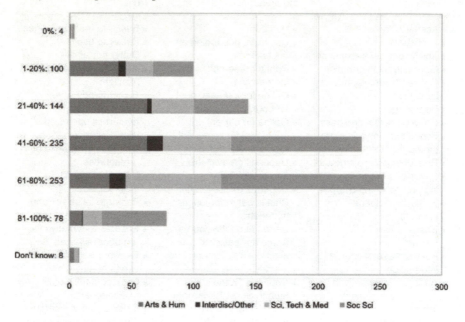

Number of respondents: 822.

20. What are the advantages and/or disadvantages of PRINT resources for your research or instruction?

Advantages of Print Resources	
More Useable	
Easy to read and digest	196
Portable	118
Ability to take notes, highlight	57
Tangible	14
Familiar	11
Multiple books open at once	8
Number of times items indicated	*404*
More Accessible	
Easy to use	34
Easy to search, nd and obtain	28
Easy to browse and nd reference	23
No technical issues	20
Easy to access	11
Easy/better to store	7
No need to photocopy or print	6
Available	4
Number of times items indicated	*133*
More Reliable	
Permanent - wont go away	25
Accurate graphics and charts	16
Durable	9
Number of times items indicated	*50*
Wider/better selection	49
Disadvantages of Print Resources	
Less Accessible	
No remote access/harder to obtain	57
Limited access	49
Not always available	40
Limited selection	21
Interlibrary loans take too long	20
Number of times items indicated	*187*
Less Useable	
Difcult to search and nd	60
uickly outdated	33
Cumbersome/bulky/heavy to carry	31
Hard to use with CMS	12
Difcult to share	9
Number of times items indicated	*145*
More Expensive	
Expensive	33
Require storage/physical space	30
Photocopying costs	11
Number of times items indicated	*74*

course management system like Blackboard.

Number of responses: 676.
This was a completely open-ended question.

21. What are the advantages and/or disadvantages of ELECTRONIC resources for your research or instruction?

Advantages of Electronic Resources
More Accessible

Any time, anywhere, immediate and convenient	315
More people can use at once	36
Better images	3
Necessary for visually impaired	2
Number of times items indicated	*356*

More Usable

Easy to search, nd, browse, and retrieve	164
Easy to share/distribute/transport	42
Ability to manipulate text, images, etc./use in CMS	42
Ability to highlight, annotate, link, bookmark, etc.	30
Easy to print/download	29
Easy to archive/organize/reference	26
Number of times items indicated	*333*

Less Expensive

No storage/physical space required	26
Cost effective	26
Reduces printing/copying/better for environment	18
Number of times items indicated	*70*

Disadvantages of Electronic Resources
Less Usable

Difcult to read onlin	79
Not portable - need to be tethered to computer/internet	36
Too much information/not always authoritative	30
Difcult to highlight/annotate, copy/paste	12
Difcult to search, nd, and retrieve	9
Difcult to use/various products are confusing	9
Need computer skills and training	9
Difcult to browse/scan	8
Have to download/difcult to download	8
Not tangible	7
Difcult to use multiple documents at once	4
Difcult to reference	4
Not e xible	2
Number of times items indicated	*217*

Less Accessible

Limited selection online	37
Not everyone has computers/connectivity	20
Copyright limitations/embargoes/printing restrictions	19
Not necessarily permanent	10
Students forget how to use the library	4
Access/authentication is cumbersome	3
Number of times items indicated	*93*

Advantages of Electronic Resources	
More Accessible	
Technical issuesdepend on technology working	45
Poor quality of graphics and images	5
Not all documents complete/materials missing	5
Easier to plagiarize/cheat	3
Number of times items indicated	*58*
Costs	
Need to print anyway/incur printing costs	29
Some resources expensive/some charge patrons	11
Number of times items indicated	*40*

Number of respondents: 686.

This was a completely open-ended question.

22. Which of the following online resources do you think are appropriate for use by your students for most of your assignments?

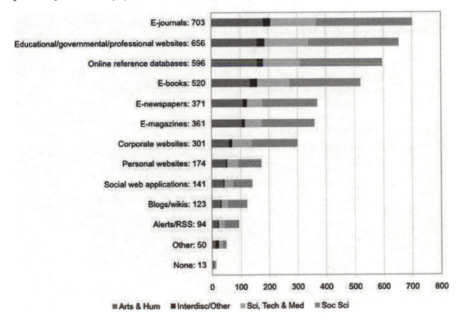

Number of respondents: 802.

Respondents selected all items that apply.

23. What types of electronic resources do you ask your students NOT to use for your assignments?

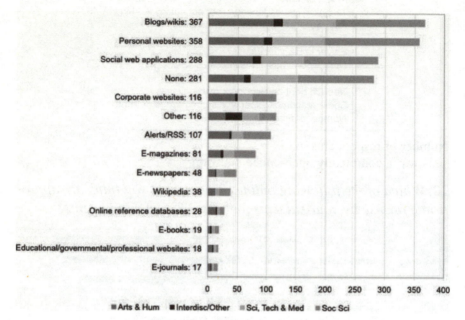

Number of respondents: 830.
Respondents selected all items that apply.

24. Are students required to use print or electronic resources for assignments in your courses?

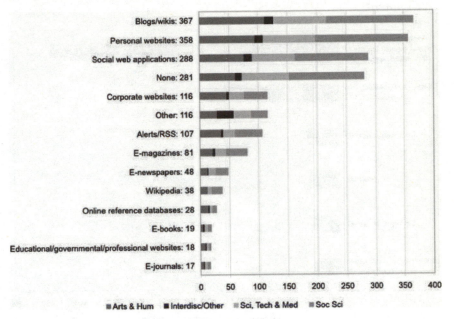

Number of respondents: 830.
Respondents selected all items that apply.

25. Where do you think students are accessing most of the information resources beyond the textbook and handout that they use for your assignments?

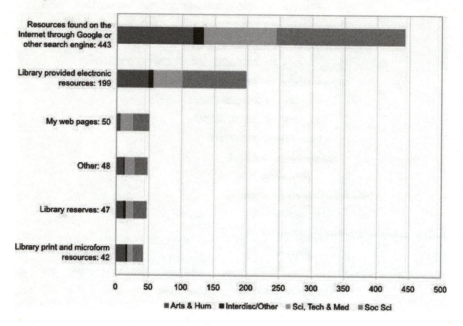

Number of respondents: 829.
Respondents selected one item.

26. What are the difficulties associated with information resources?

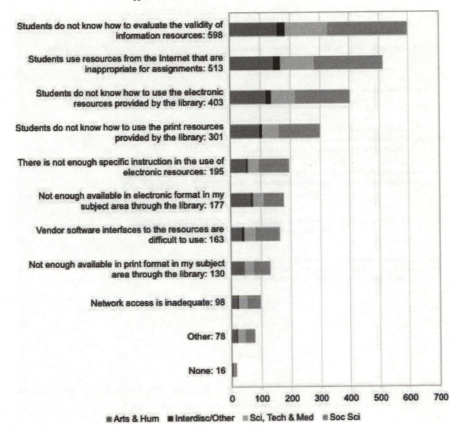

Number of respondents: 703.
Respondents selected all items that apply.

27. Of the following instruction methods for information literacy, which would you be willing to have for your course?

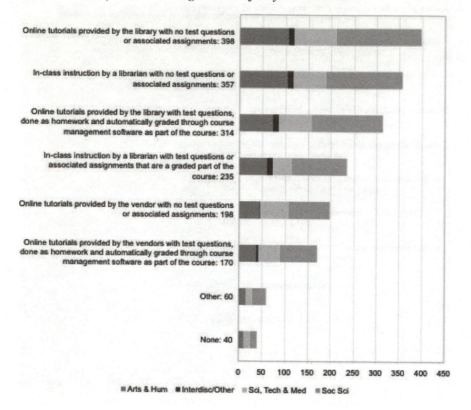

Number of respondents: 692.
Respondents selected all items that apply.
     "Other" responses include the following:

- Information literacy taught as part of the course
- Depends on the course
- Mandatory instruction for undergraduate studies
- "Rolling workshops" where people can sit in when it is convenient for them
- Assignments that require the use of electronic resources
- Expect students to have instruction before they take the class or get it on their own

- In-class instruction by a librarian with an option of test or no test
- Online tutorials provided by the library with test questions, but not graded for the course
- Online tutorials provided by the vendors that the library can modify or update as neede
- One-on-one instruction with a very knowledgeable librarian
- Printed materials so students can refer to the instructions while using the software

28. How necessary do you believe instruction in information literacy is to student research and learning?

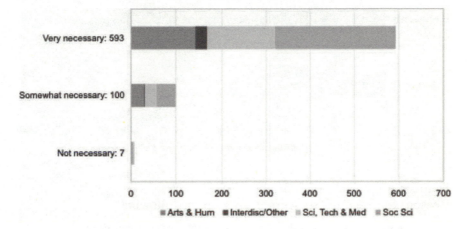

Number of respondents: 700.

29. Do technical difficulties impede use of electronic resources at your institution?

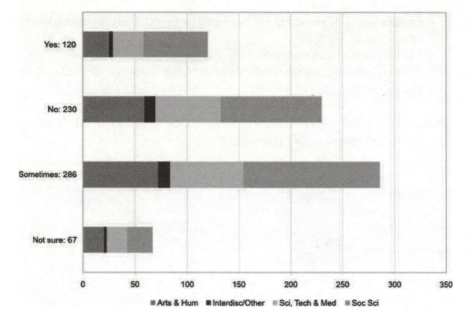

Number of respondents: 703.
Reasons for "yes" or "sometimes" include the following:

- Access and connectivity problems
- Network downtime
- Issues with course management software
- Not all students have computers
- Authentication issues
- Limited internet access
- Limited site license
- Bandwidth limitations
- Constant upgrading and maintenance issues
- Cost - students have to pay for internet access
- Difculty   logging in remotely
- Students forget passwords

- Remote access is confusing, with proxy servers, numerous passwords, etc.
- Difculty   downloading large les remotely
- Instability of vendor products
- Software compatibility issues
- Unreliable IT department
- Using vendor products (i.e., turning pages) is
- DRM restrictions

30. What do you feel would make e-book usage more suitable for use in your area?

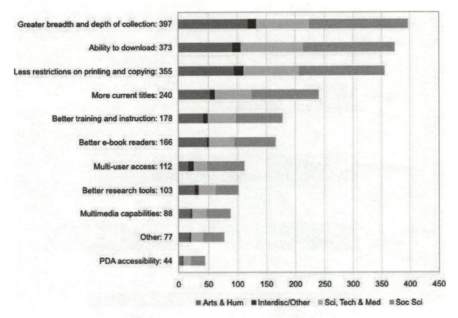

Number of respondents: 711.
Respondents selected their top three items.

"Other" responses include the following:

- Easier access/less bandwidth requirements
- No costs to students
- None—prefer print books
- Student interest
- Improved accessibility/server stability
- Linux compatibility
- More awareness and promotion of available resources
- Single platform and interface—too many vendor products are confusing
- Ability to annotate
- Available on iPod
- Better (book size) readers

- Browsable catalog
- Integration with OPAC

31. *Would you prefer your library to own or subscribe to e-books and why?*

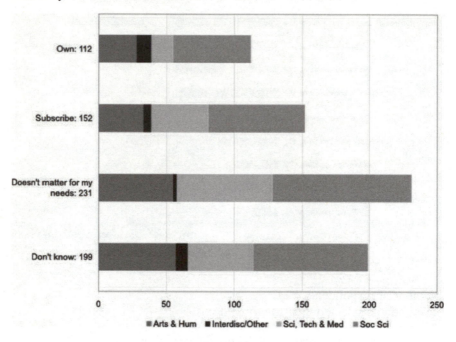

Number of respondents: 694.
Reasons "why" include the following:
Own

- Permanence
- More stable than subscription
- No restrictions on printing or downloading
- Not affected by budget cuts
- Gives the library control over the material
- Included in library catalog/can search in one place
- No recurring/rising costs associated with subscription
- Have been burned by subscription model for journals

Subscribe

- Greater flexibility
- More current materials/upgrades when new titles become available
- Access to more materials
- Available to more students
- Greater usage
- More cost effective
- Does not matter for my needs
- Access is more important than the model
- As long as there is pertinent content, the model doesn't matter
- Depends on the nature of the materials and demand
- Multi-user access, less restrictions on printing and copying, ability to download, longer access time are more important
- Whichever is more cost effective

I don't know

- Do not understand the advantages/disadvantages of owning or subscribing
- As long as materials are reliable and accessible, the model doesn't matter
- Depends on the cost
- Depends on the longevity of titles
- Depends on the type of book
- Depends on what is available
- Depends on which students would use
- Do not use e-books
- Prefer library to own print books, subscribe to journals
- Prefer print materials
- Prefer to own core materials, lease materials that go out of date quickly

COMMENTARY

11. What types of electronic resources and tools do you currently use for your research, class preparation, or instruction?

Educational, governmental, and professional Web sites ranked first in the number of faculty (89%) who indicated that they used them for research, class preparation, or instruction. This is noteworthy because it demonstrates the sea of change the Internet has facilitated in scholarly communication. These Web sites are the new phenomenon in the academic neighborhood, and they are already competing for the position as the primary source of information for research, class preparation, or instruction. The responses to question 18 concerning the preference for online versus print resources demonstrated a preference for online (50%) over print (18%). Refereed e-journals ranked a close second with 86%. Just more than 76% of the faculty surveyed selected online reference databases like encyclopedias, Statistical Abstracts, and Business Dateline. E-books had a fairly poor showing. They ranked down with personal and corporate Web sites at about 54%. This response rate coincides with the responses of the librarians in ebrary's March 2007 survey concerning usage of e-books in general. Forty-one percent found usage good to excellent while 59% found it fair to poor.

In the analysis of the ebrary survey of librarians in March 2007 (see elsewhere in this volume), I provided an explanation of the low e-book usage compared to print. Patrons compare e-books unfavorably to print books for ease of use and portability. Most patrons know how to retrieve a book from the shelf once they find it in the catalog. They do not as frequently know how to effectively use vendor e-book interfaces. And most people would prefer to read a print version of a book over an electronic version on a computer screen. I also indicated that, in my experience with patrons who learn how to use the vendor interfaces and become aware of the strengths of e-book collections (e.g., full-text keyword searching, 24/7 availability, currency, and text-handling tools), they prefer them when doing research. To this I would add another significant reason for low usage. The e-book collection has to be of a significant volume compared to the print collection for it to be worth mining for information.

For example, when a small business and education college with a collection of 40,000 mostly out-of-date print titles subscribes to an e-book collection of 30,000 mostly current titles, the e-book collection may be by far the better collection for most of the institution's student and faculty information needs. For a university with one million print titles, much of which have been specifically selected for the nuances of a more complicated set of research needs, the 30,000-title collection will be a significant addition to the collection, but it will not command the same respect.

My solution to the e-book usage problem is for publishers and vendors to provide libraries with access to very large collections along with powerful text handling tools and download capability to e-book readers such as the new offering from Sony. Charging libraries for what faculty and students use could be more egalitarian with respect to the vagaries and disparities of the diverse institutional budgets and would promote use, and the library budgets would be driven more directly by the research needs of faculty and students. Practical limits that would allow libraries to stay within budgets could be arranged through management of accounts. The way in which some libraries handle print limits is an example. A print server can manage student accounts through login identification. Page limits of library-provided printing can be set for a semester. Graduate students or faculty could have different limits. When the limit is reached, the patron is responsible for purchasing additional printing. In a similar manner, a library could facilitate access to significant e-book collections that would otherwise be beyond its means.

12. How do you currently integrate the use of e-journals into your courses?

13. How do you currently integrate the use of e-books into your courses?

Questions 12 and 13 were designed to compare e-journal and e-book usage. E-journals are used more often by faculty across the board—a total of 2,056 affirmative responses for e-journals and 1,241 for e-books. Approximately 14% of the respondents indicated that they do not integrate use of e-journals into their courses, and 36% of respondents do not use e-books for their courses. Integration of the use of e-books into teaching clearly lags behind e-journal usage. Nevertheless, the responses demonstrate that e-book and e-journal issues are very much the same.

The following are typical of concerns articulated in the comments of the open-ended responses concerning e-books:

- Do not know if they're available
- Do not know how to find them
- Not relevant to subjects taught
- Difficult to read
- Difficult to use
- Students don't have easy access to computers

The following are the open-ended responses concerning e-journals:

- Difficult to read online
- Students don't read material online

- Difficult to use
- Not aware of resources and how to find them
- Use for research, but not teaching
- Not relevant to the subjects taught
- Undergrads not capable of reading journals

Usage of e-books and e-journals by faculty in their courses is also very similar. They are both used for student research associated with the course, as assigned readings, and for faculty research and course preparation. The largest number of faculty responses for both e-journals and e-books was an affirmation of their practice of encouraging students to use e-journals and e-books for their research—68% and 43%, respectively. The second most frequent selection for e-journals and the third for e-books were for faculty use as required course readings—e-journals at 57% and e-books at 29%. The second most frequent selection for e-books and the third for e-journals was for use by faculty in research or course preparation—e-journals 48% and e-books 31%.

14. How do you find out about electronic resources available through your library?

The primary source of information for faculty about library resources is the library Web site, as attested by 81% of respondents to this question. The distant second is through personal consultation with librarians—55%. The third is through library instruction sessions—38%. Other faculty, professional, and subject area resources, and librarian classroom presentations nearly tie for fourth with 33%, 32%, and 29%, respectively. Online library tutorials (16%) and vendor tutorials (12%) constitute the remainder. Worth mentioning are the 26 of 70 open-ended comments that reported learning about electronic resources through e-mail notices from the library.

The results suggest the conundrum of current academic librarianship—the difficulty of providing comprehensive instruction. Faculty most often find out about library resources through the information provided on the library Web site. They are not being introduced to new resources comprehensively through instruction, which includes the nuances of vendor interfaces like those associated with e-books, e-journals, and reference databases.

Instruction in the effective use of online resources would likely improve usage significantly. E-journal and e-book usage, usage of reference databases such as Business Dateline, and use of general search engines such as Google would become more appropriate and effective with instruction. However, providing comprehensive instruction in the growing arena of topics becoming essential for information literacy can not be accomplished using conventional methods of information literacy instruction for faculty or students. There are not enough librarians even if information literacy were accorded a place in general education requirements. Comprehensive information literacy instruction is becoming the central challenge for academic librarianship.

15. How would you characterize electronic access to journals as compared to print?

16. How would you characterize electronic access to books as compared to print?

Questions 15 and 16 were meant to be compared. The blatantly obvious difference between e-journals and e-books is that e-journals are viewed more favorably than e-books when compared to print. E-journals are seen as providing more effective access for research (72% of responses), and they are seen as easier to use (68%) than print journals. Print books are seen as preferable to e-books for reading the entire work (79% of responses). Print books are seen as more effective for research (33% print and 27% e-books). And print is seen as easier to use for research (38% to 23%).

It is likely that effectiveness is to a large extent a factor of the breadth and depth of the collection. The responses to question 30 indicate that greater depth and breath would be the most effective way to improve e-book collections. E-journal collections commonly outstrip print collections in academic libraries. This likely contributes to the positive responses they receive as compared to print. Print book collections commonly surpass e-book collections, which in turn likely contribute to the preference for p-books over e-books. Until e-book collections compete favorably in breath and depth with print collections, they will not be taken as seriously as e-journal databases are. The message for publishers and vendors is to provide access to larger collections.

For ease of use, e-books are seen negatively compared to print in two perspectives. First, e-books are compared unfavorably to print for reading the whole work. This will be true until there are universally available e-book readers that are preferable to the comfortable and much-loved codex form of the book. Second, it is likely that research using e-books is negatively compared to print because the primary method of access is the library catalog, not the vendor interface. The strength of e-books for research becomes apparent through familiarity with the interface tools. More students and faculty already know how to use vendor interfaces for e-journals. They do not try to find e-journal articles through the library catalog. They use the vendor interfaces.

The following are samples of the open-ended comments that respondents contributed concerning their characterization of e-journals and e-books as compared to print. They are roughly supportive of the patterns of responses in the selection of responses that were provided; however, they demonstrate the broad range of individual experience with e-journals and e-books.

E-journals vs. P-journals

- Both are valuable and equally important
- Depends on the subject
- Many e-journals do not include tables and graphs in the original text
- Older works are not available online
- E-journals are not as current
- Not all journals are available online, few e-journals in my subject area
- Print journals are easier to browse and read
- E-journals are easier to find and use
- E-journals are faster
- E-journals provide greater access to more students
- E-journals are not as stable. Publishers pull content
- E-journals are only useful if you can download and print articles
- E-journals would be more useful if you could highlight text

E-books vs. P-books

- Both are valuable
- Depends on the subject
- E-books are better for research and quick reference, print books better for cover-to cover reading
- E-books are a good way to find and search books available in print
- E-book collections don't have the breadth or depth of printed collections
- E-book are easier to search
- Print books are easier to read
- Depends on the e-book functionality and interface
- E-books can be accessed remotely

- Print is more portable
- Printed books are better for complex materials with statistics and graphics
- There are too many technical restrictions on e-books (printing, number of users, etc.)

17. How would you characterize the value of search engines like Google when you are doing research or preparing instruction?

The most popular selection (53% of the respondents) characterized search engines such as Google as a "powerful tool for finding what you need" for doing research or preparing instruction. With 40% of the respondents, "occasionally useful tool" was the second most popular selection. Only 4% indicated that they thought it was not a very valuable resource.

Nearly 29% of the respondents to this question thought that Google was a more useful tool than the print resources of the library for research and instruction. Just more than 11% thought that Google was more useful than the online resources provided by the library. If the converse is valid, the library, particularly its provision of online resources, is viewed by the majority of faculty in this survey as a more useful tool than search engines like Google for accessing information resources relevant to doing research or preparing instruction. This may be comforting to librarians. However, a level of ambiguity is added when viewing these responses in the context of the responses to Question 11. The highest percentage of respondents (89%) selected educational, governmental, and professional Web sites as the electronic resource they used for research, class preparation, or instruction. Web sites are not necessarily provided through either the library or search engines. They may be accessed by following links.

The following comments, provided by the 7% that responded to "other (please explain)," offer a sampling of individual perspectives on the value of search engines like Google.

- Useful tool when used in conjunction with print and online resources the library provides
- Depends on your ability and knowledge of how to search effectively
- Usefulness depends on the type of research
- Google is not scholarly enough yet
- Google is the easiest starting point for research
- Results are not always authoritative

- Google Scholar is not as comprehensive as the library's database
- More accessible, but not necessarily more reliable or better
- Powerful tool as long as you know what you're looking for and can wade through the "junk"
- Powerful tool for searching and teaching (finding syllabi, others' research, government agency resources, etc.)

18. Do you prefer using online resources or print for your research, class preparation, and instruction?

Just fewer than 50% prefer online, 18% prefer print, and 32% have no preference. The clear preference for online resources by nearly half of the respondents is associated with particular information needs, experiences, and skills as well as the varying availability of the online and print mix of resources at their respective libraries. The following selection of responses from the 387 who included comments provides some detail for the varied experiences that comprise the preferences. The comments are listed by the preference—online, print, or no preference.

Online—50%

- Accessibility
- Availability
- Ability to access remotely
- More current information
- Students prefer online resources
- Search ability
- Convenient/fast and easy
- Scope and depth is more thorough
- Reduces costs to students
- Saves on printing/photocopying charges
- Better for distance learners
- Easier to use for instruction
- Easy storage of source information
- Ability to integrate with course management system
- Better functionality
- Can just print what you need, not the entire publication
- Can use electronic images
- Easier collation and comparison
- Durable links

- Ease of quotation
- Gives students the ability to expand their inquiries
- Saves trees
- Abstracts provided
- Necessary for visually impaired

No Preference—32%

- Use both, depending on the task
- Print for research, online for teaching
- Online for journals, print for books
- Online for current data, print for older works not available electronically
- Depends on availability and accessibility
- Depends on the length. Print is better for longer materials
- Depends on the source. Some are easier to use electronically, others in print
- Depends on the subject taught. Some have more available electronic resources than others
- Depends on the subject, available resources, and search interface
- Electronic resources are convenient, but browsing through print materials often renders information not found online
- It's the information that matters, not the format
- Online is faster, but the best sources are in print
- Print is easier to read, but online is accessible to more students
- Some print resources are unavailable online, and vice versa
- Prefer to start with electronic, then use print

Print—18%

- Easier to read and digest
- Easier to use
- Better portability
- Ability to annotate and highlight
- Can have multiple resources open and visible at once
- Do not know how to use e-resources
- Unsure of validity of e-resources
- Easier to file, track and manage
- Ensures that materials are peer reviewed

- E-resources too slow to use at home
- Greater stability—unlikely to disappear
- Less plagiarism issues
- Many required materials are only available in print
- The research process is more personal
- Print out e-materials anyway
- Students make better sense of printed materials: They read them more closely and take more notes

19. Please estimate the percentage of information resources for research, class preparation, and instruction that you access electronically as compared to print.

Estimated usage of resources skews to the electronic side. Just more than 40% of the respondents use electronic more than 60% of the time. About 30% use electronic resources less than 41% of the time. And about 30% of the respondents indicated that they use electronic and print resources in about equal measure (between 41% and 60% of the time).

20. What are the advantages and/or disadvantages of PRINT resources for your research or instruction?

Evaluating the relative advantages and disadvantages of print versus electronic resources depends on the particular resource (e.g., e-journals, e-books, or a particular vendor interface), the particular need or use (e.g., reading, reference, research), and the user's skill level with the various tools (e.g., library collection or particular vendor software interfaces). It also depends on the breadth and depth of the particular collections that are being compared. This survey catches a snapshot of faculty evaluations given the collections that they have available, their resource needs, and their skill sets. As these variables change over time, the responses will also change. With that as a caveat, I have grouped the responses in broad categories (usability, accessibility, reliability, and cost) to get some perspective on the detail.

Advantages of Print Resources

The primary advantage of print resources is their usability, which garnered 404 of the 636 comments. They were reported as easier to read in 196 responses and more portable in 118. For 57 of the respondents, it is easier or more comfortable to take notes and highlight on paper than online. Print resources are viewed as more accessible in 133 comments—ease of using (34), searching (28), and browsing (23) top the list. Reliability was an advantage for 50 faculty and 49 reported that the print collections had better selection.

Advantages of Print Resources		636
More useable		404
Easy to read and digest	196	
Portable	118	
Ability to take notes, highlight	57	
Tangible	14	
Familiar	11	
Multiple books open at once	8	
More accessible		133
Easy to use	34	
Easy to search, nd and obtain	28	
Easy to browse and nd reference	23	
No technical issues	20	
Easy to access	11	
Easy/better to store	7	
No need to photocopy or print	6	
Available	4	
More reliable		50
Permanentw ont go away	25	
Accurate graphics and charts	16	
Durable	9	
ider/better selection		49

Disadvantages of Print Resources

The primary disadvantage of print resources according to 187 responses concerned accessibility—lack of remote access (57 responses), limited access (49), availability (40), limited selection (21), and long interlibrary loan (20). Interestingly, 145 reported problems with usability, the number one advantage cited for print. They listed difficulties with searching (60), currency (33), portability (31), and coordination with online communication and resources (21).

Disadvantages of Print Resources		406
Less accessible		187
No remote access/harder to obtain	57	
Limited access	49	
Not always available	40	
Limited selection	21	
Interlibrary loans take too long	20	

less useable		145
Difcult to search and nd	60	
uickly outdated	33	
Cumbersome/bulky/heavy to carry	31	
Hard to use with CMS	12	
Difcult to share	9	
More expensive		74
Expensive	33	
Require storage/physical space	30	
Photocopying costs	11	

Course Management System like BlackBoard.

21. What are the advantages and/or disadvantages of ELECTRONIC resources for your research of instruction?

Advantages of Electronic Resources

The primary advantage reported for electronic resources was their accessibility, which garnered 356 of the 759 comments. The overwhelming majority (315) cited the ability to access electronic resources at any time from any place. Electronic resources were viewed as more useable in 333 responses, with the lion's share (164) citing the ease of searching, finding, and retrieving. They were also cited as easier for sharing and distributing (42), manipulating text and images (42), using (30), printing and downloading (29), and archiving/organizing (26). Electronic resources were viewed as more cost effective in 70 responses.

Advantages of Electronic Resources		759
More accessible		356
Any time, anywhere, immediate and convenient	315	
More people can use at once	36	
Better images	3	
Necessary for visually impaired	2	
More usable		333
Easy to search, nd, browse, and retrieve	164	
Easy to share/distribute/transport	42	
Ability to manipulate text, images, etc./Use in CMS	42	
Ability to highlight, annotate, link, bookmark, etc.	30	
Easy to print/download	29	
Easy to archive/organize/reference	26	
Less Expensive		70
No storage/physical space required	26	
Cost effective	26	
Reduces printing/copying/better for environment	18	

Disadvantages of Electronic Resources

Usability was the primary concern according to 217 of the 406 comments contributed about the disadvantages of electronic resources. The three most common comments were associated with the difficulty to read (79), lack of portability (36), and the difficulty of dealing with the volume and questionable quality of resources (30). Comments concerning accessibility were cited in 91 responses. The most prominent comments concerned the limited selection of online resources (37). Fifty-eight responses focused on the reliability of electronic resources, with the majority of those (45) addressing the dependability of technology. Concern for cost associated with printing, the expense of some resources, or fees were contributed in 40 comments.

Disadvantages of Electronic Resources		406
Less Usable		217
Difcult to read online	79	
Not portableneed to be tethered to computer/internet	36	
Too much information/not always authoritative	30	
Difcult to highlight/annotate, copy/paste	12	
Difcult to search, nd, and retrieve	9	
Difcult to use/various products are confusing	9	
Need computer skills and training	9	
Difcult to browse/scan	8	
Have to download/difcult to download	8	
Not tangible	7	
Difcult to use multiple documents at once	4	
Difcult to reference	4	
Not e xible	2	
Less Accessible		91
Limited selection online	37	
Not everyone has computers/connectivity	20	
Copyright limitations/embargoes/printing restrictions	19	
Not necessarily permanent	10	
Students forget how to use the library	4	
Access/authentication is cumbersome	3	
Less Reliable		58
Technical issuesdepend on technology working	45	
Poor quality of graphics and images	5	
Not all documents complete/materials missing	5	
Easier to plagiarize/cheat	3	
Costs		40
Need to print anyway/incur printing costs	29	
Some resources expensive/some charge patrons	11	

22. Which of the following online resources do you think are appropriate for use by your students for most of your assignments?

E-journals topped the selection list with 88% of the responses. Educational, governmental, and professional Web sites were second, with 82%. Online reference databases such as online encyclopedias, Statistical Abstracts, and Business Dateline, captured 74%. E-books picked up the fourth position with 65%. Just fewer than 50% of the respondents selected e-newspapers (46%) and e-magazines such as *Newsweek* (45%).

Given that e-books contain information similar to and as appropriate for assignments as e-journals, it would be reasonable to expect them to have a similar ranking. Explanations for the low showing of e-books compared to e-journals can be gleaned from the responses to Question 30 (What do you feel would make e-book usage more suitable for use in your area?): Most collections are too small to be very useful, e-books do not compare favorably with print books for reading, and the interfaces to some vendor databases are awkward or confusing.

23. What types of electronic resources do you ask your students NOT to use for your assignments?

Blogs and wikis take top billing for the electronic resources (44%) that respondents ask students not to use for assignments. Personal Web sites are second, with 43%. Social Web applications such as discussion boards and YouTube are third, with 35%. And 34% of the faculty responded that they do not prohibit the use of specific resources.

Courses and assignments have specific information needs that may dictate restrictions in sources. For example, the most common concern I hear from faculty is the use of personal Web sites and blogs for research papers. Often faculty members tell students that they must have peer-reviewed material. Sometimes they specifically tell them not to use Google, where students often find blogs and personal Web sites. However, other courses may encourage the use of blogs. For example, a political science course might want students to sample a variety of blogs and personal Web sites during an election. The responses to this question are helpful in that they provide librarians with an overview of the most common faculty concerns for appropriate information sources. They do not provide a general rationale for restricting any particular source of information. They merely indicate where librarians can assist faculty (i.e., with instruction of students in the selection, evaluation, and use of information resources).

24. Are students required to use print or electronic resources for assignments in your courses?

Textbooks are still the common base of the curriculum for courses and probably account for the preponderance of the 71% of the faculty, who indicated that they required use of some print resources for assignments. Just more than 70% of the faculty indicated that they require use of some electronic resources.

25. Where do you think students are accessing most of the information resources beyond the textbook and handout that they use for your assignments?

More than 50% of the respondents assume that students access most of the information beyond the textbook and handouts from search engines such as Google. Only 24% thought that students mostly used library-provided electronic resources. This is a dismal set of assumptions, though I do not believe for librarians it is unexpected.

26. What are the difficulties associated with information resources?

The top four difficulties associated with information resources concern the lack of student knowledge of information resources. Nearly 85% of respondents indicated they believe students do not know how to evaluate the validity of information resources. More than 70% believe students do not use resources from the Internet that are appropriate for assignments. And 58% and 43%, respectively, feel that students do not know how to use library electronic or print resources.

Nearly 30% of respondents indicated that they do not believe there is enough instruction in the use of electronic resources, which is curious. It indicates that faculty do not believe that instruction has, or that more will, overcome the gap in student knowledge concerning information resources. This seems a counter-intuitive position for educators to hold. I see three possible explanations. The low expectations for the effectiveness of more instruction could be explained by the hesitation on the part of faculty to assert that librarians are not providing adequate instruction. In most academic settings these days, instruction in information literacy has dramatically increased. Library faculties are stretched to the limit in their efforts to provide comprehensive instruction in the growing list of topics in which all students should receive instruction. The second explanation concerns student choice. Faculty may assume that the primary problem is student seduction by the Google phenomenon. It is the easiest thing for students to do, and they are not likely to change with further instruction. The third explanation is that faculty members believe the problem is student lack of subject area knowledge when doing research rather than information illiteracy.

Whatever the explanation for the discrepancy between the high number of responses concerning student lack of knowledge as a problem and the relatively low score for lack of instruction being a problem, I believe student information illiteracy could be significantly ameliorated through comprehensive information literacy instruction. In the typical hour- to two-hour library instruction session, it is common that only a portion of students who need instruction receive it. Those who do receive instruction have generally been introduced to a small portion of the topics associated with the growing array of topics that need covering. And of that group, many have been on the tour multiple times and seen the same small portion of instruction in the basics. Access to the students is driven by the requests of the faculty associated with particular courses so students get the same lecture in multiple classes. Comprehensive instruction in information literacy for all incoming students is generally not the norm for most colleges and universities at this time. The result is that only a portion of the student population is exposed to a small portion of library resources and concepts associated with information literacy in the context of the rapidly changing information environment.

The shift in information access because of the Internet has increased the need for instruction in the rapidly expanding global information sphere. The days of a library tour that centered on the catalog and how to find things in the library are gone. Appropriate topics for information literacy include concepts of peer review, evaluation of information resources, thoughts on plagiarism, instruction in citing resources, the presentation of a variety of search strategies, instruction in e-journal and e-book database interfaces, the selection and use of search engines, the use of tools like those provided by Serials Solutions, and instruction in a host of proprietary and open access information databases. The list continues to expand as more resources relevant to the curriculum continue to appear and evolve more sophisticated interfaces to a growing complexity of data structures.

The magnitude of the information literacy needs may also be the explanation for why instruction is not reported by faculty in the above question as the answer to the lack of student knowledge concerning information literacy. There is no apparent solution to a problem that seems so overwhelming. The problem, I believe, is information illiteracy in the context of the new information sphere. The solution is comprehensive integration of information literacy horizontally and vertically throughout the curriculum.

27. *Of the following instruction methods for information literacy, which would you be willing to have for your courses?*

Only 6% responded with none. The large majority of the faculty indicated that they were in favor of some form of information literacy instruction as part of their courses. The favored method of information literacy instruction is the least intrusive—online tutorials selected by 58% of respondents. They require no class time and have no associated tests or assignments. An additional benefit is that online tutorials expand the reach of the limited library faculty, which opens an avenue to comprehensive information literacy instruction. It would be reasonable to expect that faculty would not want to give up class time or impact their subject area assessment strategies, as information literacy is related to but outside of the course subject areas. I would argue, however, in favor of some form of assessment that constituted a small portion of the course grade, perhaps multiple choice questions that could be automatically graded and posted through course management software such as Blackboard. More than 45% of the faculty responding to this question agreed. They selected the option for online tutorials with graded assessment as part of the course. Students to a large extent weigh the effort they give to learning on the scale of probable impact on their grade. In my experience, it has been demonstrated very clearly that few students will even participate in non-mandatory library instruction. And those who participate in mandatory instruction are likely not paying much attention unless they believe it will impact their grade.

28. *How necessary do you believe instruction in information literacy is to student research and learning?*

The responses to this question provide a measure of the growing awareness of the underlying need for information literacy. Nearly 85% of the respondents indicated that it was very necessary. Almost 15% indicated somewhat necessary. Less than 1% thought it was unnecessary.

29. *Do technical difficulties impede use of electronic resources at your institution?*

Nearly 60% of the respondents indicated that technical difficulties impede use of electronic resources at their institutions at least some of the time. For 33% of respondents, technical difficulties are not a problem. The following is a sampling of some of the comments provided by 179 faculty who selected "yes" or "sometimes."

- Access and connectivity problems
- Network downtime
- Issues with course management software
- Not all students have computers
- Authentication issues
- Limited internet access
- Limited site license
- Bandwidth limitations
- Constant upgrading and maintenance issues
- Cost—students have to pay for internet access
- Difficulty logging in remotely
- Students forget passwords
- Remote access is confusing, with proxy servers, numerous passwords, etc.
- Difficulty downloading large files remotely
- Instability of vendor products
- Software compatibility issues
- Unreliable IT department
- Using vendor products/turning pages is slow

30. What do you feel would make e-book usage more suitable for use in your area?

Greater breadth and depth of collection garnered the top response position, with 56% followed by the ability to download (52%) and less restriction on printing and copying (50%). Just fewer than 34% suggested adding more current titles. Finally, 25% of the responding faculty noted the need for better training and instruction. If we as librarians assume that it is still important to make sure students know how to use the library's catalog, instruction in the use of the more complicated vendor e-book interfaces should also be considered a must.

31. Would you prefer your library to own or subscribe to e-books and why?

About one-third of respondents indicated that it does not matter for their needs, and 29% indicated that they did not know why it would matter. In other words, for 62% this is a non-issue. The responses to question 30 make it clear that their concerns are for greater breadth and depth of the collection, the ability to download e-books, and less restrictive printing and copying however it is accomplished.

CONCLUSION

The most notable aspect of faculty usage of electronic and print resources for research and instruction was the strong preference overall for using electronic resources. Approximately 50% prefer electronic versus 18% for print. For 72% of the respondents, e-journals provided more effective access than print, and 68% found them easier to use. Reading an entire book or extensive sections of it was an obvious exception for 79% of the respondents who preferred print. The electronic resources that faculty thought were most appropriate for the majority of their assignments were e-journals (88%); educational, governmental, and professional Web sites (82%); online reference databases (74%); and e-books (65%). This closely reflected the preferences faculty reported for their own usage.

The responses by faculty over e-book and e-journal concerns and usage are very similar with the notable difference that e-books lagged behind in usage. Faculties want access to more resources and better tools for searching and using, and many do not like reading online. They are used both for student and faculty research, as assigned readings, and for course preparation.

The overwhelming majority of faculty (85%) viewed instruction in in-formation literacy as very necessary. Almost 15% saw it as somewhat necessary, with fewer than 1% viewing it as unnecessary. A majority of the faculty (58%) preferred the least obtrusive form of instruction for their classes—online tutorials with no assessment. Approximately 45% of the faculty selected tutorials with assessment.

The clearest message from this survey for publishers and vendors is to increase the breath and depth of collections, to provide portable reading devices, and to evolve continually more powerful research tools. For li-brarians, the message is aggressive pursuit of the electronic resources most relevant to the curricula of their institutions and comprehensive instruction for their effective use.

Academic E-books: Supply Before Demand in the Life Sciences?

Barb Losoff

INTRODUCTION

The advent of electronic information has affected all elements of information gathering, from discovery to publishing: "Whether people like digital media or not, reading and literacy are being redefined by the arrival of digital technology" (Ziming, 2005, 701). Studies have shown that library users check out e-books, but just how they are used remains unclear. According to Rowlands, "It is the users who will drive the e-book story forward" (Rowlands, 2007). Exactly how the e-book will look and feel is another question. Tony Horava, in *Against the Grain*, stated that "a few years from now we will conceive of the term 'author' and 'book' in radically new ways, as scholarly communication evolves to meet new expectations and opportunities" (2007, 1). In the life sciences (chemistry, biology and medicine), books have been considered a secondary or peripheral resource. However, "Relevant information exists not only in journal and news formats, but also in books which are coming into their own as research resources in our electronic information environment" (Ojala, 2007, 51). The introduction of the e-book within higher education "could lead to a paradigm shift influencing e-learning, research and the nature of academic publishing" (Rowlands, 2007).

LITERATURE REVIEW

The growth of electronic media is transforming the information landscape, with more than 93% of all new information being digitally created (McLuckie, 2005). E-books have the potential to become a much larger player and "are coming into their own as research resources in our electronic information environment" (Ojala, 2007, 51).

A working definition of e-books is "any piece of electronic text regardless of size or composition (digital object), but excluding journal publications, made available electronically (or optically) for any device (handheld or desk-bound) that includes a screen" (Armstrong, Edwards, and Lonsdale, 2002). The e-book market has grown rapidly since 2004, with revenues up 23% in 2005 along with a 20% increase in published titles (University College London, 2006). In spite of the marked increase, a report from 2006 found that worldwide e-book sales represent about 1% of the increase in U.S. book sales but less than 1/20th of 1% of total U.S. book sales (Crawford, 2006). The introduction of a single standard for e-books released by the International Digital Publishing Forum (IDPF) in December 2006 will undoubtedly be a boon to e-book publishing and sales. The Open eBook Publication Structure Container Format "will allow publishers to release a single standard file into their sales and distribution channels and will also enable consumers and library patrons to exchange unencrypted ebooks and other digital publications between reading systems that support the new standard" (Rogers, 2006, 28).

User studies have identified an important niche for e-books in distance education and reference. A report from 2003 found that students were interested in using e-books and that e-books enhanced the "interaction between educators and students when dealing with teaching and learning materials" (Shiratuddin, Landoni, Gibb, and Hassan, 2003, in Texas Digital

Library). Studies have shown that reference materials offer significant value to users in the e-book format (McLuckie, 2005). Reference materials found in collections from Knovel Library, Wiley InterScience, and Springer provide access to prestigious scientific publishers, including CRC Press and McGraw-Hill. Functioning as aggregators, these vendors often provide enhanced features such as interactive tables and graphs, full-text searching, and hyper-links (McLuckie). Other advantages to users of these Web-based reference e-books are portability, availability (24/7), multimedia connectivity, simultaneous access, and continuous content updates.

The downside for the user is the difficulty of extended reading from a computer screen. The back-lit technology is fatiguing to the eye and apparently the brain. A 2005 study found that "undergraduate students who read online text find it to be more difficult to understand, less interesting," and they even considered the authors less credible than when reading the printed version (Thomas, 2007). Printing from e-books has been another obstacle for the user owing to the various constraints protecting copyright and revenues that restrict copying.

Newly designed e-book readers with organic light-emitting diodes (OLEDs) and electronic paper displays may be just the impetus for an e-book revolution. Sony's E-book Reader introduced in the fall of 2006 uses a new digital ink display that "provides paper-like reading comfort and long battery life" (Hane, 2006, 22). Sony's Reader is similar to a paperback, approximately 6 inches long, 9 ounces in weight, with a leather cover that folds back for reading comfort. Light is required for reading as the display is not backlit. The Sony Reader can hold up to 80 books, and additional e-books can be purchased from Sony's CONNECT eBook Store stocked with 10,000 titles. Additional features include free RSS feeds from CONNECT and the ability to listen to unencrypted MP3. The cost of the Reader is approximately $350. Although there is interest by academic librarians who have tested the Reader, it is not designed for college-level work, lacking hyperlinks and multimedia capability. Sony is looking into the best way to approach the higher education market, according to David Seperson, a product manager for the Reader (Young, 2006).

The question remains whether a single-function device such as the Sony E-book Reader without Internet connectivity will actually satisfy the users, particularly when studies have indicated that users want integration of all electronic devices (Thomas, 2007). As society becomes more interconnected, a stand-alone device, even one with hyper-links, music, and portability, may not significantly fulfill users' e-reading requirements. Enter the Kindle, Amazon.com's e-book reader introduced in November

2007. Like the Sony Reader, the Kindle is 6 inches in length and utilizes a high-contrast, low-power screen technology (Mossberg, 2007), but the real innovation of the Kindle is wireless connectivity (Levy, 2007). The Kindle holds more than 200 books with titles accessed directly from Amazon.com without first downloading to a computer. Amazon has more than 90,000 titles available at $9.99 per title. The Kindle's Internet connectivity includes options for electronic editions of 11 newspapers (including the *New York Times*), eight magazines, and 300 blogs for monthly fees (Wildstrom, 2007). The price of the Kindle is high at $399, which may pose a barrier to consumers. Whether the Kindle will impact higher education remains to be seen, as limited wireless connectivity still runs contrary to the academic model of resource integration. Another alternative in the e-book evolution are advances in the software for reading e-books on the computer. Adobe has released a new version for managing and reading digital publications that, according to the company, "is an improvement to the Adobe e-book reader and an answer to the confusing proliferation of e-book formats" (Cross, 2006, 13).

As e-books gain footing in the academic endeavor, librarians need to know not only what e-book users read but why and how (Levine-Clark, 2006). A study from the University of Denver Penrose Library found only 7.1% read the entire book, with 56.5% reading a chapter or article within a book and 36.4% reading a single entry or a few pages (Levine-Clark). The author noted a study in 1985 that found the majority of science scholars (75%) read only small sections of print books. Users' interactions with e-books reflect similar use patterns compared to print books, following Francis Bacon's adage, "Some books are to be tasted, others to be swallowed, and some few to be chewed and digested" (Ojala, 2007, 49).

Another study coming from the United Kingdom will hopefully shed new light on users' interactions with e-books. The SuperBook Project originated with e-journals applying "deep-log analysis of the digital 'fingerprints' left by the users of e-journals" (University College of London, 2006). Dave Nicholas, at the School of Library, Archive and Information Studies, University College of London (UCL) and his colleagues are applying the same methodology to e-books. The premise of the study is that expanded availability of e-books may drive a shift in user behaviors.

This study will "evaluate awareness of, and attitudes towards e-books, the impact of e-book intervention on learning, book usage, satisfaction with e-book content, and whether, as a result of these interventions, users demonstrate different patterns of study from the non-users" (Rowlands, 2007). The virtual scholars will be UCL students, researchers, and staff utilizing an e-book collection of more than 3,000 titles from Oxford Scholarship Online, Wiley Interscience, and Taylor & Francis. The study began in November 2006 and will run one year. Interconnectivity may in fact be an essential attribute for any e-book. As the SuperBook study in the United Kingdom unfolds and the e-book readers are put through their paces, perhaps a more precise picture of readers and their books will begin to emerge.

METHODOLOGY

Assessing content of e-book packages in relation to faculty research and teaching is a necessary task for subject bibliographers. At the University of Colorado at Boulder (CUB), selected life science faculty were contacted in a small exploratory survey in order to gauge interest, use, and content considerations for e-books. Twelve life science faculty members at CUB were asked to respond to a short survey (see Appendix for list of survey questions). Eight faculty members completed the survey, including four biologists, two biochemists, and two chemists.

RESULTS

Of the eight respondents, only two had used e-books. A comment by one faculty member who had not used e-books stated, "Part of making it useful would be awareness. I am not currently aware of what e-books are available!"

Faculty members were asked about the types or genre of books that would be useful in e-book format. All eight CUB faculty selected review literature as more significant than reference materials. Course material preparation was selected by the two faculty members as their main purpose for e-book use, followed by research and general reference. One respondent indicated an interest in using e-books for general reading.

When asked whether book content from prestigious publishers was as important to their research/teaching as journal literature the faculty members were evenly split. Of those who said "no" to the question, two qualified their answers: "No, generally books are considerably out-of-date by the time they are published." And, "No, but there are exceptions." A comment from a faculty member who said yes to this question stated, "Yes, in particular Wiley—in chemistry they are the 'premier' publisher at the present time."

Seven of eight faculty members were in favor of purchasing e-books rather than print from notable scientific publishers. The faculty member not in favor of electronic over print commented, "No, I don't like reading on a computer screen; however if it were possible to print selected chapters that might be nice." A comment from a faculty member who was in favor of the e-book over print qualified that: "Yes, provided there are no unreasonable restrictions on access, nor a price system that is based on the number of users," and "Any good material online beats the physical because of access. However, the user must be able to save the materials as PDF and must not have to deal with cumbersome page-at-a-time access or page-at-a-time printing. I know they don't want me to download the whole book and have it on my disk. However, that is exactly what I do when I get a journal article online. I download the whole thing to my computer as a PDF and then I read it as I will."

The final question addressed the integration of e-book content into research databases and whether that might influence research/teaching? Slightly more than half the faculty members said "yes," two members were unsure, and one said "no" to this question. One commented, "Yes, without doubt the research landscape is being changed in terms of information access, and the more information that becomes electronic the easier it will become to integrate knowledge across a large timeframe." Another commented, "It would make it easier to study several authors' explanations of basic concepts, without having aging editions piling up in my office. So it would influence my teaching. It would also help me answer student questions when my own off-the-cuff answer is not quite enough."

Faculty members were encouraged to provide additional comments, one of which was "I think the most important priority now for the science holdings is to extend our electronic coverage of journals back in time. It is extremely frustrating to look for an article and find that our electronic access only began in the 1990s." And another commented, "Looking up information in an electronic book might be quicker and more successful than paging through the tables of contents and indices of heavy paper text books."

DISCUSSION

In the life sciences, e-book purchases have generally fallen into the guidebook, handbook, and reference categories. The faculty members at CUB placed review literature above standard reference materials. This interest in subject reviews was noted in a statistical review of CUB

NetLibrary life science titles in 2006. Of the 1,681 titles users checked out, many were in-depth subject overviews. The CUB faculty survey confirmed that natural histories, trends-in, and annual reviews all serve a purpose for the user. This information is useful for CUB subject bibliographers for expanding the life science e-book collection beyond reference materials.

A common complaint from users is the lack of awareness about e-books (Croft and Bedi, 2005; Milliot, 2007), and this was indicated in a faculty comment from the survey. With e-book expenditures increasing, marketing these resources should be a requirement. Libraries need to promote e-books to "particular user groups through targeted and structured strategies" (Tedd, 2005: 72).

CUB faculty identified e-book use in relation to course material preparation as their choice of purpose. Studies have shown students of distance education rely on e-book course materials and that their studies are enhanced by using e-books (Shiratuddin et al., Texas Digital Library, 2003). The survey responses indicate that e-book material is useful in course preparation for both on-campus education and distance education.

The exchange of information and research in the sciences, in general, is dominated by journal literature. In an effort to gauge the role of books in research, the question to the faculty was whether book content was equally important to their research/teaching as journal content. The faculty responses were evenly split: four agreed, and four disagreed. This question might reflect the differences in disciplines, with books having different impact levels depending on the separate disciplines (i.e., chemistry, biology, and the like). Faculty conducting medical-related research might prefer electronic access to both print journal and book content while biologists primarily rely on electronic journal content for their research.

It is more than a question of content; there is the consideration of what each life science discipline values in relation to research/teaching, as indicated by one of the survey respondents who addressed the need of archival journal coverage. If book content traditionally has not been as important as journal literature, could that change with e-book full-text search capabilities? There are several aspects to this question that require a deeper analysis using a user/discipline-centered approach. Bennett and Landoni (2005) addressed the need for a user-centered approach when considering e-books, by utilizing a four-dimensional vector: content, format, purpose, and use. E-book design then "becomes a two-step process, in which an analysis of user requirements yields a user profile that may then be utilized to develop the optimum format" (Bennett and Landoni, 11).

Publishers are developing subject-based collections, but the question concerning content remains. What is the criterion for inclusion, and how does that translate to the particular research needs of individual academic institutions? A question posed by Wicht from her article "Buying Ebooks" asks "How can my users repurpose the content? (*Library Journal*, 2006). Without informed selection for content, these pre-established packages may include titles that do not further the research goals of the institution. A study at UCL in 2007 evaluating how users find books noted that a "one-size-fits-all solution would not seem to be a good idea" and that librarians and publishers "might do well to segment their offerings in a much more sophisticated way" (Rowlands, Nicholas, Jamali, and Huntington, 2007, 22). The e-journal bundles offered to academic libraries were billed as a cost-effective means to acquire greater access to scholarly literature. The bundles were static with no ability to repurpose content. Many libraries experiencing reduced budgets in conjunction with journal pricing inflation found they could not cancel titles from these pre-set packages. The lesson learned from this less-than-ideal arrangement was the need for "fluid" package arrangements, with the ability to adapt to institutional change.

Given the option of purchasing e-books over print, the faculty preferred the electronic book, although with qualifications. CUB faculty expect e-books to allow simultaneous access, with the ability to print and download complete chapters, and suggested that publisher pricing systems based on FTEs were unreasonable. The e-book model emulated by NetLibrary, the "one e-book/one user model" (Algenio and Thompson-Young, 2005, 116), has been unsatisfactory, and yet it is still the predominant model as NetLibrary is one of the largest e-book aggregators. Printing from the NetLibrary collection confounds the user with one-page-at-a-time print conditions, as was indicated in the faculty comments. Bennet and Landoni called for change, alleging that NetLibrary has long since "been dictating the rules of engagement" and has "shown too little of a sign of wishing to listen to user concerns" (2005, 11). Libraries are now being offered new e-book models based on content, unlimited users, and the ability to download chapters or even entire books.

Springer introduced in 2006 its new e-book packages with full-text capability, multimedia functionality, concurrent access, permanent purchase, and downloading capabilities. The e-book packages are subject-based, with content fully searchable along with its e-journals through the SpringerLink platform. Springer's platform fees are based on number of FTEs, contrary to the expectation of the CUB faculty member. Springer may find that even after publishing a more useful, searchable, downloadable e-book, it has priced them too high. In October 2007, the Max Planck Society (MPG) of Germany, a prestigious scientific research organization with more than 80 research institutes, cancelled its subscription to all 1,200 Springer e-journals. The MPG, as reported by Sietmann (2007), found that "an analysis of user statistics and comparisons with other important publishing houses had shown that Springer was charging twice the amount the MPG still considered justifiable for access to the journals, and that the 'justifiable' rate is still higher than comparable offers of other major publishing houses" (Heise Zeitschriften Verlag, 2007). Although details remain undisclosed, in February 2008 Springer renegotiated with MPG on the pricing and functionality of the Springer e-journal packages (Library Journal Academic Newswire, 2008). Certainly the prestige of MPG influenced the outcome; however, this highly publicized case provided a valuable lesson. Product research is necessary, and librarians need to have a voice in tailoring e-packages.

The final question attempted to gauge the future, whether the integration of e-book content into research databases would influence the faculty's research/teaching. This question resulted in answers that varied; although half the faculty were in agreement, several were unsure. This is unknown territory, although It appears that e-book content has the potential to become more of an integral part of research than the print counter-parts. Integration of full-text book content into research databases may facilitate the rediscovery of the book. As stated eloquently by a CUB chemist who bears repeating, "Without a doubt, the research landscape is being changed in terms of information access, and the more information that becomes electronic the easier it will become to integrate knowledge across a large timeframe" (Phillips, 2007).

CONCLUSION

The CUB faculty indicated that e-books have the potential to enhance their research/teaching. Full-text searching in e-books may breathe new life into life science research, allowing book content and data to be mined online along with e-journal literature. Continued studies, such as the SuperBook Project, on how users find books, read books, and use books will provide a foundation for strategic library acquisitions. Librarians must take the initiative to convey user expectations to publishers, thereby ensuring that demand for e-books informs the supply.

REFERENCES

Algenio, E., & Thompson-Young, A. (2005). Licensing E-Books: The good, the bad, and the ugly. *Journal of Library Administration, 42*(3–4), 113–128.

Armstrong, C., Edwards, L., & Lonsdale, R. (2002). Virtually there? E-Books in UK academic libraries. *Electronic Library and Information Systems, 36*(4), 16–27.

Bennett, L., & Landoni, M. (2005). E-Books in academic libraries. *The Electronic Library, 23*(1), 9–16.

Crawford, W. (2006). Why aren't ebooks more successful? *EContent, 29*(8), 44.

Croft, R., & Bedi, S. (2005). E-Books for a distributed university: The Royal Road University case. *Journal of Library Administration, 41*(1–2), 113–137.

Cross, L. (2006). E-Book reader as best seller. *Graphic Arts Monthly, 78*(11), 13.

Hane, P. J. (2006). The new e-book readers. *Information Today, 23*(10), 22–24.

Horava, T. (2007). The renaissance of the eBook: Transformations and question marks. *Against the Grain, 19*(2), 1–16.

Levine-Clark, M. (2006). Electronic book usage: A survey at the University of Denver. *portal: Libraries and the Academy, 6*(3), 285–299.

Levy, S. (2007). Can it kindle the imagination?; We read the fine print on Amazon's new gadget. *Newsweek, 150*(22), 64.

McLuckie, A. (2005). E-Books in an academic library: Implementation at the ETH Library, Zurich. *The Electronic Library, 23*(1), 92–102.

Milliot, J. E-Books need visibility. Retrieved August 14,2007, from <http://www.publishersweekly.com/article/CA6460298.html> R.R. Bowker Co.

Mossberg, W. S. (2007, November 29). Amazon's kindle makes buying e-books easy, reading them hard. *Wall Street Journal* [Eastern edition], p. B1.

Ojala, M. (2007). Searching by and for the book. *Online, 31*(2), 49–51.

Phillips, A. (2007). Questions on "academic e-books: Supply before demand in the life sciences? A Personal Interview/Survey. 21 Oct. 2007.

Rogers, M. (2006). IDPF releases ebook standard. *InfoTech*, 131(20), 28.

Rowlands, I. SuperBook: Planning for the ebook revolution. Retrieved March 15, 2007, from <http://www.ucl.ac.uk/slais/research/ciber/superbook/> University College, London.

Rowlands, I., Nicholas, D., Jamali, H. R., & Huntington, P. What do faculty and students really think about e-books? Unpublished manuscript. University College, London.

Shiratuddin, N., Landoni, M., Gibb, F., & Hassan, S. E-Book technology and its potential applications in distance education. Retrieved March 2, 2007, from <http://journals.tdl.org/jodi/article/view/jodi-99/89> Texas Digital Library.

Sietmann, R. Max Planck Society terminates licensing contract with Springer Publishing House. Retrieved October 19, 2007, from <http://www.heise.de/english /newsticker/news/97652> Heise Zeitschriften Verlag.

Tedd, L. A. (2005). E-Books in academic libraries: An international overview. *New Review of Academic Librarianship, 11*(1), 57–59.

Thomas, S. (2007). Another side of the e-book puzzle. *Indiana Libraries, 26*(1), 39–45.

Together Again: Springer, Max Planck Agree to New "Experimental" Deal. Retrieved May 12, 2008, from <http://www.libraryjournal.com/info/CA6528977.html> Library Journal Academic Newswire.

Wicht, H. Buying Ebooks. Retrieved October 8, 2007, from <http://www.libraryjournal.com/article/CA6322021.html> Library Journal: netconnect.

Wildstrom, S. H. (2007, December 3). A new chapter for the e-book? Amazon's Kindle includes a wireless connection and eliminates the need for a computer. *Business Week*, 4061, p. 74.

Young, J. R. Even with improved screens, e-book devices not ready for college. Retrieved February 7, 2007, from <http://chronicle.com/weekly/v53/i17/17a03301.htm> *The Chronicle of Higher Education*.

Ziming, L. (2005). Reading behavior in the digital environment: Changes in reading behavior over the past ten years. *Journal of Documentation, 61(6), 700–713*.

APPENDIX

Survey Questions on "Academic E-Books: Supply Before Demand in the Life Sciences?"

1. Have you used electronic books?
2. What types of life science electronic books would you use?
   a) Reference materials
   b) Technical books
   c) Review literature on a particular subject
   d) Manuals
   e) Other
3. For what purpose would you use life science electronic books?
   a) Research
   b) Lecture preparation
   c) Course material preparation
   d) General reference/data
   e) General reading
   f) Other
4. Do you consider the book content of publishers such as Wiley, Springer, and Elsevier as important to your research/teaching as the journal articles?
5. If books published by notable scientific publishers were available electronically would you favor the electronic over the print?
6. Do you think the integration of electronic book content into academic research databases will influence or enhance your research/teaching?

The University of Pittsburgh Study in an Electronic Environment: Have E-books Changed Usage Patterns of Monographs?

Rickey D. Best

INTRODUCTION

In the 32 years since the completion of the University of Pittsburgh study on the use of library materials, we have seen a migration in the format of materials from print to electronic. Whereas in 1975 electronic books were unheard of, today they are readily available for purchase. While the pressures of growing collections and budgetary constraints still exist for libraries, a question exists as to whether the basic premise of the Pittsburgh study and of Trueswell's 80/20 rule[1] still hold true. In the digital environment, with the added convenience of accessing a book electronically at any time, is the premise that a few titles comprise most of the usage still true? The hypothesis of this article is that the premise of the 80/20 rule and the Pittsburgh study holds true regardless of the format of the material. Within the electronic environment a majority of the titles will not be accessed and a small proportion of the titles will be responsible for the majority of access.

THE PITTSBURGH STUDY

In 1975, the University of Pittsburgh received a grant from the National Science Foundation. The study was conducted "to develop measures for determining the extent to which library materials (books/monographs and journals) are used, and the full cost of such use."[2] Conducted and written at a time of budget constraints and pressures from growing collections, the study examined book use in the Hillman Library and journal use in other branch libraries. The penultimate goal, as described in the background of the study, "was to develop a cost benefit model of some critical library operations in terms of use of materials."[3] Among the issues facing libraries described in the study, we find the same pressures existing more than 30 years later. Libraries are still facing the pressures of inadequate budgets and limited space. A potential panacea—the electronic book and journal— have appeared within the mix of resources acquired by libraries. But has the format change resulted in usage changes? If so, do libraries move to purchase access to more electronic book titles?

LITERATURE REVIEW

Since libraries have been collecting books, administrators have wanted to be assured that their expenditures have been justified by usage. Trueswell (1969) noted that 80% of the circulation requirements were satisfied by approximately 20% of the library's collection.[4] Trueswell went on to argue that 90% of the circulation requirements could be met with a collection in which "about 50 percent of the present stack holdings could readily be identified as all books that have circulated one or more times in the last four years."[5] Fussler and Simon (1969) in their study of the use of books in large research libraries utilized the following assumptions:

"1. The recorded circulation use of books is a reasonably reliable index of all use, including the unrecorded, consultative, or browsing use of books that are common to major research libraries;

2. There are certain patterns in the use of books that are common to major research libraries;

3. Within homogenous subject areas and types of books (that is, monographs and serials), use is a suitable initial criterion for segregating materials into different levels of accessibility;

4. Economic factors may make it highly desirable to segregate books, on the basis of their value and use, into two or more levels of accessibility."[6]

The articulation of the predictability of future use from past use is consistent with Trueswell's study.

The University of Pittsburgh study conducted by the Dr. Allen Kent et al. aimed to develop a cost-benefit model based upon usage. The results of the study confirmed the arguments of Trueswell, Fussler, and Simon in demonstrating that past use is an adequate predictor of future use in a print environment. As noted by Bulick, Sabor, and Flynn in the second chapter of the Pittsburgh study, "a very small portion of the collection of the library collection of book titles accounts for the major portion of the circulation use."[7] Hardesty, in two separate studies, conducted collection use studies at two small liberal arts colleges[8] utilizing the Pittsburgh methodology. Hardesty's approach confirmed the findings of the Pittsburgh study that "external circulation data can be utilized with a high level of confidence to measure total book use, since the books that were used in-house, placed on reserve, or requested by other libraries on interlibrary loan were predominantly the same books that were circulated to Pittsburgh students and faculty."[9] In Hardesty's studies at DePauw University and Eckerd College, an assumption was made to treat each circulation as having equal value. The issue of usage of electronic books has been dealt with by Hughes' study of monographs in the digital library.[10] In the study conducted by Hughes at Columbia University, she noted that usage of the online books fell within Trueswell's distribution projection, with 21% of the titles accounting for 66% of the usage.[11]

The AUM Study

In order to answer the assumptions posed by Trueswell and Kent et al. (i.e., that a majority of usage in achieved by a small percentage of the

total collection, in an electronic environment), the Auburn University at
Montgomery (AUM) Library conducted a survey of usage of its electronic
book holdings to determine whether use was consistent with the patterns
determined by Trueswell and the University of Pittsburgh. A branch campus of Auburn University, AUM holds separate accreditation from the
Southern Association of Colleges and Schools. The University consists
of five academic schools (business, education, liberal arts, nursing, and
sciences) with 17 undergraduate and 14 graduate degrees. Enrollment at
the university in fall of 2007 was more than 5,000.

The Library itself at AUM consists of a collection of 300,000+ monographic titles and some 2,200 current periodical subscriptions. Because of
space limitations within the library, the library has focused diligently on
providing electronic access to a wide variety of resources, both in terms
of books and journals, in order to provide the student body and the faculty
with convenient access to the collections. In acquiring electronic books,
the Library has participated in the licensing of access to the NetLibrary
shared collections offered through the Southeastern Library Information
Network (SOLINET). The AUM Library has licensed six of these shared
collections, which comprise nearly 58,000 titles.

The shared collections within NetLibrary include university press as
well as association and for-profit publishers. The subject areas covered in
the collections include agriculture; the arts; biology and life sciences; business, economics and management; chemistry; computer science; earth sciences; education; general works and reference; history; home economics;
language and linguistics; law; library science and publishing; literature;
mathematics and statistics; medicine; networking and telecommunications;
philosophy; physics; political science; psychology; religion; science (general); social sciences (general); sociology and anthropology; sports and
recreation; technology, engineering and manufacturing; and travel and
geography. The collections are balanced to reflect interest of academic,
corporate, school, and public libraries.

Within its study, AUM followed Hardesty, Kent, et al. in equating each
access to an electronic book as being equal. Unlike previous studies, however, with e-books one no longer must consider browsing usage nor exclude
reference materials. Unlike print titles, no consideration was required to
be given to titles loaned through Interlibrary Loan. Because there are no
discrepancies caused by in-house use of titles, each access of an electronic
book serves as an accurate recording of total use. While Hardesty's observation that "recorded circulation statistics may be more appropriate for
measuring the undergraduate use of a college library"[12] may be true, in the

current electronic environment of accessing NetLibrary, we do not collect information on user status. Thus we cannot determine the specific amount of usage by undergraduates, graduate students, and faculty.

AUM Data Collection

Because each of the six NetLibrary shared collections was loaded into the AUM Library catalog in a staggered fashion, it was determined to examine the usage data annually for each of the collections. The University of Pittsburgh study found "that any given book purchased had only slightly better than one chance in two of ever being borrowed. When a book had not circulated within the first two years of ownership, the chances of its ever being borrowed were reduced to only one in four."[13]

In examining the usage data for AUM, it becomes clear that the first year of access provided to the specific collections is an introductory period: Students are locating the titles and slowly integrating use of the collections into their research. Each of the collections contains unique titles, so the usage patterns differ based upon the utility of the titles for the students' research. In this regard, the electronic title is no different than the print. Only those titles useful for student research will be used. A limitation placed on the user by the shared collections is that a title is not available for check-out by multiple users at the same time. To address this issue, SOLINET licensed access to multiple copies of some titles for which usage was expected to be heavy.

In examining the AUM Library data, we see that it conforms to the findings of Hardesty and the Pittsburgh Study in that most books "circulated little or not at all during the approximately five-year time period."[14]

As one can see by the data in Figure 1, annual usage over the NetLibrary collections 1 and 2 increases slowly but steadily for the first three years of the availability of the collection, then generally has a slight drop the fourth year followed by an increase in the fifth year. While there is no clear and apparent reason for this fluctuation, it is entirely possible that user needs for access to titles vary by course assignments over the years. It is interesting to note the success of collections 3 and 4 in terms of use of the titles included. The average number of titles accessed during the first four years of availability of Collection 3 was 1,539. For Collection 4, the average number of titles accessed in the first three years of availability was 1,161.

FIGURE 1. NetLibrary Shared Collection Usage by ear

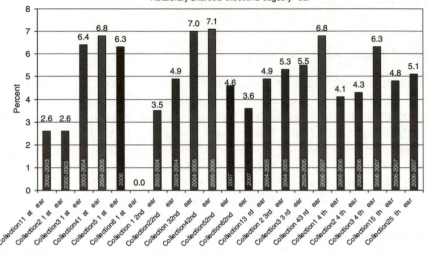

NetLibrary SharedC ollectionU sageb y ear

Overall, the data indicate an upward growth in the percentage of titles accessed following the first year. In examining the access data, we find that over the life of the collections' availability, 83.1% of the NetLibrary holdings in AUM's collections have never been accessed. This is significantly higher than the approximately 40% total cited by Kent, Montgomery, and Williams for titles added during a one-year period that are never used.[15]

Table 1 shows the percentages of titles accessed, the equivalent of print titles circulating. The data conform to the Pittsburgh Study and Trueswell's 80/20 rule. For the AUM Library, the overall percentage of titles accessed was 19.31%, versus 80.69% not accessed. Thus, a few titles do constitute a majority of usage in the digital environment. Table 1 shows the percentage of titles accessed per collection over the life of the collections availability at AUM. The collection with the largest percentage of titles accessed was Collection 3, with 25.28% of the titles accessed.

In examining usage by title, a number of titles had significant access. One-half of the titles were in a discipline where one would assign a higher value on the currency of information: computer science. Three of the most heavily used titles were in literature, where historical review has value. Of the remaining titles, one was in business and one in the social sciences (general) category. Neither of these titles appears to require immediacy of

TABLE 1. NetLibrary Shared Collection Usage by the AUM Library Users

NetLibrary Shared Collections	Titles Accessed	Accessed	Number of Accesses	Average Access per Title Accessed	Percentage Not Accessed	Total Number of Titles
Collection 1	3,261	19.93	6,337	1.94	80.07	16,362
Collection 2	2,448	22.09	5,235	1.78	77.91	11,079
Collection 3	2,936	25.28	6,159	2.09	74.72	11,610
Collection 4	1,663	21.09	3,483	2.09	78.91	7,882
Collection 5	838	10.93	1,686	2.01	89.07	7,660
Collection 6	131	3.59	236	1.80	96.41	3,639
Total	**11,277**	**19.36%**	**23,136**	**2.05**	**81.64%**	**58,232**

157

access to retain value. The top 10 titles, in terms of access and their subject fields, were:

Accesses	Title/Author	Publication Date	Subject
239	Visual Basic 6 from Scratch/Robert Donald	1999	Computer Science
111	Perspectives on Cormac McCarthy/Edwin T. Arnold	1999	Literature
89	Learn Pascal/Sam Abolrous	2000	Computer Science
81	Visual Basic.Net By Example/Gabriel Oancea	2002	Computer Science
77	Understanding Flannery OConnor/Margaret E. hitt	1995	Literature
71	Practical C++/Robert McGregor	1999	Computer Science
66	Real Estate Investing from A to / m. Pivar	2004	Bus., Mgt. & Econ.
59	Marriage of Heaven and Earth/Randall Clack	2000	Literature
57	Absolute Beginner s Guide to Databases/ .V. Petersen	2002	Computer Science
56	Media Effects: Advances in Theory & Research/ . Bryant	2002	Soc. Sci. (General)

Of the titles, five were in computer science, three in literature, one in business, and one in social sciences. Table 2 shows that the top 10 subject areas over the life of the collections in terms of access at AUM are, somewhat surprisingly:

TABLE 2. Top Ten Subject Areas by Number of Times Accessed

1. Literature	3,699
2. Business, Economics & Management	3,670
3. Social Sciences (General)	3,325
4. Computer Science	2,920
5. Medicine	2,403
6. Education	934
7. Arts	922
8. History: orld & General	696
9. Law	645
10. History: United States	578

Table 3 shows the distribution of access for the collections over the time they have been accessible.

TABLE 3. Access Rates

Times Accessed	Percentage of Times Accessed	Number of Accesses	Number of Titles
0	83	0	47,221
15	15	14,499	8,772
610	1	4,249	567
1115	.002	1,628	122
1620	.001	1,002	56
2125	.0003	450	20
2630	.0004	761	27
3135	.0001	326	9
3640	.0001	270	7
4149	.0001	461	10
5059	.00007	226	4
66239	.001	734	7
Total 24,606	**99.01137%**	**24,606**	**56,822**

The figures here confirm the findings of Trueswell and the Pittsburgh Study for AUM. Eighty-three percent of the titles available in an electronic format were not used at all. Fifteen percent were used between one and five times, and slightly more than 1% were used six times or more. Though the AUM study differs from those conducted by Hardesty at DePauw University and Eckerd College in that the AUM study analyzed use across a larger sample of books (i.e., the entire NetLibrary collection), similarities do exist among usage at DePauw and Eckerd and AUM.

Hardesty provided an analysis of a year's circulation data broken out by subject classification.[16] To provide a comparable analysis with Hardesty's data, a comparison was conducted examining the print circulations from the Eckerd University Library in 1984–1985 with print circulations and e-book accesses from the AUM Library. In Table 4, the data for AUM show number of circulations for print/and accesses (e-books) for 2006, the latest year for which there are complete data. In examining the data from Eckerd College and comparing them with that of AUM, Table 4 shows some interesting correlations. Remembering that Eckerd College is a bachelor's level institution and AUM is classified as a master's (L) by the Carnegie Foundation, one would expect differences in the curriculum that would impact library usage.

In analyzing the data in Table 4, we can see a reasonable correlation in the humanities. Specifically for the circulations for classes in the humanities,[17] the percentage of print circulations at Eckerd was 45.3%. Print circulations

TABLE 4. Circulations/Accesses for 2006 by LC Subject Classication

LC Subject Classications	Eckerd College Print Circulations by Subject	Percentage AUM Library Print Circulations by Subject	Percentage AUM NetLibrary Collections Access by Subject
A (General orks)	23(0.6)	12 (0.0)	1 (0.0)
B-BD (Philosophy)	967 (2.7)	190 (0.8)	69 (1.1)
BF (Psychology)	1,380 (3.9)	584 (2.6)	96 (1.5)
BH-B (Aesthetics-Ethics)	391(1.1)	30 (0.1)	20 (0.3)
BL-BX (Religion)	2,219 (6.3)	578 (2.5)	172 (2.8)
C-CT (History: General)	372 (1.1)	90 (0.0)	26 (0.4)
D-DX (orld History)	2,441 (6.9)	1404 (6.2)	222 (3.6)
E (American History)	1,518 (4.3)	1098 (4.8)	305 (3.3)
F (U.S.-Latin American History)	389 (1.1)	367 (1.6)	143 (2.3)
G-GB (Geography	114 (0.3)	12 (0.0)	26 (0.4)
GC (Oceanography)	123 (0.3)	1 (0.0)	4 (0.0)
GF (Human Ecology)	78 (0.2)	4 (0.0)	26 (0.4)
GN-GT (Anthropology	334 (0.9)	5 (0.0)	94 (1.5)
GV (Recreation)	526 (1.5)	537 (2.3)	70 (1.1)
H-HA (Social Sciences-Statistics)	190 (0.5)	143 (0.6)	12 (0.2)
HB-HC (Economics)	1,068 (3.0)	144 (0.6)	62 (1.0)
HE-HF (Transportation-Commerce)	819 (2.3)	787 (3.5)	270 (4.4)
HG (Finance)	567 (1.6)	92 (0.4)	65 (1.0)
H (Public Finance)	80 (0.2)	25 (0.1)	2 (0.0)
HM-HV (Sociology)	2,380 (6.7)	1888 (8.4)	492 (8.1)
HX (Socialism-Communism)	389 (1.1)	62 (0.2)	17 (0.2)
- X (Political Science)	1,229 (3.5)	594 (2.6)	150 (2.4)
- X (Law)	444 (1.2)	438 (1.9)	94 (1.5)
L-LT (Education)	817 (2.3)	1400 (6.2)	188 (3.1)
M-MT (Music)	851 (2.4)	559 (2.4)	153 (2.5)
N-NX (Art)	1,524 (4.3)	798 (3.5)	53 (0.8)
P-PB (Classical Languages & Literature)	391 (1.1)	251 (1.1)	89 (1.4)
PC (Romance languages)	57 (0.2)	54 (0.2)	9 (0.1)
PD (Scandinavian languages)	17 (0.1)	2 (0.0)	0 (0.0)
PE (English language)	160 (0.4)	89 (0.3)	25 (0.4)
PF (German languages)	8 (0.1)	13 (0.2)	2 (0.0)
PG-PH (Slavic languages)	162 (0.4)	73 (0.3)	2 (0.0)
P -PM (Oriental, Asian, African Languages)	139 (0.4)	41 (0.1)	6 (0.1)
PN (General Literature & Drama)	784 (2.2)	1038 (4.6)	314 (5.1)

(Continued on next page)

TABLE 4. Circulations/Accesses for 2006 by LC Subject Classication *(Continued)*

LC Subject Classications	Eckerd College Print Circulations by Subject	Percentage AUM Library Print Circulations by Subject	Percentage AUM NetLibrary Collections Access by Subject
P (French, Italian & Spanish Literature)	1,072 (3.0)	276 (1.2)	98 (0.1)
PR English Literature	1,422 (4.0)	1830 (8.1)	272 (4.4)
PS (American Literature	1,258 (3.5)	3012 (13.4)	649 (10.7)
PT (German Literature)	257 (0.7)	53 (0.2)	17 (0.0)
P (Children s Literature)	471 (1.3)	0 (0.0)	1 (0.0)
(Science: General)	281 (0.8)	92 (0.4)	22 (0.3)
A (Mathematics & Computer Science)	839 (2.4)	562 (2.5)	457 (7.5)
B (Astronomy)	441 (1.2)	25 (0.1)	10 (0.1)
C (Chemistry)	561 (1.6)	65 (0.2)	19 (0.3)
D (Physics)	652 (1.8)	38 (0.0)	14 (0.2)
E (Geology)	256 (0.7)	5 (0.0)	5 (0.0)
H- P (Biology)	1,192 (3.6)	483 (2.1)	142 (2.3)
R (Microbiology)	68 (0.2)	48 (0.2)	9 (0.1)
R-RB (Medicine: General)	392 (1.1)	281 (1.2)	151 (2.4)
RC (Internal Medicine)	578 (1.6)	663 (2.9)	243 (4.0)
RD-R (Medicine: Specialization)	304 (0.8)	962 (4.2)	198 (3.2)
S-S (Biology)	235 (0.7)	64 (0.2)	30 (0.4)
T (Management Engineering)	58 (0.2)	20 (0.0)	34 (0.5)
TA (Engineering: General)	15 (0.1)	9 (0.0)	20 (0.3)
TC (Hydraulic Engineering)	35 (0.1)	2 (0.0)	3 (0.0)
TD (Environmental Technology)	130 (0.4)	2 (0.0)	2 (0.0)
TE-T (Engineering Misc.)	34 (0.1)	8 (0.0)	9 (0.1)
T -TL (Electrical Engineering)	87 (0.2)	41 (0.1)	112 (1.8)
TN-TP (Mining & Chemical Engineering)	67 (0.2)	11 (0.0)	14 (0.2)
TR (Photography)	75 (0.25)	79 (0.3)	6 (0.0)
TS (Production Management)	19 (0.1)	9 (0.0)	20 (0.3)
TT (Handicrafts)	35 (0.1)	3 (0.0)	19 (0.3)
TX (Home Economics)	94 (0.3)	17 (0.0)	54 (0.8)
U (Military Science)	202 (0.6)	81 (0.3)	29 (0.4)
V (Naval Science)	38 (0.1)	11 (0.0)	1 (0.1)
Library Science	116 (0.3)	141(0.6)	124 (2.0)
Total	*35,376 This gure is incorrect. Actual total is 34,369	22,458	6,063

at AUM were 51.6%. Additionally, 39.4% of the electronic circulations was in the humanities classes. For the social sciences, the print circulations at Eckerd equal 30.75%, while AUM print circulations equal 30.5%. E-book circulations in the social sciences at AUM equal 29.6%, comparable to the print circulations in the social sciences. In the sciences and health-related fields, at Eckerd the print circulations equal 16.7%. AUM's print circulation in the sciences equaled 14 % of the circulations, and the electronic book access equaled 21%.

Interestingly, in the disciplines of math, AUM's print circulations were comparable to the circulation patterns at Eckerd (2.5 for AUM vs. 2.4 for Eckerd). Access to e-books, however, showed that 7.5% of the e-book titles accessed at AUM were in mathematics. In the field of medicine/nursing, both AUM print and e-book circulations were significantly higher than the circulations at Eckerd (8.3 in print for AUM, 9.6 e-books circula-tion, versus 3.5 in print for Eckerd). This significant difference can be tied to AUM having a school of nursing, which Eckerd does not, along with a program in medical technology which, again, Eckerd does not. Overall, there seems to be a reasonable correlation between the per-centage usages of e-books at AUM with those of the print collection. Both collections match the discipline area usage identified by Hardesty at Eckerd.

CONCLUSION

Through an examination of the usage data of the NetLibrary collections held by AUM, the data confirm the hypotheses that a small proportion of the titles are responsible for the majority of access regardless of format. Trueswell's 80/20 hypothesis is substantially confirmed. Similar to the findings of Hughes, 19.36% of the titles in the NetLibrary collections at AUM accounted for 49% of the access. William A. Britten, in his article "A Use Statistic for Collection Management: The 80/20 Rule Revisited," cites the argument against using circulation statistics by noting that "A high level of disuse can be said to be the price of scholarly potential."[18]

In the 30 years since the Pittsburgh Study was completed, libraries still purchase materials to support "scholarly potential." Acquiring electronic books is no different from acquiring the print counterpart in terms of the potential value of the title in question to the study body and the faculty. At AUM, the usage of the NetLibrary collections is consistent with the proposition that few books provide for the majority of use.

REFERENCES

1. Kent, A. (1979). *Use of library materials: The University of Pittsburgh Study*. New York: Marcel Dekker, Inc., and Trueswell, R. W. (1969). Some behavioral patterns of library users: The 80/20 Rule. *Wilson Library Bulletin, 43*, 458–461.
2. Kent, 1.
3. Kent, 1.
4. Trueswell, 458.
5. Trueswell, 459.
6. Fussler, H. H., & Julian, L. S. (1961). *Patterns in the use of books in large research libraries* (pp. 3–4). Chicago: University of Chicago Press, 1969.
7. Bulick, Stephen, Sabor, William N., & Flynn, Roger. (1979). Circulation and in-house use of Books. In Kent, A. *Use of library materials: The University of Pittsburgh Study*. New York: Marcel Dekker, Inc.
8. Hardesty, L. Use of library materials at a small liberal arts college. *Library Research, 3*, 261–282, and Hardesty, L. (1988) Use of library materials at a small liberal arts college: A replication At Eckerd College of the 1978 University of Pittsburgh Study. *Collection Management*, 1981;*10* (3–4), 61–80.
9. Galvin, T. J., & Kent, A. (1977). Use of a university library collection. *Library Journal, 102*, 2317–2320 (specifically p. 2318).
10. Hughes, C. A. (2001). The myth of 'obsolescence': The monograph in the digital library. *portal: Libraries and the Academy, 1*(2), 113–119.
11. Hughes, 117.
12. Hardesty, L. (1981). Use of library materials at a small liberal arts college. *Library Research, 3*, 262.
13. Kent, 10.
14. Hardesty, 1981, 266.
15. Kent, 201.
16. Hardesty, 1988, 68–72.
17. Classes calculated as being in the Humanities included B-BD; BH-BJ; BL-BX; C-CT; D-DX; E; F; M-MT; N; P-PB; PC-PT (Note: AUM does not classify juvenile literature in the PZs). Classes in the Social Sciences include: BF; G-GB; GF; GN-GT; GV; H-HA; HB-HC; HE-HF; HG;HM-HV; HX; J-JX; K-KX; L-LT; TR-TX; U; V and Z. Classes in the Sciences include Q; QA; QB; QC; QD; QE; QH-QP; QR; R-RZ; S-SK; T-TP.
18. Britten, W. A. (1990). A use statistic for collection management: The 80/20 Rule revisited. *Library Acquistions: Practice & Theory, 14*, 188.

Mission Possible: E-books and the Humanities

Tony Horava

When e-books are discussed in an academic setting, it is often assumed that the primary appeal will be in the sciences and professional fields such as management. Though it is true that students and professors in STM disciplines have been among the earliest adaptors (seeing that they have become quite comfortable with e-journal searching and browsing), there is certainly a case to be made for e-books in other research areas. Humanities fields, once the sole bastion of the printed book and the study of primary manuscripts, have taken a mixed and tentative approach to e-books. The first part of this article will discuss the unique challenges that e-books pose for humanities researchers, in the context of scholarly communication and the nature of humanities research. The second part will examine implementation and management challenges. Humanities e-book collections at the University of Ottawa, Canada will serve as a backdrop for this discussion. Computer-based e-books, rather than portable devices, will be examined.

The paradox of e-books is readily apparent—for every point there is a counterpoint. E-books provide convenient 24/7 access from the desktop, but interfaces can be difficult to navigate. They allow patrons to save, print, and download, but the digital rights management (DRM) restrictions imposed by various e-book aggregators and publishers are a constant thorn. E-books offer browsing, but patrons don't browse an e-book the way they do a print book. E-books provide a wealth of new access, but ownership is often not included in the bargain. E-books provide durable links, links to reviews, and inclusion of supplementary material in audio-visual formats, but many patrons prefer to print out the pages that interest them. Libraries acquire e-book collections that greatly augment their holdings, but acquisition and cataloguing procedures need to be carefully honed to take into account a format that doesn't correspond to the traditional print world. Licensing of e-books can assume many shapes and require time-consuming negotiations, as standard models have not yet emerged. Libraries develop access strategies that promote visibility and integration into teaching and research but face the challenge of defining measures of success, in terms of usage or collection development.

Humanities e-books are widely available today, but determining what to acquire opens a Pandora's box of issues related to collection development, budgeting, teaching and research expectations, and access challenges. The use of digital reference works has become commonplace, but the digital monograph has received a much more limited level of acceptance. Overlaying all of these issues is the budgeting conundrum—how to budget appropriately for e-books in an information environment exploding with new opportunities? How to prioritize e-books in the humanities? These are a few realities of the current landscape.

HUMANITIES FACULTY

Characteristics

The vast majority of faculty today were schooled in a print culture in which discrete objects were studied. Documents or manuscripts were viewed and analyzed on an individual basis, often involving travel, grant funding, and creative research techniques. It was assumed that the text as an artifact was paramount and that the scholar's role was to develop an intimate understanding of texts and ideas in their cultural and intellectual milieu. The availability online of scholarly archives, image databases, illuminated manuscripts, audio and video files, blogs, and the use of social networking technologies has meant that different media have a more prominent role in scholarly discourse than ever before and representations in various media that can be contextualized in ways that were never possible before. This could include collocating different editions of a work and its variants; assessing paintings, songs, and oral transcripts with primary source documents; or performing textual analysis and data mining on a large body of work to examine linguistic, syntactic, and culturally defined patterns of speech and thought.

Visualizing and juxtaposing relationships between objects has led to new interpretations and modes of inquiry. This of course is set against the explosion of research databases, online archives, and Web sites that allow the scholar to easily search, browse, and retrieve large amounts of information relating to a specific author, work, period, or movement. Repurposing knowledge and creating new contextual meanings has never been easier, assuming that one has awareness of and access to the relevant resources. Preservation of the scholarly record in digital form is a critical challenge for everyone. The ACLS Commission on Cyberinfrastructure for the Humanities and Social Sciences points to the urgency of the issues:

> The needs of humanists and scientists converge in this emerging cyberinfrastructure. As the importance of technology-enabled innovation grows across all fields, scholars are increasingly dependent on sophisticated systems for the creation, curation, and preservation of information. They are also dependent on a policy, economic, and legal environment that encourages appropriate and unimpeded access to both digital information and digital tools. It is crucial for the humanities and the social sciences to join scientists and engineers in defining and building this infrastructure so that it meets the needs and incorporates the contributions of humanists and social scientists.[1]

There can be no doubt that this will revolutionize scholarship. Cyberinfrastructure implies a layer of tools, practices, standards, and support that is essential for the research enterprise. As the generation of graduate students from the past 10 years moves into the ranks of academe, they will bring new concepts of what is considered scholarly output for purposes of tenure and promotion. These students will have been schooled in the virtues of electronic theses submission, open-access publications, and the widespread availability of digital research resources and workflow tools to capture, share, and manipulate information. Freely available text analysis tools such as TAPoR (tapor.ualberta.ca) and Collex (www.nines.org) are providing transformative abilities for humanities scholars to make and share new discoveries. These have opened doors of research that were not previously possible, simplifying and synthesizing resources that were once disparate and kept in separate silos. The veneration for the printed monograph, engrained in generation after generation of humanities scholars, will begin to give way to new forms of scholarly communication considered legitimate. These will be articles and books published online, multimedia works, open-access publications, and collaborative ventures of many kinds.

The envisioned Scholarly Collective at the University of Minnesota addresses the need for a new infrastructure to support scholarship in the humanities:

> Our proposed Scholar's Collective would address the dual challenge of creating useful tools for humanities scholarship, while simultaneously creating capacity for collaboration. The methodology we recommend would focus on creating incentives for adoption of these new tools through graduate student–faculty research partnerships... The scope of the Scholar's Collective addresses two significant cultural shifts in humanities scholarship. The first is the research practices of scholars who depend on electronic media and tools for individual and collaborative work but whose research methods have not yet successfully incorporated techniques to manage a hybrid information environment. The second is the increasingly social dimension of new online environments.[2]

If this pattern is emulated elsewhere—and I believe it will be—we can expect to see an easier transition to the new model. When this transformation really takes root, it can be expected that the print monograph will begin to lose its predominance in scholarly discourse, and a greater coexistence between print and electronic will develop, although the print will remain dominant and prestigious for many years to come. Collaboration will become integral to research, and the growing legitimacy of digital forms of research will have profound implications for collection development in academic libraries. There will be less emphasis on acquiring print books and more emphasis on assuring that a wide range of resources, largely digital, will be made available. The Google Book Search project, now developing a critical mass of participation and content from almost thirty research libraries (as at October 2007), is a sure sign that e-books will play a growing role in academic discourse and in how books are accessed. Regardless of how one feels about the legal controversies, this huge collection of out-of-copyright books is challenging libraries to find innovative ways to deliver monograph literature to its patrons. Expectations are changing rapidly as Google is increasingly seen as a partner rather than a foe.

Young faculty are developing their research profiles and advancing their careers in a digital age wherein new ways of sharing and analyzing primary and secondary sources and new ways of publishing are having a profound effect on shaping their expectations of what a research library is supposed to be. As this generation progresses through the ranks, we can expect to see their influence grow and a consequent impact on how e-books are used and supported. Twenty or thirty years from now, will the debate over book formats in the humanities have shifted? I'll speculate that there will be a much wider consensus on book formats and that this will develop from the ways in which faculty teach, research, and publish.

Humanities publishers, uncertain today about which business models to pursue, will move away from the unsustainable model of producing a print run of several hundred copies to a more distributed approach that embraces new technologies of production and dissemination, including print-on-demand, pay-per-view, and access across various aggregator systems. In this era of mergers and acquisitions, many smaller publishers will be absorbed by larger entities. University presses are under tremendous pressure to become financially self-sustaining, to exploit digital distribution technologies and new business models; this is not an arena wherein the humanities have the greatest appeal or traction. Their very purpose of credentialing scholarship and conferring prestige in a competitive publishing environment are under much debate. Rice University Press (⟨http://ricepress.rice.edu/⟩) is a good example of a press that is reinventing itself as a digital scholarly publisher offering monographs in the humanities and social sciences in an affordable manner, using open-source software and Creative Commons licensing. Print-on-demand will complement the digital format, and partnerships with other university presses will support the publishing of backlogged works. Whenever politically feasible, university presses and libraries should make common cause in order to combine their areas of expertise in the publishing enterprise. The Ithaka report, "University Publishing in a Digital Age," notes that "There are natural partnerships between the press and the library due to their complementary skills and assets."[3]

Trends and Issues

There are several trends and issues that are worth highlighting. The rise of the image in our wired world has important implications for how we see the relationship between print and other media, particularly in the humanities. Mitchell Stephens argues that:

> the video revolution is, by my reckoning, humankind's third major communications revolution, and the disruptions occasioned by the first two—writing and print—are surprisingly similar to those we are experiencing now. The stages in which the new technologies were adopted seem comparable, as does the profundity of the transformations they cause. Even the anxieties and anger sound familiar.[4]

There can be no doubt that this has profound implications for the humanities, where the printed word is the core around which meaning, form, and scholarly discourse have intricately developed. For the monograph, the medium is the message—the form profoundly influences the patterns of thought, analysis, and values that underpin the creation of new knowledge. It would seem that the advent of the e-book implies a radical break with the past at both a conscious and an unconscious level in how we engage with ideas and existing scholarship and how we communicate with colleagues. The ramifications for a text-anchored culture are only now beginning to be felt. Stephens wrote in 1998, when the impact of the Web was only moderately felt in comparison with today's ubiquitous presence. How literacy is being influenced by the shift to a visual culture is a much large question that is especially critical to the humanities.

The Report from the MLA Ad Hoc Committee on the Future of Scholarly Publishing noted several key concerns in relation to e-book publication:

> Several questions about electronic publishing are still not resolved. First, electronic book publication does not necessarily reduce costs, a major portion of which are connected with the editing process. Second, electronic book readers and software programs designed for reading electronic documents on personal computers have not been standardized, and different systems

may not become compatible for many years yet (Lynch, 'Battle'). Third, we need mechanisms that will guarantee the permanence of electronic publications, given that digital storage systems continue to undergo complex changes (Besser 157–158). And fourth, some observers fear that large conglomerates will end up owning and controlling the content of electronic sources (Lynch, 'Battle'), thus making access to this mode of publication more difficult for scholars in the humanities, whose work often does not have immediate or obvious practical use value. . . . Most urgently, we need to address the issue of peer review for electronic publication in the humanities, whether of monographs and specialized books or of articles in online journals.[5]

Here are five points of disquietude: the costs of e-books; the lack of standardized access across online readers and devices; the durability of content; the fear of monopolistic control of the intellectual property; and the centrality of peer review (which is equivalent to the time-honoured approach to print books). All of these issues are perfectly valid and reflect the impact of technology and market forces on traditional approaches for the dissemination and permanence of scholarship. The fact that these issues are being addressed by various associations, publishers, and libraries signifies that there is recognition of how essential it is to respond to these concerns in order to successfully develop an e-book model. It is also worth noting that the MLA Task Force on Tenure and Promotion recommended that "Departments and institutions should recognize the legitimacy of scholarship produced in new media, whether by individuals or in collaboration, and create procedures for evaluating these forms of scholarship."[6] This is certainly a sign of changing times amid the cautionary notes above. Legitimizing new media, such as e-books, for the tenure and promotion process will have major consequences for academic discourse and reward structures.

Peer review has been a cornerstone in the scholarly ecosystem for more than 300 years. While the peer review system is imperfect, it is better than any alternative and has well served the academic community for ensuring the advancement of knowledge according to accepted standards. The exceptions to this situation—much played in the media—only highlight the general applicability of the rule. The new forms of digital scholarship in the humanities will need to come to grips with peer review to ensure that quality control remains integral to the publishing enterprise.

The vast impact of interdisciplinarity needs to be underlined. Today it is commonplace that humanities scholars work in a climate of awareness of contiguous disciplines not only in other humanities research areas but in the social sciences, science, engineering, law, and medicine. Discipline-specific norms and practices are exposed to new modes of analysis and new ways of approaching research problems and methodological issues. Though many humanities scholars work independently, as their predecessors did, there are many more working in collaborative teams. One good example at the University of Ottawa is the Piano Pedagogy Research Laboratory. This is a highly multidisciplinary initiative to study piano learning and performance.

> Computer science engineers, cognitive psychologists, neuroscientists, audio-visual specialists, software developers, and musicians have joined together to share their knowledge and expertise with the objective of providing the research equipment and the research protocols that would allow a better understanding of the complex skill that is piano learning.[7]

This hub has led to numerous teaching and research activities, cross-institutional collaboration, public lectures, various papers, and a forthcoming book.

Funding agencies in the humanities are placing greater emphasis on collaborative approaches, national and international participation, the creation of research that is relevant to social issues, the building of knowledge at the confluence of multiple domains, and the presentation of results in widely accessible forms and in different media. All of these factors tend to favor the development of the e-book, which is tied to technological approaches for wider dissemination of research. The development of Gutenberg-e in collaboration between the Mellon Foundation, Columbia University Press, and the American Historical Association is a shining example of how scholarly monographs can be published with high production standards in digital format. Time will tell whether this is a model that others will adopt. The California Digital Library's eScholarship Editions (⟨http://content.cdlib.org/escholarship/⟩) provides access to 2,000 scholarly e-books, many in humanities disciplines.

Scholarly associations, where humanities faculty work together for the benefit of their discipline, face difficult choices about their future. Lynch has noted that:

> One of the first things you need to talk about is what are the priorities in a scholarly communications program being run out

of the society. Is the priority broadest dissemination, meaning open access? Is the primary goal revenue? Or is the priority really innovation in modes of scholarly communication, which may take you to a very different place than open access?[8]

In this landscape, humanities associations need to forge a well-crafted strategy by considering their mission, their resources, and their sustainability. What is the best way to disseminate knowledge, contribute to the advancement of the discipline and its professional members, and maintain financial viability? There are enormous tensions at play and no easy answers. The crisis in monograph publishing is a reality with which humanities associations need to come to terms. Many factors—economic, political, technological, and educational—have led to this crisis. There are opportunities to develop digital scholarship, such as e-books, that will have a large impact on the future viability of publishing and dissemination of research in the humanities. Each association has to consider its mission in light of the new modes of scholarly communication and the stakes in partnering with a major publisher or vendor, or in resolutely deciding to remain independent.

On a different level, it is important to consider the nature of reading experience in the digital age. It is clear that the cognitive process of reading text from a screen, rather than reading a physical object page by page, with all of the tactile and sensory differences, is enormously different. The nature of holding and reading a physical object creates a personal experience that can't be duplicated in an electronic environment. The pervasive impact of the Web on the development of language is another major area of cultural change. The reality that language is becoming much more fluid, non-prescriptive, and technological has an influence on our experience of reading. If McLuhan were alive today, he would surely have lots to say about the pervasive influence of the e-book on the habits of a humanities scholar in the 21st century. If the medium really is the message, then the digital medium adds a value of legitimate repurposing that greatly influences how the e-book content is used. Morineau's functional analysis of the ability of print and e-book formats to transmit information indicates something major about the cognitive difference between the two:

> The results obtained show that the function of encoding knowledge is comparable to that which occurs with a paper book, thus permitting a similar level of comprehension of the information (humour of the text, quantity of data recalled from memory).

Nevertheless, because the electronic book is functionally closer to a computer than a traditional book (because of the support's inherently multi-functional nature) it does not provide the external indicators to memory that the classical book does, in that it does not serve as an unambiguous index to indicate a field of knowledge on the basis of its particular physical form. The sensory-motor evaluation of supports has allowed us to show the strong relationship that exists between the sensory-motor representation of the user and his/her treatment of the information content of the paper book or e-book.[9]

The questions of memory and form are but two facets of this sea-change and are challenges that will need to be further investigated and understood as we move forward in the digital era. As memory is an intricate element of learning and communication, how will the personalized experience of the printed text can replaced by the customization of an e-book? Are the two equivalent? There are qualitative and experiential differences to consider. It is useful for librarians to be aware of issues related to the learning and cognitive impacts of e-books, as these matters are very germane to the mission of our institutions and the alternative ways in which teaching is delivered to many students. Not enough is known about the pedagogical outcomes in postsecondary education using digital materials, particularly as this affects the humanities, where sustained argument is essential for presentation of ideas and issues. As time passes, there will certainly be more investigation in this area.

The ACLS Humanities E-book project notes that "Each year the world community creates five exabytes of new information, including scholarship, in stored media in the form of paper, film, magnetic, and optical media . . . . This figure is expected to grow by 30% a year. Only one-tenth of one percent of this material is created in print."[10] The sheer volume of this output leads to questions of access, stewardship, and evaluation of content. We are at a crossroads in terms of how scholarly communication is produced, and the e-book falls squarely into this debate. E-books will frequently be citing works available only in print, whether owing to copyright issues or lack of resources to digitize, and this will create its own challenges. There are enormous implications for preserving our printed cultural heritage and being able to use it for scholarship and dissemination of research, but coordinated initiatives are only beginning to emerge, and these require more involvement than just the library world to succeed. A broad coalition of stakeholders is required. Ventures such as Portico and

CLOCKSS are promising, but their focus has been on ejournal literature rather than e-books.

Partnerships

In this context, it is clear that e-book collections, however defined, will lead to profound methodological changes in the ways that humanists think, research, and present new knowledge to the world. The analytical tools (e.g., advanced indexing tools, modeling and simulation tools) and the dizzying ability to combine primary research documents and objects in new contexts have implications for the nature of the scholarly monograph as a sustained argument that can only be understood in a linear fashion (i.e., from beginning to end). The Web-based world is standing this paradigm on its head, and it won't be long before non-linear multimedia and digital scholarly works in the humanities gain sufficient credibility to coexist on a par with traditional print counterparts. This will have a much more profound impact on the humanities than the social sciences, or law, science, or medicine, for the humanities have been intimately grounded in the printed word as the root of knowledge, understanding, and inspiration. The digital book inherently has a dynamic form that encourages the updating of arguments and inclusion of supplemental content; this is contradistinguished from the fixed form of the printed text.

It is not too surprising that the humanities have been slower to adapt to the revolution underway in university teaching and research. In only a decade, e-book collections have made enormous transformations for practices for some humanist scholars, but this will become more ubiquitous as time passes. The relationship between computing and the humanities has led to new ways of envisioning and explaining the past, and thereby informing our understanding of cultural and social issues that involve visual layers of meaning. There is an intensifying synergy occurring between computing centers and various humanities programs and researchers, thus transforming the way research is conceived and undertaken.

The University of Virginia Institute for Advanced Technology in the Humanities is a good example. Its goal:

> is to explore and develop information technology as a tool for scholarly humanities research. To that end, we provide our Fellows with consulting, technical support, applications development, and networked publishing facilities. We also cultivate partnerships and participate in humanities computing initiatives with

libraries, publishers, information technology companies, scholarly organizations, and other groups residing at the intersection of computers and cultural heritage.[11]

One of the current projects is "Mapping the Dalai Lamas" which aims to:

> integrate digital texts of classical Tibetan-language biographies with digital animated maps, timelines, and images to present significant events in the lives of the Dalai Lamas as well as to reveal hitherto unnoticed connections between biographical events, geographic location, social and historical context, and literary and rhetorical expression.[12]

Innovative linkages between religious texts and the socio-cultural landscape in which they were created leads to new understanding of the past, and this is indicative of the new research culture in which the humanities are developing. There is no doubt that these developments are blurring the line between e-books and other types of documents and objects and throwing into question the definition of the monograph as a scholarly work painstakingly created by a lone scholar, in a fixed form. It is also evident that the silos of scholarly research and popular culture are rapidly vanishing; for example, photos, oral histories, advertising, cartoons, Web sites, blogs, and magazines of all sorts can be legitimate sources of research. Kirschenbaum reflects upon the challenges and complexities of working with literature in the new world of scholarship:

> The wholesale migration of literature to a born-digital state places our collective literary and cultural heritage at real risk. But for every problem that electronic documents create—problems for preservation, problems for access, problems for cataloguing and classification and discovery and delivery—there are equal, and potentially enormous, opportunities. What if we could use machine-learning algorithms to sift through vast textual archives and draw our attention to a portion of a manuscript manifesting an especially rich and unusual pattern of activity, the multiple layers of revision captured in different versions of the file creating a three-dimensional portrait of the writing process? What if these revisions could in turn be correlated with the content of a Web site that someone in the author's MySpace network had blogged?[13]

The future holds enormous potential for new forms of content analysis and data mining leading to discoveries that were hitherto impossible. This is an exciting development that needs to be balanced by the pressing need for curation of digital research and with the need to develop access and context-rich discovery mechanisms. E-book collections, as a key layer of scholarship, exist in the same sphere of potential and fragility that is common to all digital works in the cultural record.

Kevin Kelly examines the issue from the view of repurposing content and adding value in the Web world we inhabit:

> What is the technology telling us? That copies don't count any more. Copies of isolated books, bound between inert covers, soon won't mean much. Copies of their texts, however, will gain in meaning as they multiply by the millions and are flung around the world, indexed and copied again. What counts are the ways in which these common copies of a creative work can be linked, manipulated, annotated, tagged, highlighted, bookmarked, translated, enlivened by other media and sewn together into the universal library. Soon a book outside the library will be like a Web page outside the Web, gasping for air. Indeed, the only way for books to retain their waning authority in our culture is to wire their texts into the universal library.[14]

As it is quite unlikely that the cultural record will be fully digitized anytime soon, the humanities need to address the thorny issues of resource discovery and collaboration in a hybrid world where content mashing is the norm. While it is somewhat premature to assume that physical books will be "gasping for air," in terms of visibility there is no doubt that humanist scholars will need to adapt their research and methodological strategies in light of these realities. The print and digital realms can be seen almost as different languages requiring a complex translation process to coherently integrate different ways of knowing and learning.

LIBRARY IMPLEMENTATION ISSUES

Licensing

Much has been spoken and written about the complexities and frustrations of licensing e-book collections. There are subscription options;

purchase options; pay-per-view options; patron demand-driven models; and various combinations such as lease to own and selecting purchase or lease on a subject collection basis. Access models that limit the e-book to a single concurrent user, or to an annual number of accesses, have caused headaches. Libraries have educated publishers about the importance of perpetual access and contract language for ensuring these options. Libraries have invested major time in negotiating the intricacies of licenses with publishers or vendors and in coming to terms with the implications of leasing versus ownership. Library negotiators have dealt with defining rights and responsibilities, definitions of authorized users and permitted uses, cost models involving print and electronic formats, legal clauses to mitigate risk, material format issues, and renewal options. Allen McKiel, commenting on ebrary's global e-book survey, states that: "The intertwined relationship between print and electronic marketing strategies combined with the growing complexity of e-marketing models exacerbates an already tense relationship between librarians and publishers. Trust is a valuable asset for success in an arena of uncertainty."[15]

Libraries have had to adapt their workflows to publishers and vendor's models, rather than the other way around. MARC records are sometimes available, sometimes not. The quality and source of the records have been important issues as libraries try to incorporate e-book cataloguing into the standard workflow. Acquiring a collection of several thousand e-books has required cataloguing services to build loaders and develop processes for integrating these titles into the catalogue as efficiently as possible. Acquisitions units have to set up new accounts and workflow procedures with multiple vendors and publishers for acquiring e-books, and this adds new layers of work for capturing the relevant information in ILS systems and for reporting and payment purposes. Developing parallel procedures to print acquisition has been time consuming and complex for libraries. Collections librarians who negotiate agreements have had to confront a smorgasbord of licensing options.

DRM systems that monitor and tightly limit printing and downloading have led to endless frustration for library staff and patrons. The frequent nonexistence of interlibrary loan provisions has led many to question the value of e-books in a collaborative and open information environment. Technical issues such as browser plug-ins and two-step authentication systems have necessitated time and energy from systems staff to enable access. It is essential that publishers and vendors take a long hard look at their business and technology models to simplify the acquisition process and provide wider access to e-book content for authorized users. DRM in an academic environment to protect intellectual property needs to be rethought. We need to insist on the unacceptability of DRM systems and to apply copyright provisions (fair use) as the benchmark for usage rights in e-books licensing agreements. Library staff are very responsible in investigating excessive downloading and in sensitizing patrons to their responsibilities in using licensed commercial content. Threats to intellectual property are much more likely to originate outside of the university than within it.

The Shared Electronic Resources Understanding (SERU) is an emerging initiative that aims to reduce the onerousness of licensing by developing an informal benchmark for agreement, and this is highly laudable. However, it remains to be seen how e-book publishers and vendors will respond to this opportunity. There are also various model licenses available for use, but these were created with the periodicals marketplace in mind and need adaptation to suit the e-book format. As time progresses, publishers will likely become comfortable with informal arrangements as opposed to the time-consuming process of formal licensing. The possibility of litigation between libraries and publishers to resolve issues seems evermore remote.

For the humanities, libraries greatly prefer the purchase model to the subscription option, as the titles are expected to be of enduring value, much as a print book. Questions about new editions or supplementary material need to be considered—how will this be addressed? It is unusual to find an e-book purchase agreement that doesn't require an annual access fee to ensure continued access, thus invoking budget commitments. Publishers and vendors need to be aware that e-books represent a sea-change in how collection development and collection management are understood, particularly in the humanities. Publishers see the academic sector as a growth market and, not surprisingly, new e-book offers are popping up on a regular basis.

Publishers need to examine their economic assumptions about the academic marketplace. Delays between print and electronic publication are a serious problem—how many publishers are moving toward a digital production workflow? Publishers fear the cannibalization of print revenue streams but underestimate the bounce effect of backlists suddenly being available online. Knowing what is available in what format from which vendor is an ongoing challenge for selectors and inhibits a more responsive uptake of the e-book. Pricing, of course, is a hot-button issue. Greater flexibility in purchasing models is important and unbundling the electronic from the print to recognize the economies of scale in the digital format. This in turn links back to the publisher's production model. The scale of the e-book phenomenon, and the significant overhead in implementation and maintenance, mean that libraries cannot afford price models that are grounded in the print. Scalability means a more affordable costing model that recognizes the efficiencies of digital production. And this raises the difficult question of whether the print monograph is an endangered species or not.

Access

MARC records were acquired in order to make the titles available in the catalogue via 856 links. This is vital in enabling discovery and visibility of e-books, as the catalogue is still a central access point for learning about library resources. Keyword searching retrieves e-titles, which means that students discover e-books without having to search for a specific format. Studies have indicated that catalogue access is one of the drivers behind successful promotion and high usage of e-books. MARC records are sometimes included in the e-book collection, and sometimes there is an additional—and large—price tag attached. Vendors need to be sensitive to the fact that libraries require full MARC records when acquiring e-book collections and that this be included in the proposal. While some will argue for the death of the catalogue, it is more likely that the library holdings will remain an integral element of the library's portfolio of resources. However, it will be absorbed or layered into new discovery tools that include Web-based resources and external resources. Libraries have not been able to exploit the richness of MARC record data for resource discovery. The ability of these new tools to enable faceted searching, relevancy ranking, and user-generated tagging will enable richer access to e-book metadata than ever before and better exposing this metadata is essential for increasing usage.

The Web site is also central to an e-book strategy. At the University of Ottawa, we offer a descriptive A–Z database listing. The e-book collections are included in this page, as they are searchable databases. As the database page has high visibility and is considered prime real estate on the Web site, students and faculty often access e-book databases through this route. Subject librarians link can link to these collections on their subject-speciality Web pages or course pages. We have also developed a promotion page for e-books under a "How To" link on the main library page. This provides information on the different ways of searching for e-books in the catalogue, either individually or as a collection. We offer a page explaining how to create persistent links to e-resources such as e-books. As faculty become more familiar with this process, they will be incorporating these links into course Web sites and other course material to be shared with students. Librarians actively promote e-book collections in information literacy programs and through research assistance and reference service. Federated searching holds much promise in allowing patrons to effectively find e-books across different collections and across different formats, but we are in the early days of federated searching. There are various technical complexities in federated searching, such as security issues, response time, and the availability of connectors, that need to be addressed before this can become a viable solution. Staff workload and ongoing maintenance are not insignificant issues either.

Developing a critical mass of e-books is an important objective. This means that the patrons searching for library resources will receive meaningful and numerous hits, on a par with print materials, and this will build awareness and familiarity. E-journal searching across large publisher collections has become commonplace with astonishing rapidity. In today's world, how can we develop an awareness that scholarly e-book collections are far from being free? It is important to instill an understanding of costs, scale, and budgeting. We decided to create a Web page that highlights the fact that several million dollars per year are spent in e-resources, many of which are e-book collections. This step can help instill a better understanding of the nature of scholarly information in digital form.

Can scholarly e-books be made available for PDA and other mobile devices? To achieve greater visibility and impact, we need to make e-books accessible in ways that fit in with patrons' habits for acquiring and using information. While there will certainly be technical and security issues to consider, it is important for publishers and vendors of e-books to move in this direction, as libraries need to focus on delivering content in ways that are student-focussed.

Integration is a buzzword that is regularly heard in discussions about e-books. Integration with catalogues, with Web sites, with federated search tools, and with information literacy programs, is a basic requirement. To achieve maximum exposure and impact, libraries are developing integration strategies for their e-book collections. Evidence so far indicates that the catalogue is the primary access and discovery tool for e-books. We also need to ask, How do we define success? What level of usage and what critical mass of anecdotal evidence will allow us to say that the financial and staff investments have paid off? There is no doubt that a significant percentage of faculty in humanities need to see the value of e-books for teaching and research and actively promote their use before any indicators of success can be realized.

Budgeting

E-book collections wreak havoc on the traditional distinction between serials and monograph budgets. Neither beast nor fowl, they fall into a hybrid zone that requires careful consideration of how the budget is allocated, as there are implications at the format and subject level, both for one-time and ongoing commitments.

Historical collections, such as *Early English Books Online* and *Eighteenth Century Collections Online*, are acquired as a major one-time cost with an annual access fee. This requires two budget expenditures, one of which is ongoing. On which budget codes should these be paid? How are they to be funded in light of many other pressing priorities for collection development? We have a multi-library environment, and we chose to pay the one-time costs from a central monograph fund dedicated to electronic resources. The ongoing access fee is paid from a central serials fund. These monies are taken off the top of the budget, and the remaining monies are allocated to the libraries according to a process and formula that takes into consideration the various supply and demand factors. However, this remains much more of an art than a science.

The issues become more complex when one considers e-book collections of current titles. Are they one-time purchases or ongoing commitments? Are they to be paid on monograph or serial funds, in relation to format and budget control? This blurs the lines of traditional notions regarding budget allocation and requires schools to think in new and creative ways. If a current e-book collection is an ongoing commitment, how does this affect the monograph allocation for the disciplines concerned? Can one sustain the commitment in the long term? It may not be simple to determine which disciplines are affected and to what degree. What about print equivalents? No one wants to pay twice for the same content, but are researchers in the humanities prepared to give up their cherished print copies and go solely digital? This will vary enormously depending on the culture within the faculty, but it is essential to ask this question as our role is to support the teaching and research requirements of the university community.

Slicing the pie into thinner slices can mean that reductions elsewhere need to be made. Can a library afford to duplicate print *and* electronic? On principle, we like to think that we shouldn't pay twice for the same content, but there are occasions when it seems necessary. It can also be argued that the value-added search and linking features, remote accessibility, integration with other resources, and inclusion of supplementary content in other formats (video, audio, and data) make the e-book a fluid work separate from its print counterpart. However, there is no easy consensus on this issue. In what situations are we prepared to pay twice for the same content, when humanities faculty prefer the time-honoured print copy, even when the aggregated e-book collection is demonstrated to them? Many libraries have had to cut back on their print monograph acquisitions in recent years owing to budget pressures. This means that the e-book needs to clearly demonstrate its value and relevance in the context of scarce financial resources.

The impact on approval plans needs to be carefully considered as well. Approval plans for print titles are commonplace in academic libraries today. This practice has been developed and refined over the past 30 years or so, in response to the need for more efficient ways of delivering appropriate books. If one subscribes to a publisher's e-book collection on an annual basis, does the library decide to eliminate the print titles from a vendor approval plan, and how does one avoid duplication? Michael Levine-Clark notes that "In order for e-Books to be successfully and meaningfully integrated into the approval process, approval vendors need to have a significant amount of frontlist e-Books available to them at the time of publication."[16] This may work in the STM arena, where researchers are quite happy to use the virtual library, but it is an entirely different matter where humanists are concerned. Dialogue and consultation, both within and without the library, will be important to find solutions that work for everyone. This also points directly to the challenges raised by the Big Deal in regards to e-books. Does a library need every book published by a given publisher? If 80% or 90% are judged relevant, is it more cost-effective to acquire the whole collection? What is the tipping point? And how does one justify these decisions to faculty, especially in relation to their attachment to print? The budget impact of allocating scarce resources to a large-scale e-book collection needs to be carefully considered, especially considering that some faculty may require specialized primary sources that are available only in print.

Collection development strategy is important. Can one make a long-term commitment to an e-book collection, in terms of content and budget? The curriculum, the teaching technologies, and desired learning outcomes have to be taken into account. If not, the work of licensing, acquiring, cataloguing, and promoting could be in vain. In the humanities, this question has particular resonance, as books are seen to be at the heart of the collection, and the physical library is usually seen as their laboratory.

The "journalization" of e-books is widely evident—they are being packaged and sold as collections that require annual renewal, and yet e-books are not serials in the typical sense. They are one-time publications, as are print monographs. There is an expectation, however, that new content will be added as it becomes available, just as in the journal world. From a budget viewpoint, e-books that are acquired as ongoing collections need to be financed as an annual renewal, and the costs can be quite high. Producing collection management reports for e-books can be a challenge as well, for this depends on how the titles are entered into the acquisitions system (e.g., coded as books or serials and entered as individual bib records or not) and the tools available for extracting the data. The muddying of the boundaries between serials and monographs has profound consequences for how we conceive of e-books and absorb them into the library's various workflows and reporting structures. If the e-book package subscription were cancelled, researchers would quickly notice that new titles are no longer being added, and collection development issues would be raised. In an era wherein e-book collections can be acquired or eliminated with great rapidity, how are libraries prepared to deal with the contingency of losing a collection? Is there a viable fallback strategy?

Usage

The University of Ottawa has acquired a number of well-known e-book collections in the humanities, both retrospective and current. There are approximately 330,000 e-book titles available to the university community, most of which were acquired as collections. Some were acquired consortially and others independently. While conventional wisdom would lead one to expect low usage, the reality is more nuanced.

This collection includes monographs in philosophy, religious studies, political science, and finance. We own approximately 1,100 titles. In a 1-year period, there were about 1,000 printed pages viewed ("full-content units requested"). Oxford explains that full-content units requested are "the number of entries viewed. For long articles split into sections, each section counts as a separate 'content unit.' For Oxford Scholarship Online, five print pages viewed online counts as one 'Full-content unit.'"[17] This terminology is hardly self-evident. There were 538 searches and 6,709 Web pages viewed, for an average of 12.4 pages per search (Fig. 1). This would indicate that patrons are using this resource for quick reference or targeted searching.

Early English Books Online is a collection of works published in English between 1475 and 1700, as well as works published in other languages in Britain and her dependencies. There are about 125,000 titles. There were 1.54 PDF downloads per search, and slightly more than 7 document or page image views per search. There were approximately .09 documents or

FIGURE 1. Oxford Scholarship Online

Time period	Sessions	Full-content units requested	Web pages requested	Hits	Searches
August 2006– August 2007	1,076	5,023 (equals 1,004 pages)	6,709	80,519	538

page image views per title, which could be attributed to a very selective need for certain works or pages within works. Interestingly, there were 624 searches that returned no hits, which could be owing to the user's lack of familiarity with the database or lack of relevant results (Fig. 2).

FIGURE 2. Early English Books Online (EEBO)

Time period	Sessions	Searches	Document /page image views	PDF full-text downloads	ASCII full-text views	Searches returning no hits
August 2006– August 2007	1,569	1,636	11,476	1,059	437	624

Eighteenth-Century Collections Online offers approximately 135,000 works published in English between 1701 and 1800, as well as works published in other languages within Britain and her dependencies. The number of sessions and searches is significantly higher than for its counterpart, EEBO, as is the number of downloads. This likely reflects the research interests of faculty and graduate students. It is interesting to note the wide difference between the number of full-text records downloaded and the number of all retrievals including citations and abstracts. This would reflect a lot of filtering and analysis before relevant results are found (Fig. 3).

The ACLS Humanities E-book Project is an expanding collection of current and retrospective monographs in various humanities disciplines, with core strength in History. There are currently about 1,500 titles. The number of searches is similar to EEBO above. However, if one considers the relatively small size of the collection, there were approximately eight page or image views per title, which is much higher. The table of content views indicates that a minority of patrons use this as a means of navigating the text (Fig. 4).

FIGURE 3. Eighteenth Century Collections Online (ECCO)

Time period	Sessions	Full-text records downloaded	All retrievals (including citation & abstracts)	Searches
August 2006— August 2007	4,419	4,373	26,654	28,006

FIGURE 4. ACLS Humanities E-book Project

Time period	Searches	TOC views	Page/image views	Text views
September 2006–August 2007	1,525	84	12,398	47

NetLibrary offers current e-books across all subject areas. We own about 7,000 titles that were acquired mostly through consortial agreements. Usage statistics are very basic (Fig. 5). "Access" is defined as a session that is more than 10 minutes in length. Humanities books (history, literature, philosophy, religion, and arts) accounted for 18.2% of the total usage, which is quite strong in comparison with social sciences at 2,264 accesses and business, economics, and management at 1,996 accesses

FIGURE 5. NetLibrary

Time period	Total number of accesses	'Humanities' accesses
Aug 2006 – Aug 2007	9,728	1,802

We own 15 collections in the Alexander Street Press portfolio, acquired via our national consortium, the Canadian Research Knowledge Network in January 2006. These provide primary source material (books, diaries, letters, correspondence, reports, etc.) in a number of humanities or social sciences disciplines. Being a recent acquisition, it is impressive to see that 4,550 pages from 1,426 sessions were viewed during a 12-month period (Fig. 6). The high number of hits (almost 20,000) indicates that patrons are searching these databases quite extensively in order to pinpoint the resources that are important to them. This also reflects upon the wide scope and range of these databases.

FIGURE 6. Alexander Street Press

Time period	Sessions	Pages	Hits
June 2006–June 2007	1,426	4,550	19,769

We have acquired two sets of e-books from the Gutenberg-e project, for a total of 16 works. The usage numbers are quite modest, which could attest to the limited size of the collection and lack of awareness among patrons in history and related disciplines. Over an 11-month period, there was an average of 10 sessions and 34 page views per month (Fig. 7).

FIGURE 7. Gutenberg-e

Time period	Unique visitors	Sessions	Page Views	Searches
August 2006–June 2007	101	110	382	62

These snapshots reflect a level of usage that might surprise those who believe that research e-books have no role to play in the humanities. While these numbers don't indicate who the patrons are and how successful they were in using e-book collections, it is at least clear that there is significant usage in the university. The historical collections in particular have drawn major attention from patrons, as they have discovered how much easier it is to consult a Web database than deal with the frustrations of manipulating microfilm and paying for print copies. The high numbers of pages viewed for ACLS indicates that current e-books are also of value, and this goes against conventional wisdom. These figures also indicate that we are still far from the day when usage reporting for e-books is presented in a standardized format. Vendors need to make more efforts in this area in order to enable us to compare collections in a consistent manner.

This also raises the thorny problem of comparing usage of print books with e-books. Matthew Ismail asks, "As we buy more and more e-Books and e-Book collections, can we continue to treat these and our print books as fulfilling two separate needs in our collection? If we cannot say that they differ in function, in other words, can we evaluate them by the same standards?"[18] I would argue that e-books are different in function, as a result of being distinctly different in how they are read, how they can interact with other types of research, and how they can be manipulated. Search interfaces and functionality influence usage in ways we don't fully understand yet. The technological reshaping of scholarly content has profound implications for use and research practices and expectations. New metrics are needed. The studies that exist to date demonstrate the differences between how print and electronic are used, by both students and faculty, but the value for learning outcomes needs to be better understood. We are only at the beginning of this process.

HUMANITIES FACULTY COMMENTS

In an informal survey, various professors have given feedback to the author on their attitude toward e-books. One who teaches Shakespeare explained how she had to read Russian translations of Hamlet on the Web for a thesis examination, as the library didn't own them. As well she directs students to read full-text parodies and adaptations of Shakespeare on the Web. Another who teaches Judaic Studies explained that the only e-book she uses is the *Encyclopaedia Judaica*, as none of her other texts are available. An English professor referred me to a site of literary works published by students. Another English professor commented on the research value of Eighteenth Century Collections Online and how much easier and more convenient it was than using interlibrary loans. A classics professor explained that he occasionally browsed an e-book for a specific reference but doesn't like the format of e-books. Other faculty use the historical collections mentioned above and refer their students for coursework. It is certainly the case that available e-books in the collection don't cover various areas of faculty research interest and don't cover works in foreign languages or particular editions with scholarly apparatus. Therefore print is still the primary resource for many of them.

CONCLUSION

E-books have a role to play in the humanities, but this is evolving as faculty and student expectations change and as the scholarly communications landscape is being profoundly altered. A library's choices in supporting or not supporting digital monograph publishing in the humanities will help decide the future of these forms of dissemination, and by extension the choices available to authors. Partnerships with university presses, involvement in digital publishing initiatives, and open-access publication will have an important role as well. The impact of e-books on the economics of publishing has been less dramatic in the humanities than elsewhere;

however, the endangered state of the academic monograph is a barometer of complex realities in the face of transformative change. At bottom lie two questions: What are the values by which the humanities wish to define themselves in the digital information era? How do these values translate into a coordinated plan of action for sustaining scholarship, when principles of public good and knowledge dissemination clash with questions of economic viability? Creative models that promote the values of scholarship in a sustainable manner are essential.

Libraries are gaining hard-won experience in integrating e-books into their collections and workflow practices. While there are some who bemoan the arrival of the e-book and others who see it as the source of endless excitement, the truth probably lies somewhere between. There are strengths and weaknesses, opportunities and pitfalls. In the immediate future, print and electronic monographs will coexist in an uneasy marriage for scholarship and publication. In the not too distant future, though, I expect the digital form could prevail. This will have seismic consequences for the traditional form and use of the academic monograph as a vehicle for scholarly communication. The key drivers will be greater depth of e-book collections; better usability of e-book platforms; more integration with course delivery; more standardization in business models and sustainable pricing; pervasiveness of scholarly activity and collaboration via the Web; generational change among faculty; and the Google effect. The expectations of new generations of web-savvy students will play a large role as well. The very definition of "book" will undergo a major overhaul as a vehicle for linear sustained arguments and will eventually become a dynamic digital work that gains legitimacy for purposes of teaching and for tenure and promotion purposes. For libraries, the technological and budgeting challenges will remain significant, and in some cases extremely daunting. At the University of Ottawa, there has been an important uptake for the e-book collections, but more assessment needs to be done in order to judge the degree of success of this usage. How does it compare to equivalent print works in the humanities and in other areas of research such as science, business, or medicine? How do we ensure that e-book usage translates into successful learning outcomes? Most importantly, how will the shift from text-based to multimedia scholarship affect how knowledge in the humanities is created, learned, taught, and disseminated? This will need to be understood in terms of the changing educational expectations and teaching technologies in the academy. There will be a much more nuanced and powerful relationship between the humanities and technology, as scholars come to view technology as providing an essential framework for conducting their research, developing new methodologies, synthesizing knowledge, and uncovering new associations of ideas between past and present. Campus IT departments and technology teaching services will be essential partners in this process.

The paradigm shift of a collection being defined by various types of access arrangements rather than physical ownership onsite is gradually being assimilated by staff at all levels. For humanities professors, however, the shift is harder to absorb. The future for e-books in the humanities will need to be much more finessed than in the sciences and medicine. The related issues of preservation, discovery and usability, analytical tools, and pedagogical value are integral to the success of e-books. The mission is possible, but the way is filled with challenges and question marks. We are reinventing humanities collections as we are reinventing our libraries—and the ride has endless surprises and opportunities. Samuel Johnson once remarked that "Books that you may carry to the fire and hold readily in your hand, are the most useful after all."[19] In today's wired world, it isn't clear how we hold books anymore. In the era of the digital multimedia text, the question of what we have gained and lost is a significant philosophical and practical issue. Thus the reinvention continues . . .

NOTES

1. American Council of Learned Societies Commission on Cyberinfrastructure for the Humanities and Social Sciences, "Our Cultural Commonwealth" <http://www.acls.org/cyberinfrastructure/acls.ci.report.pdf> Retrieved October 11, 2007, 47.

2. University of Minnesota Libraries, A Multi-Dimensional Framework for Academic Support: A Final Report June 2006. <http://www.lib.umn.edu/about/mellon/UMN Multi-dimensional Framework Final Report.pdf > Retrieved October 11, 2007, 56.

3. Laura Brown, et al. University Publishing in a Digital Age *Journal of Electronic Publishing* 10 (3) 2007 <http://www.ithaka.org/strategic-services/Ithaka%20University%20Publishing%20Report.pdf> Retrieved December 3, 2007, 17.

4. Mitchell Stephens, The Rise of the Image the Fall of the Printed Word <http://www.nyu.edu/classes/stephens/rise%20of%20image%20-%20Intro.htm> Retrieved September 14, 2007, 1.

5. Modern Language Association. MLA Ad Hoc Committee on the Future of Scholarly Publishing. "The Future of Scholarly Publishing" <http://www.mla.org/pdf/schlrlypblshng.pdf > Retrieved October 3, 2007, 9–10.

6. Modern Language Association. MLA Task Force on Evaluating Scholarship for Tenure and Promotion: Executive Summary <http://www.mla.org/pdf/task_force_tenure_promotio.pdf > Retrieved October 3, 2007, 3.

7. Piano Pedagogy Research Laboratory, University of Ottawa. Multidisciplinary Research Teams <http://www.piano.uottawa.ca/orientation4_en.html> Retrieved September 30, 2007, 1.

8. Scott Jaschik, Publishing and Values. Inside Higher Education. <http://www.insidehighered.com/news/2007/08/22/anthro> Retrieved October 5, 2007, 1.

9. Thierry Morineau, et al. (2005). The emergence of the contextual role of the e-book in cognitive processes through an ecological and functional analysis. *International Journal of Human-Computer Studies*, *62*, 346.

10. ACLS Humanities E-book Project, Introduction–The New E-book: A Digital Portal. <http://www.humanitiesebook.org> Retrieved September 14, 2007, 1.

11. Institute for Advanced Technology in the Humanities, University of Virginia. <http://www.iath.virginia.edu> Retrieved September 14, 2007, 1.

12. Ibid, Retrieved September 14, 2007, 1.

13. Matthew Kirschenbaum. Hamlet.doc? Literature in a Digital Age *The Chronicle Review*, <http://chronicle.com/weekly/v53/i50/50b00801.htm> Retrieved August 21, 2007, 4.

14. Kevin Kelly, Scan This Book! *The New York Times*, May 14, 2006. <http://www.nytimes.com/2006/05/14/magazine/14publishing.html?n=Top/News/Business/Companies/Wikipedia&pagewanted=print> Retrieved October 15, 2007.

15. Alan McKiel, ebrary Global E-book Survey <http://www.ebrary.com/corp/collateral/en/Survey/ebrary e-Book survey 2007.pdf> Retrieved October 1, 2007, 8–9.

16. Michael Levine-Clark, (2007). Electronic books and the approval plan: Can they work together? *Against the Grain 19*(2): 20.

17. Oxford University Press, private communication to the author, June 15, 2007.

18. Matthew Ismail, (2007). Can we integrate electronic resources into our allocation formulas? *Against the Grain 19*(2): 14.

19. John Bartlett, "Familiar Quotations" 10th ed., 1919. <http://www.bartleby.com/100/249.112.html> (accessed October 11, 2007).

REFERENCES

ACLS Humanities E-Book Project. Introduction: The new e-book: A digital portal. Retrieved September 14, 2007, from <http://www.humanitiesebook.org>.

American Council of Learned Societies Commission on Cyberinfrastructure for the Humanities and Social Sciences, Our Cultural Commonwealth 2006. Retrieved October 11, 2007, from <http://www.acls.org/cyberinfrastructure/acls.ci.report.pdf>.

Brown, Laura, et al. (2007, Fall). University publishing in a digital age. *Journal of Electronic Publishing*, *10*(3), 1–60.

Ismail, Matthew. (2007, April). Op Ed: Can we integrate electronic resources into our allocation formula? *Against the Grain*, 19(2), 60–61.

Jaschik, Scott, Publishing and Values. *Inside Higher Education* Retrieved October 5, 2007, from <http://www.insidehighered.com/news/2007/08/22/anthro>.

Kelly, Kevin, Scan This Book!" *The New York Times*, May 14, 2006. Retrieved October 15, 2007, from <http://www.nytimes.com/2006/05/14/magazine/14publishing.html?n=Top/News/Business/Companies/Wikipedia&pagewanted=print>.

Kirschenbaum, Matthew. Hamlet.doc? Literature in a Digital Age *The Chronicle Review*. Retrieved September 28, 2007, from <http://chronicle.com/weekly/v53/i50/50b00801.htm>.

Levine-Clark, Michael (2007, April). Electronic books and the approval plan: Can they work together? *Against the Grain*, 19(2), 18–22.

McKiel, Allen (2007). *ebrary Global e-Book Survey*. Palo Alto, CA: ebrary, MLA Ad Hoc Committee on the Future of Scholarly Publishing. The future of scholarly publishing. Retrieved October 2, 2007, from <http://www.mla.org/pdf/schlrlypblshng.pdf>.

MLA Task Force on Evaluating Scholarship for Tenure and Promotion. Executive summary. Retrieved October 2, 2007, from <http://www.mla.org/pdf/task force tenure promotio.pdf>.

Morineau, Thierry, et al. (2005). The emergence of the contextual role of the e-book in cognitive processes through an ecological and functional analysis. *International Journal of Human-Computer Studies*, 62, 329–348.

Stephens, Mitchell. *The Rise of the Image the Fall of the Word*. <http://www.nyu.edu/classes/stephens/rise%20of%20the%20image%20-%20preface. htm> Oxford University Press: Oxford, 1998.

University of Minnesota Libraries. A multi-dimensional framework for academic support: A final report, June 2006. Retrieved October 11, 2007, from <http://www.lib.umn.edu/about/mellon/UMN Multi-dimensional Framework Final Report.pdf>.

University of Ottawa, Piano Pedagogy Research Laboratory. Four principal functions. Retrieved October 5, 2007, from <http://www.piano.uottawa.ca/orientation4_en. html>.

Moving from Book to E-book

Reeta Sinha
Cory Tucker

INTRODUCTION

In the last five years, electronic books have slowly become commonplace in academic libraries. Owing to an increase in their popularity, electronic books are now offered in databases, subject collections, and on a title-by-title basis by most publishers and several aggregators. At the University of Nevada, Las Vegas (UNLV) Libraries, an initiative was undertaken to purchase electronic books in specific disciplines in which program growth was evident. This article discusses UNLV's experience as the library developed its electronic books collection and how electronic books are now used at the library. In addition, the authors consider the impact of electronic books on libraries in the areas of collection management, selection and acquisitions workflow, collection assessment, and working with vendors.

LITERATURE REVIEW

Analyzing the literature, several articles serve as case studies for academic and public libraries and usage of electronic book collections. One example of such an article is a case study by Hernon, Hopper, Leach, Saunders, and Zhang (2007). The authors examined search behavior and use patterns of undergraduates in economics, literature, and medicine with regard to electronic books. The study showed that undergraduates limited their research to library databases and unless electronic books were included in these databases or recommended by a professor, they were not used very often. The study illustrated the fact that libraries must be cognizant of how students gather and use information. A second study by Bailey (2006) measured electronic book usage at Auburn University in Montgomery, Alabama. It found that electronic book usage increased during 2002–2004, while use of the library's print collection decreased. The study also found that electronic books in the subject areas of business, computers, literature, social sciences, and medicine were the most used. Other case studies include Dillon (2001), Chu (2003), Ismail and Zainab (2005), Hughes and Buchanon (2001), Gunter (2005), and Langston (2003). For public libraries, there have been case studies including those by McKnight and Dearnley (2003) and Dearnley, Morris, McKnight, Berube, et al. (2004).

An article by Dooley (2007) describes the experience of purchasing electronic books at University of California-Merced. The author discusses the establishment of the library in 2005 and how the library emphasized electronic materials for its collections, except for books due to significant barriers that existed for electronic books at the time. Dooley goes on to describe how the library did begin to purchase different e-book collections over the next few years, including those supplied by ebrary, NetLibrary, EBL, and MyiLibrary. The Dooley article emphasizes how the library is now looking into e-book-only collections for specific disciplines as previous barriers to establishing e-book collections have been overcome.

Other articles written about e-books discuss issues related to cataloging and licensing. An article written by Martin (2007) talks about the challenges associated with cataloging e-books, focusing primarily on how e-book content is integrated into library online catalogs. Martin discusses the Machine-Readable Cataloging (MARCs) records provided by e-book vendors and how the quality of the records varies from vendor to vendor. The article also presents issues related to cataloging principles and workflow as e-books are processed by cataloging units. In an article by Rice (2006), the author broaches the concept of licensing e-books and the wide array of licensing agreements. Rice states there are three basic models for e-book licensing, with one additional model that stands apart from the rest. The three basic models include a print model, the database model, and the free or open-access model. The notable exception is a non-linear lending model based on a certain number of "loan instances" per year.

BUILDING AN E-BOOK COLLECTION FOR THE UNLV LIBRARIES

UNLV has changed quite a bit from the one-building campus in the desert when it was established in 1957. Since that first class of 300 students, the student population has grown to more 28,000 in the university's first 50 years. Growth at UNLV has meant more than new students, however. Each year more new faculty, new academic programs and buildings—including a state-of-the-art library—have been added. Since the 1990s, particularly, scores of new academic programs across all disciplines have been implemented at UNLV at the graduate level, from a doctoral degree in the fine arts to the opening of a new campus housing a dental school, a cancer institute, and a biotechnology center. The UNLV Libraries have responded by adopting new approaches to budget allocation and collection development, focusing on providing access to information resources in multiple formats. Under a mandate to transition from print-based collections to those that are primarily electronic, the Libraries moved from a collection of fewer than 20 electronic resources in 1998, composed mainly of index and abstract databases, to more than 200 full-text databases, e-journal collections, and other e-resources by the end of fiscal year 2004–2005. By July 2005, UNLV library users had access to 16,000 journals. Fewer than 10% of these were in print format, with most of the growth in the e-journal collection occurring over a period of two years. The growth rate of UNLV's e-book collection during this period, however, was not as dramatic.

2000–2001: Getting Our Feet Wet

UNLV's e-book collection began in earnest with the acquisition of a shared NetLibrary collection purchased through a regional consortium in 2001. The collection consisted of approximately 2,000 titles covering a broad range of subject areas. Other e-books acquired by the library around the same time included online reference works such as the World Book Online, a few CRC Handbooks and, in 2002, Oxford Reference Online. By the fall of 2002, although use data for e-books were not collected or analyzed consistently, there was little, if any, evidence that e-books were being used or even in demand by UNLV students and faculty. Consequently, despite a push to build online book collections within the library, there was, understandably, reluctance on the part of subject librarians to divert a portion of their monograph allocations toward the purchase of e-books. Other obstacles to integrating e-books into the library's collection included issues for the user related to the e-book reader, such as a single-use, check-out model and, for the librarians, a separate workflow to review and select individual e-book titles. For a campus serving a large population of undergraduate students and students who attended classes on a part-time basis or in the evening, it seemed incongruous that books available online 24/7 were not being used or popular. A closer examination of the shared collection, however, showed that most of the titles in the collection were published in the late 1990s or even earlier. More recent and new books were available only in print form at the library.

2003–2004: Build That Critical Mass and They Will Come

Given the lack-luster experience with e-books initially and increasing pressures on staff and budget resources owing to growth at UNLV, experimenting with e-books was not high on the priority lists of most at the library. During fiscal year 2003–2004, however, the Collection Development (CD) department proposed to conduct a pilot project to give e-books another chance at UNLV. The project centered on the idea that if the library built a critical mass of e-books—newer titles in specific subject areas—and increased its marketing and user education efforts, it would see an increase in use and demand for e-books. CD would spend its funds so as not to impact the subject allocations of liaisons and after one year, usage of e-books would be evaluated.

Starting in the fall of 2003, the library took advantage of NetLibrary shared collections being offered at the time to build its e-book collection quickly. The library focused on medical, information technology, and business administration titles. A shared collection including a broad range of subjects was also acquired. Also, as publishers made e-books available, either in collections or title-by-title, the library acquired more e-books throughout the year. Examples include but are not limited to scientific-medical-technical titles published by Marcel Dekker, the History E-Books Database (upon the recommendation of a UNLV faculty author), Elsevier book series online, and assorted online reference works by major publishers. By the end of fiscal year 2003–2004 approximately 3,500 e-books, mainly supplied by NetLibrary, had been added to UNLV collections. MARC records provided by vendors were loaded into the library's Online Public Access Catalog (OPAC), and while there were few focused marketing efforts related specifically to e-books, subject Web pages listed newly cataloged titles on a monthly basis, including new e-books.

After one year, a review of vendor-supplied usage data showed more than 400 "check-outs" for NetLibrary titles. The overall number of accesses for NetLibrary titles was approximately 2,200, an impressive number given that library users still had not verbalized a preference for e-books. As expected, the highest number of accesses was for titles related to computers, nearly 31% of total accesses for the 12-month period. More surprising, however, was the 27% of total accesses for titles in literature, the arts, and social sciences given efforts by the library to acquire e-books in science and business-related academic areas demonstrating program growth at UNLV. Only about 14% of e-book accesses related to business and medicine titles. Without the benefit of user surveys or other concrete information, it was concluded that the relatively high use of e-books in literature and the social sciences was due to term paper assignments in introductory level courses for UNLV's large undergraduate student population.

2004–2005: E-books Integrated into the Collections

Fiscal year 2004–2005 marked a turning point for the UNLV Libraries with regard to e-book collection development. Usage data was certainly a contributing factor—it was difficult to say that e-books weren't being used at UNLV when the data indicated otherwise. It was harder still to say so when most users seemed to have come across the library's e-books on their own, through the online catalog via a subject search, or while navigating the library's e-resources Web listings. As new faculty joined UNLV during the year, liaisons began to hear of requests for the library to look at e-book aggregators faculty had access to at their previous institution. By fall of 2005, UNLV libraries had added 24,000 e-books via ebrary's Academic Complete Collection.

2007: Where Are We Now?

At UNLV, the library routinely acquires both print and electronic books. One of the more recent collection development efforts related to electronic books focused on the reference collection. The library noticed a significant drop in the use of its print reference materials in the library over the previous two years. In addition, the library, concerned with space issues, began looking at the print reference collection as a logical collection to save space and money. For these reasons, UNLV Libraries has aggressively been purchasing online reference collections that include the content of print materials showing high use. The library is also reviewing online reference collections that will be useful for new and existing programs.

Another area in which there has been an increased effort to purchase electronic books is in the health sciences. The Nevada System of Higher Education has made health sciences a priority, and UNLV has seen its health sciences program grow exponentially since 2003. In the last three years, UNLV has opened a new campus that houses several health sciences departments. This off-site campus has no brick-and-mortar library facility available to those who are located there and, owing to the fact that previously purchased health sciences e-books have experienced high use, UNLV Libraries has recently purchased e-book collections in the biomedical sciences.

THE IMPACT OF ELECTRONIC BOOKS ON LIBRARIES

Electronic Books and Library Users

One of the most significant ways in which e-books have impacted libraries relates, not surprisingly, to the library patron. Despite access to thousands of recently published e-books, many library users at UNLV still seem to prefer print books over electronic. This appears to be due mainly to two factors. First, library users are still getting used to the notion that books are actually now available online. This is, of course, less of an issue with younger users because so many have used e-books in high school or while surfing the Internet and are generally more aware of their existence. User satisfaction or lack thereof with the software required to read books online may also affect a student or faculty member's decision to choose print over online books. An example of this is how some e-book readers require the user to download a plug-in, while others do not. The tools available in the e-book software will also impact the user, especially if the tools create obstacles to browsing through or searching for an e-book.

How e-books available from the library are accessed can be a major issue for library users as well. It is vital that libraries receive (or create) cataloging records as they would for a print book so the e-book title can be included in the library's online catalog. Of course, receiving vendor-supplied MARC records has its own problems. Consistency or standardization of MARC records among vendors is necessary for the library to maintain database integrity—the quality of records in the online catalog. The availability of MARC records immediately upon purchase and receipt of data is critical to acquisitions and cataloging workflows as well. In one instance at UNLV, the vendor did not provide MARC records until six months after access had been granted to a large e-book collection the library had purchased. This sort of delay, without any penalty to the vendor who had received payment in full from the library, does not inspire confidence in those libraries that are looking to build e-book collections.

The marketing of e-books by libraries has been a significant issue ever since e-books appeared on the horizon. As with other electronic resources, library marketing efforts are vital to promoting e-books. Some libraries have done an outstanding job of this, while others have not. Not only is it important to have e-books in the library's online catalog but if a library has invested in purchasing large e-book collections for the benefit of its users, these collections need to be highlighted and easily accessible in different areas of the library's website. Additionally, subject librarians must make students and faculty aware of e-books that are available in specific disciplines, showing users not only how easy electronic books are to access and use but, for faculty, librarians must also how e-books can be integrated into the teaching curriculum. This can be done easily through library instruction sessions when presenting other electronic and print resources available at the library.

Electronic Books and Collection Development

Electronic books have had several implications in the area of collection development in academic libraries during the past few years. Initially purchasing collections offered by publishers and aggregators, libraries are moving to selecting individual titles. As this happens, first and most important, the library needs to establish collection development policies for mixed format collections—how will selectors determine the preferred format for a book if it's available in multiple formats? Is it even possible to set a policy; will the library always prefer the first option to be the print edition (or the electronic), for example? Will the preferred format vary from subject to subject? Or, particularly during the period of transition, does the library prefer to have a book in both formats? Selectors also need to consider whether traditional selection criteria for print books also apply to electronic books or are there additional factors to consider, such as the e-book reader, licensing terms for the content, and the ease of providing access to e-books via website and/or the online catalog?

Another issue that selectors face is how to avoid duplication. When buying electronic books, either individually or through collections, it is vital that the library not purchase an e-book twice, which may happen quite easily. Not only is there considerable overlap between the e-book aggregators—the same titles available in more than one e-book supplier's collections—but as book vendors offer e-book titles individually, the library may already have purchased a title through a collection offered by an aggregator or the publisher. In either case, de-duplication must be possible and easy to accomplish when purchasing individual titles through vendors such as YBP, Coutts, or Blackwell's. If a library sets up an e-book ordering service with vendors, the book vendor and/or e-book supplier should be able to load lists of e-book titles currently held by the library into the vendor title database and ordering system so selectors do not inadvertently order e-books the library has had access to through another source.

Budget allocation for e-books is one of the more complex issues facing collection development librarians. Depending on the demand for e-books at an institution and the collection development policy, if one has been established for e-books, the library needs to determine how much of the budget should be set aside for print books and for e-books. Beyond the amount to budget, the method by which these allocations are made also needs to be decided. Should the library divert existing funds, for example, allocated for print books toward the purchase of e-books? Or should the library create a new fund line for e-books? Each library needs to develop a budgeting method based on its environment, its users, and the pace with which it wants to incorporate e-books into the library's collections. At UNLV, the library has decided to observe expenditures over the coming fiscal year to determine where and how money is being spent on e-books by liaisons.

All of the above decisions need to be made as academic libraries face dwindling materials budgets. So, where should cuts in funding occur? Traditionally, the book budget was sacrificed in the face of increasing cost for subscription-based resources. In this new environment, does the library treat e-book funds as it did print book budgets? For example, in certain disciplines, if faculty and students prefer journals and the library decides the budget for "books" is reduced to save journals, will this cut impact the budget for e-books as well, or just print books?

Electronic Book Workflows

E-books have had a significant impact on a number of workflows in libraries, but selection, acquisitions, and cataloging may have been affected the most. As discussed earlier, subject liaisons and collection development librarians now have another format option to choose from as they perform their collection development duties. However, once selected, are e-books treated in acquisitions like print books? At UNLV when the library purchased collections from e-book aggregators from 2003 through 2005, Collection Development and the library's Electronic Serials librarian handled most of the tasks that needed to be completed. Now that librarians there are selecting most e-books via GOBI, the online order system of the library's book vendor, the workflow of selectors and acquisitions staff is similar to that of purchasing a print book. For technical services, though cataloging is an activity that is already performed for print books and other library materials, considerations with e-books include but are not limited to the source of the MARC record, the quality of MARC record, and the additional workload in already strained departments.

Electronic Books and Collection Assessment

To evaluate book collections, the methods used for print books and e-books are similar. For both formats, some measure of use is preferred. At UNLV, data on usage for print books are provided by the circulation department. Use data are gathered for external usage (checkout) and internal usage (re-shelving books). For e-books, use data are provided by the vendor and are gathered quarterly by collection development staff. From these data, monthly use is calculated.

There are a number of options available to academic libraries for evaluating e-book use, but most are impacted by data made available by vendors.

UNLV Libraries have been collecting use statistics for electronic resources, including e-books, since 2003. The good news for the library has been that each e-book supplier has been able to send it use statistics for individual books. The bad news is the lack of consistency in the data among e-book vendors. For example, NetLibrary usage reports provide LC classification numbers for its titles whereas ebrary does not. So, in order to examine e-book use for ebrary titles, UNLV has had to use the ebrary record number and match it with the bibliographic record in the library's online catalog to obtain the LC number. On a more positive note, it helps the library that its e-book aggregators supply usage reports for each of the subject e-book collections offered. Data such as these, if they are readily available, makes it relatively easy for libraries to assess in which disciplines e-books are used more often, which, in turn, will help librarians make purchase decisions in the future.

Finally, in addition to use, assessment of the book collections, print and electronic, may include, as the UNLV Libraries have done, analyzing the year of publication to determine the period of research and/or how old the books are that patrons are using.

Electronic Books, Libraries, and Vendors

Library vendors who have traditionally supplied academic libraries with print books seem to have also struggled with the emergence of e-books as a format during the past few years. Recent developments, however, demonstrate some progress and, for libraries, the impact has been both positive and negative. Regardless of the vendor, ordering e-books through book vendors seems to have become easier as all major vendors have developed mechanisms and/or relationships with aggregators or publishers to sell electronic books. For example, UNLV currently purchases books through YBP Library Services using the vendor's online title database and ordering system GOBI. With both print books and e-books in the system, librarians can visit one place to review, select, and order titles in either format. When UNLV set up its e-book account with the vendor, it loaded UNLV's previously purchased e-book titles from NetLibrary and ebrary so that GOBI informs the librarian not only whether a print edition of a title has been purchased by the library already but now whether the library has already purchased the e-book, thus avoiding duplication (and wasting precious book funds). Also, in order to streamline the selection process for e-books, the library requested YBP to create an approval profile for e-books based on UNLV's print approval plan profile. By doing so, librarians receive electronic notification of new e-books in profiled areas for librarians to review and order. With both print and e-book expenditures in one system, when it is time to evaluate approval and firm order activity, UNLV will be in a good position to assess the impact of e-books not only on the monographic budget as a whole but on collection activities as they vary from subject to subject.

On the negative side, publishers and vendors have not made it easy for librarians, who are already suffering from "choice overload." While it's true that in the print world, a library could always order a book direct from the publisher or from its book vendor, pity the poor librarian who now has to decide where to get that e-book a faculty member has requested. A single e-book title may not only be available by the publisher and an e-book aggregator but may be available from the library's vendor, if the vendor offers e-books. If the title is offered by an e-book aggregator and the library doesn't have access to that aggregator's titles, the library can't fulfill the faculty member's request. The e-book may also be available from the library's subscription agent or it may be included in a full-text database, or in an e-book collection, but one that is only from the publisher. However, titles in a collection may or may not be available individually.

As price may not vary from source to source and librarians have several vendors and the publisher trying to sell the same e-book, what becomes the basis for the decision? Is it the e-book reader or satisfaction with the vendor's service, the ease of ordering, or some other factor? Who makes these decisions? Traditionally, acquisitions staff were charged with determining the best source for a book. Will this decision now be made by selectors or Collection Development? Finally, while it may desirable from a workflow perspective to select and order e-books via the library's primary book vendor system, if the vendor has contracted with only one e-book aggregator, or with a few publishers' offerings, the library may be forced to go back to the dark days of direct ordering from publishers.

CONCLUSION

This article provided a general overview of issues many libraries face when integrating electronic books into a print-based collection. Using one academic library's experience over a period of five years, the authors described the impact on virtually every unit in the library as it built an e-book collection, from budget allocation and technical services workflows to introducing e-books to library users and dealing with publishers, aggregators, and vendors. As more and more libraries engage in this process, the authors feel a number of issues need to be addressed by publishers and vendors to facilitate e-book collection development and acquisitions. These include but are not limited to the following:

- Licensing agreements: Standardize and simplify agreements (if licenses are needed at all!);
- Collections: Do not force libraries to purchase every book by a publisher or none at all; do not offer some titles in collections and exclude others—title-by-title acquisitions must always be an option, whether through the publisher, vendor, or aggregator;
- E-book readers: Develop readers that are painless for the user and library to use; and
- E-book content: Content should be platform-neutral so that a library should not have to purchase multiple platforms (and library users should not have to learn to navigate each one).

What will the next five years bring? There are definitely more questions than answers at this point. What further impact will e-books have on library collections and workflows? Will users demand more electronic book content from libraries? Will the impact of e-books on library collections and expenditures be similar to that of electronic journals—that is, will e-books begin to replace print books? Probably not; however, this emphasizes the need for librarians, working together with publishers and vendors, to develop efficient and effective methods to develop and manage collections that include books in both print and electronic formats for decades to come.

REFERENCES

Bailey, T. P. (2006). Electronic book usage at a master's level i university: A longitudinal study. *The Journal of Academic Librarianship, 32*, 52–59.

Chu, H. (2003). Electronic books: Viewpoints from users and potential users. *Library Hi-Tech, 21*, 340–346.

Dearnley, J., Morris, A., McKnight, C., Berube, L., Palmer, M., & John, J. (2004). Electronic books in public libraries: A feasability study for developing usage models for Web-based and hardware-based electronic books. *New Review in Information Networking, 10*, 209–246.

Dillon, D. (2001). E-books: The University of Texas Experience, Part I. *Library Hi-Tech, 19*, 113–124.

Dooley, J. (2007). From print to electronic: The UC Merced experience. *Against the Grain, 19*(3), 22–26.

Gunter, B. (2005). Electronic books: A survey of users in the UK. *Aslib Proceedings: New Information Perspective, 57*, 513–522.

Hernon, P., Hopper, R., Leach, M. R., Saunders, L. L., & Zhang J. (2007). E-book use by students: Undergraduates in economics, literature and nursing. *The Journal of Academic Librarianship, 33*, 3–13.

Hughes, C. A. & Buckanan, N. L. (2001). Use of electronic monographs in the humanities and social sciences. *Library Hi-Tech, 19*, 364–375.

Ismail, R. & Zainab, A. N. (2005), The pattern of e-book use amongst undergraduates in Malaysia: A case of to know is to use. *Malalysian Journal of Library and Information Science, 10*, 1–23.

Martin, K. E. (2007). Cataloging eBooks: An overview of issues and challenges. *Against the Grain, 19*(1) 45–47.

McKnight, C. & Dearnly, J. (2003). Electronic book use in a public library. *Journal of Librarianship and Information Science, 35*, 235–242.

Langston, M. (2003). The California State University Library E-book pilot project: Implications for cooperative collection development. *Library Collections, Acquisitions, and Technical Services, 27*, 19–32.

Rice, S. (2006). Own or rent? A survey of eBook licensing models. *Against the Grain, June*, 28–30.

New Types of E-books, E-book Issues, and Implications for the Future

Aline Soules

INTRODUCTION

With new technological capabilities, it is common to replicate existing practices in a new setting. To date, the evolution of the e-book has primarily followed that pattern. The majority of today's e-books are simply print books presented in an e-environment. Their chapters may be searchable and navigable in a different way from the print world, but other features, such as the ability to "dog-ear" or "mark" portions or pages, are print concepts and terminology.

With a growing understanding of how the print book adapts to new technologies, however, authors and creators are taking the format into a new realm. The e-book is evolving into something that could never appear in print, and innovators are experimenting with new ideas. In some cases, these creations are not always recognizable as e-books, and there are those who wonder if the term *book* is applicable in any way, but the roots of these inventions are in the book, even as their creators take off in different directions.

HARDWARE

These experiments, however, while pushing the edge of innovation, are still bound to available technology, particularly hardware. One major challenge for the now-"traditional" e-book has been sustainable e-reading. In 2006, the Sony Reader digital book was described as "the first E-ink-equipped e-book reader in the U.S.,"[1] an important technical leap forward in readability with a display Sony describes as "almost paper-like."[2] Physically, the reader is easily handled with a long-lasting, rechargeable battery and extensive memory. In addition to e-books, it also handles other formats from PDF files to blogs to audio files,[3] but the technological discovery of e-ink is what brought the hardware closer to providing truly sustainable e-reading.

The success of this product, however, is still in question, as Sony has dropped the price significantly since its launch. Now, we have Amazon Kindle, "an electronic device that [Jeff Bezos] hopes will leapfrog over previous attempts at e-readers and become the turning point in a transformation toward Book 2.0."[4] Logging on to Amazon.com in late November, 2007 (and presumably through the pre-holiday marketing season) takes the shopper not to the regular home page but to a letter from Jeff Bezos and a link to the $399 Kindle sales page with messages from supporters such as Toni Morrison. This is the heavy-duty marketing machine in action. Also equipped with e-ink technology, the reader has features that are similar to Sony's product. There are two big breakthroughs. One is access to the content that Amazon.com has already established, along with the inclusion of different content (e.g., subscriptions to newspapers, magazines, and the like that are beamed automatically into Kindle) and the ability to sell that content relatively cheaply. The other is the wireless connectivity that enables the content to be beamed in. "This isn't a device; it's a service," according to Bezos.[5]

Ultimately, a separate reader may not make sense, as the new BlackBerry or Treo or the latest "all-in-one hand-held device" is developed with better visibility, a way of expanding the screen, and other features. For individual consumers, there may be two important tests—whether it will hold all our best loved or much needed books and whether we can read comfortably in bed! For creators of new types of e-books, this technological challenge drives them to create works that are either short in duration (i.e., mini-e-books, or delivered in small "bites").

E-BOOKS TODAY

One way around the reading challenge is to focus on content that is designed to be consulted rather than read from beginning to end. A reference book, for example, is more viable in e-format than a full-length novel. Other factors that make e-books more generally acceptable are the continuing replicas from the print world that provide familiarity (dog-earing, marking text), technology-based activity that is familiar from other software programs (cut and paste, download, print, annotate), and capabilities from other sources such as databases (searching, jumping from one chapter to another, saving, e-mailing, formatting for citation). The biggest advantage the e-book offers, however, is the anytime, anywhere accessibility that users love in the database and Web worlds.

As an example, think of the quintessential print book—*Encyclopedia Britannica*. This multi-volume reference book is now *Britannica Online*, and you'd be hard pressed to consider it the same creature as its original. Now an e-reference title, this transformation behaves like a database with full-text content. Open it and you'll find that the content is essentially the same, although it is easier and faster to offer new entries; that there are links to a blog and more content outside the e-book; and that you can search both *Britannica* and the *Merriam-Webster* dictionary (two e-books in one). Conduct a search and choose an entry from the results list, and you'll get an article or a portion of the full article that you would previously have read in print. The hierarchy of the content is provided, allowing you to see where this information fits in the bigger picture of the larger article or category.

In the library, if we are not simply buying or renting print books in e-form, we are acquiring emulations of the database world that we have come to know well. We rent or buy e-books or e-book packages from NetLibrary, ebrary, Safari, et al. Some titles now include audio and video clips. With the packages, we may get both books we want and books we don't (as the vendor secures publisher contracts and, by default, the overall selection), but we are buying or renting individual titles in increasing numbers, either separately or within the packages. At this point, we have built a critical mass, making it more likely that e-book titles will show up in user query results in our Online Public Access Catalogs and enable them to be a more familiar part of the information landscape. This helps to build e-book readership or, at least, e-book use. Users, however, still expect these "books" to behave in the same way as their print counterparts, and they don't necessarily envision them as something potentially different. They see the anytime, anywhere access and search capability as part of the delivery rather than the e-book. They may or may not see e-reference titles as books at all, even though, as librarians, we are conscious of their monographic roots.

FROM THE PAST TO THE FUTURE OF THE E-BOOK

So what happens next? Or what has been happening while we have been busy dealing with the e-books with which we are now familiar?

In 2002, I attended a Digital Literature Festival in Santa Barbara, California. One presenter was Ted Padova, who worked with Adobe Acrobat software, enhancing text in a variety of ways. He moused over a piece of text in a history book to bring up an image, then an action clip of a battle. I don't remember the exact subject matter but, suddenly, history moved from dates and the rote memorization of the 13 causes of some war to a story of people and passion. Computers could already handle that type of information, although there were challenges; today, they can handle the information with ease and more effectively through links, clicks, and mouse-overs. We can enjoy animation, graphics, font—all embedded. Computers can also handle the file sizes involved.

Non-Profit Experiments

Experiments have been going on for a number of years, as can be seen in the list of projects sponsored by the Institute for the Future of the Book.[6] The Institute is "a New York-based think tank dedicated to inventing new forms of discourse for the network age." It has a blog called if:book that "covers a wide range of concerns, all in some way fitting into the techno-cultural puzzle that is the future of ideas. When [they're] not writing this blog, [they] build open source software and lead publishing experiments with authors, academics, artists and programmers." It is funded by the MacArthur Foundation, affiliated with the University of Southern California, and located in Brooklyn, New York.[7]

Its CommentPress project has been a key foundation for many other projects:

> For far too long electronic documents have been saddled with ill-fitting metaphors from the realm of print: e-books, e-ink, e-paper etc. Publishers expect us to purchase, own and consume e-books (or articles, papers, journals) in basically the same way we do paper books, failing to reckon with the fact that texts take on different values and assume different properties when placed in the digital environment—especially when that environment is part of a network. Institute for the Future of the Book was founded in 2004 to, among other things, try to redress this failure of imagination by stimulating a broad rethinking—in publishing, academia and the world at large—of books as networked objects.
>
> CommentPress is a happy byproduct of this process, the result of a series of "networked book" experiments run by the Institute in 2006-7. The goal of these was to see whether a popular net-native publishing form, *the blog*, which, most would agree, is very good at covering the present moment in pithy, conversational bursts but lousy at handling larger, slow-developing works requiring more than chronological organization—whether this form might be refashioned to enable social interaction around long-form texts.[8]

The first of these projects was McKenzie Wark's *GAM3R 7H30RY*. Wark's style of writing in small sections facilitated online discussion and became an example of the idea that books can be created by many authors. The subject of this networked book is the critical theory of games, and the public helped to write it. They commented in "digital 'margins' that allowed "a stream of unabashed conversation."[9] Wark used the comments from this two-way dialogue to create his book. During that time, the hope was that it would "be an unprecedented hybrid authorship,"[10] and that hope came to fruition. The print version that emerged was published by Harvard University Press in 2007 and "includes an edited selection of comments from the Version 1.1 web edition,"[11] which is still online. Wark then mounted Version 2.0 on the site and took more comments, but now he says he is moving on to other things.[12] On the Web site, however, there are now visualizations to explore and other forums. In libraries, catalog entries provide links to an electronic table of contents, another emerging feature for books in general, and on the Harvard University Press Web site, you can listen to a short interview with McKenzie Wark.[13] Harvard University Press also contracts with ebrary for its standard e-books, although at this time of writing, Wark's book is not listed.

Of the Institute's other projects, *Sophie* was designed "to open up the world of multimedia authoring to a wide range of creative people. Originally conceived as a standalone multimedia authoring tool, *Sophie* is now integrated into the Web 2.0 network,"[14] enabling streaming documents and the embedding of various media and objects and the use of live dynamic text fields for comment (again via CommentPress). In July of 2007, an early release was made available for downloading.

Readers can explore the Institute's other projects at their Web site.[15] These projects make use of techniques that involve others in digital conversation and comment and offer educational opportunities for debate and thought among the participants.[16] They also offer authors a chance to engage in an iterative process of writing, comment, re-writing, idea testing, more writing—all enhanced by digital conversation. The Institute also solicits proposals for larger-scale publishing projects to "be developed with an editorial board that will also function as stewards of the larger network."[17]

The Institute has also supported various visual projects or art e-books. The Gates project, an Experiment in Collective Memory, was a joint project of Flickr and the Institute to "remember" Christo and Jeanne-Claude's Gates Central Park project via pictures from voluntary contributors. These were either photographs or manipulations of existing photos. The blog enabled comments and discussion that, in turn, influenced how the "collected content" was used.[18] In this case, the collective creation was not synthesized by a particular author or a particular group of authors but remained in the hands of the contributors. In June, 2007, an entry stated that the project would be dormant while plans were made for the archive. The entry further noted that there were "3,564 photos collected under the 'gatesmemory' tag in Flickr."[19] The final entry on the Institute Web site is an August, 2005 link to an online lecture about the Gates by John Weber, Director of the Tang Museum at Skidmore College. When I contacted Dr. Weber about the project, he noted that it had been more than 10 years since the original Gates project.[20] Currently, this appears to be finished, although its final form is in multiple pieces located in multiple places.

In IT IN place, the artist presents still images for comment and has been doing so since February, 2005. The last entry I viewed was on October 27, 2007, which is unlikely to be the last entry in this ongoing e-book of images. There's a link to the same images on Flickr and also a "Vimeo" site with an invitation to upload videos to that site for free. There are video examples to view.[21] When you view the images on the blog, you see that there are a minimal number of comments, which raises the question: If they give an e-book on a blog and no one comes, does it really exist?

Some projects are pure experiments, some are author-driven, some are open to the collective imagination, some are designed to appeal to niche audiences, some are designed for the public at large—they are all hybrids of Web, content, and software, each element combining and enriching and informing the other. Some are successful, some less so, but all of them push the envelope and test the limits of what is possible.

Mysteries and Desire: Searching the Worlds of John Rechy is part of another project called the Labyrinth Project. It is described as an "interactive memoir in three sections."[22] "Memories" offers a "three dimensional representation of Rechy's subjectivity," "Bodies" offers a "gestural" interface, and "Cruising" allows you "to control the rhythmic mix of movements, music, setting and commentary." This e-book is for sale at $39.95. This is one of three e-books available from the Annenberg Center for Communication at the University of Southern California. To quote from its web site:

> Working at the pressure point between theory and practice, the Labyrinth Project is a research initiative on interactive narrative, directed by Martha Kinder, at the Annenberg Center for Communication at the University of Southern California in Los Angeles. In pursuing its primary goal of expanding the language, art, culture and theory of interactive narrative, the project has produced a series of electronic fictions with three award-winning artists well known for their experimentation in non-linear narrative who had not previously worked with electronic multimedia: novelist John Rechy and independent filmmakers Nina Menks and Pat O'Neill. Participating in the conceptual design and production, these artists collaborated with the Labyrinth core creative team, headed by writer-producer Marsha Kinder, art director Kristy H.A. Kang, and interface designers Rosemary Comella and James Tobias, with a supporting crew of students from the USC School of Cinema-Television.[23]

There are other e-book projects of a very different nature, projects that at first glance appear less adventurous than the above examples, but which are equally experimental and deeply rich in content. Examples can be seen in e-book archives. Disciplines such as history and literature are particularly served by these efforts.

The Library of Congress American Memory project is a library of multiple "collections," within which are topics, within which are e-books of various types—documents, images, media—all searchable, all linked to sites for teachers, and all connected to a librarian for assistance.[24] This archive is continually growing via various forms of e-books and is another example of how it is difficult to be sure that an e-book or a collection of e-books is finished. People may stop working on it, as is the case with Wark's book or the Gates project, but someone might take a fresh interest and start up again.

Another example is the Whitman Archive.[25] Funding is provided by government agencies and universities, and there is an effort to gather donations in order to create a permanent endowment for the project. This e-book has two named editors, project staff that includes scholars and a librarian, and an advisory board. The sections of the site serve as forms of online chapters (e.g., manuscripts, criticism, images, audio, bibliography) and the site carries all the authority of the scholarship that has been and continues to be invested in its creation. The images section is reminiscent of an art exhibition catalog.

These various e-books are direct communications from the creators to the users, an aspect that makes them particularly valuable in addition to the high scholarship which they represent.

Commercial Endeavors

While non-commercial efforts may struggle for funding and must rely on the generosity of foundations, universities, and donations, the commercial world is trying to make e-books viable under the drive of profit. This is a different type of challenge and results in slower development of experimental types of e-books.

Publishers' current attempts at transformation are focused on reference titles, as described with Britannica Online earlier in this chapter. The advantage is that most reference titles are not designed to be read cover to cover, by-passing the whole readability issue. Some publishers are further ahead than others with these conversions and are planning or implementing new e-only titles. Gale's Virtual Reference Library, for example, provides a platform for its full range of transformed e-titles, and each library's site is populated with its particular subscriptions. Titles are available for students throughout their educational experience (e.g., Kids InfoBits for the K-5 crowd) or the many titles provided to the higher-education market. On the site, the "edition" and "year of publication" are given, and these titles carry both an ISBN and an e-ISBN. Once the publisher puts the material online, it's a simple step to engage in continuous or frequent updating. Once that happens, are they still e-books? Or are they more like e-serials? Gale is staking its future on its virtual e-reference collection, currently the highest revenue goal for the company, according to product manager Erin Sullivan.[26]

Thomson Gale also offers its Business Plans, a collection of actual business plans written by entrepreneurs seeking funding throughout North America. Rather than collecting them into a print book, Gale is making them available to business people when and where they're needed. Other business e-books include encyclopedias of business, management, and small business.

Many Alexander Street Press products are reminiscent of the Library of Congress American Memory project. They offer collections of e-books within their databases. Media elements enhance music and performing arts, transcripts from therapy sessions provide original material in Primary Sources in Counseling and Psychology, and the list of benefits extends to every discipline. These, too, are moving from the traditional book concept to a more fluid evolution with new e-book portions added as available.

An alternate commercial approach is to work the advertising model, à la Google. Services like SpiralFrog "offer music, videos, and, in one case, books for free in exchange for users having to view advertising. For businesses like music and book publishing, which are largely transactional, experimenting with an ad model is fresh territory that could ultimately deliver a new revenue stream."[27]

University presses are also getting into the act. According to its Web site, Rice University "has re-launched its university press as an all-digital operation."[28] After a fairly extensive experimentation stage, the press has chosen this approach to deal with the economic and other challenges of scholarly publishing. Traditional peer review and editing remain, but "rather than waiting for months for a printer to make a bound book, Rice University Press's digital files will instead be run through *Connexions* for automatic formatting, indexing and population with high-resolution images, audio and video and Web links."[29] A creative force behind this idea was Rich Baraniuk, a professor who was dissatisfied with the textbooks available to him. Again, this is a blend of Web, content, and free software tools to foster the evolution of the material through development, manipulation, and continuous refinement.[30] In addition, there is a focus on open source. Economically, Rice wants to focus on fields impacted by high costs, such as art history or medical diagnostics, but from a scholarly perspective, the Press is interested in fostering new models of scholarly work that use text, media, and Web in a composite whole. This goes back to Ted Padova's early work with Adobe Acrobat in 2002, work that was an early forerunner of what many scholars are now seeking to implement in this now-richer technological framework.

DEFINITION OF AN E-BOOK

By this point, you are probably wondering whether all these experiments and resulting titles can really be described as books, e- or otherwise. They contain everything from text to images to audio to video, all in varying degrees. As part of the interview process, I chose not to ask interviewees about their definitions of an e-book until late in our conversations. While they knew the purpose of the interview, I still wanted them to consider their works without the constraints of a "label."

As expected, interviewees tended to base their e-book definitions on the area or areas of their own focus. In some cases, the definitions were primarily technical, requiring that the creation be initiated digitally and primarily published digitally but with no restriction on content or the presentation of that content. In some cases, the definitions were quite narrow, with a view of the e-book as an electronic equivalent of the print version. One interviewee considered the e-archive as a whole new entity; another thought of it as simply a new e-edition. To some, the very term "e-book" was a problem. In one case, e-reference was the preferred term because, for that individual, the e-book carried the baggage of requirements for equipment/hardware for viewing and problems related to checking in and checking out e-copies. In another, it was suggested that only librarians are hung up on this terminology. For some, the e-book is merely a rite of passage between the print book and something as yet not invented. For one person, it is an "experience of reading; for another it a "constellation of possibilities," a definition I found most appealing as I envisioned the open road of e-adventure that will take us to new experiences and expand our minds with new thoughts, images, and stories. That definition comes full circle, in a way, because wasn't the printed book just that—a way to expand and explore beyond ourselves as we turned each page? Now, instead of turning a page, we click a mouse or engage with the material in some other way.

It is important to note the point that only librarians care about the term "e-book." Just as users haven't cared in the past whether the information comes in a book/monograph or serial/periodical, so they probably don't care about the form of the information they encounter online. What they want is the information that they need or are interested in pursuing, that is presented in an engaging way, that is available anywhere and anytime, and that is affordable.

PASSIONS, CHALLENGES, AND ISSUES

For this article, I interviewed 28 authors, creators, editors, publishers, vendors, and librarians who are involved in these new types of e-books, eliciting perspectives on various passions, challenges, and issues, along with very different emphases reflecting the divergent worlds in which the interviewees live and work. I am very grateful to all the interviewees for their time and thought on these topics.

The Appendix provides the questions I used with each interviewee.

Benefits

Many non-commercial experiments are connected to the academic world. It is part of the research endeavor of a number of faculty members in a wide range of disciplines. There are so many facets available in the creation of these complex materials that there is room for very varied and exciting collaborations, as attested to by the list of participants in some of the projects described above. Artistically, the world has exploded with opportunities to offer original materials on a much wider scale. Those materials can be new creations, as with *Gamer Theory* or *Mysteries and Desire*, or they can be primary materials such as are provided by the American Memory project or the Whitman archive. The increased accessibility of content and the expansion of when and where it can be accessed are among the most important shifts in our creative world.

Another wonderful aspect of this process is in the new relationships possible between creators and those who come to the material. There has always been some form of feedback on print books, whether it's a formal book review or letters to editors or some other communication, but it has been much more asynchronous and much less frequent than it is now. When you consider the decision of the Gates project to leave the collective creation in the hands of the contributors and Wark's *Gamer Theory* process of involving participation in the creation of the work, it is clear that these new paradigms change the nature of the creator/"reader" relationship significantly.

These wonderful aspects of e-books and e-book experiments are not without their challenges. The use of the word *passions* in the heading for this section is deliberate. Those involved in this process are clearly passionate about their projects. They face significant challenges, both in the creation of these works and also in the environment in which they live and work.

Economics

More than one interviewee spoke of the costs involved in these projects. In one interview, David Goldberg, professor at the University of California and Director of its system-wide Humanities Research Institute, spoke of the work on his new book and how he kept "stumbling across images that were deeply connected to his thoughts,"[31] but he also discovered that it is too expensive to get rights to images and that even if he secured the rights to use the material, his publisher would be faced with impossibly high production costs. Goldberg will develop a Web site to go with his book and will include URLs throughout the book, but this will not be the same as fully integrating images into the text.

One of the first costs, therefore, comes at the very beginning of the cre-ation process. The intellectual property issue came up over and over again with interviewees of all types. This issue is too complex to explore in depth in this chapter, but, as Goldberg pointed out, it is part of the economy of the creation and publication of e-books, and part of the politics of publishing as well. There are no easy answers and it will impact significantly what will ultimately be possible. The Whitman archive has a separate chapter called "Conditions of use."[32] A quick glance reveals the complexity of the issues. The site explains fair use and provides a form to request permission along with a list of contributors. There are extensive details on what to request and from whom. The form is only for materials described as being under the archive's copyright. Requests for other materials must go to contributors, including public and private libraries and special collections that presumably have requirements that differ from one to the other. These processes require time, money, persistence, and patience.

Scholarly Choices

How is information chosen for e-books? Google has been digitizing books for some time and doing so on a large scale, but the choice of what to digitize has been largely arbitrary from a scholarly perspective.

The libraries with whom Google has contracted may influence digitization decisions, but intellectual property constraints, the easy availability of some titles over others, the condition of physical copies, and other factors also affect what is and is not digitized. As has probably always been the case, the development of new content is based on the particular passions of creators with some constraints from the outside world, while conversion of old formats to new is influenced by the expediency of what's available, what's technologically possible, and what's economically viable. Knowing this, it would be a wonderful pipe dream if we could foster some collective discussion on this subject. These constraints also affect the much smaller experimentations. Creators, such as Wark and Rechy, may largely avoid this particular problem, but authors such as Goldberg experience it, as do those working with archival e-books.

Audience

The audience, if you can still call it that, is shifting. As was seen above, there can be challenges in getting people to a blog, like the IT IN place project, but there are also unexpected audiences for material as well. In my interview with Matt Cohen, a contributing editor to the Whitman archive, he mentioned that there are some 22,000 hits a day from secondary schools.[33] The Whitman archive is a particularly scholarly endeavor that comes from a higher education research environment, but teachers and students are drawn by the opportunity to make Whitman come alive through his work, his images, and even a recording (there is a "36-second wax cylinder recording of what is thought to be Whitman's voice reading four lines from the poem 'America'").[34] This raises the question of why one site draws participants and one doesn't—content, presentation, ease of navigation, search algorithms, marketing, support for constant updating and change, the possibilities are many. E-books are more complex to create than print books because content, technologies, editing, and marketing must each be effective and also be successful in combination.

The audience factor is growing not only because of their involvement in actual creation, but also because we know more about them through the unprecedented tracking capabilities of the online world. If a site like the Whitman archive gets 22,000 hits a day from secondary schools, what might that do to the archive's choice of direction? With its funding sources and the "contained" subject focus, it may or may not make a difference in this case, but for commercial enterprises, audience is everything because audience translates into profit. While the popularity of titles in the print world influences the choice of future projects, there have usually been a few editors and publishers willing to take a chance on a marginal project. With narrower profit margins and a capability to dissect an audience's characteristics to the finest detail, such projects will either disappear or have to be picked up by the non-commercial world. The popularity contest with relevance ranking is now in full force.

Another audience issue is language. While print books at a certain level of success have been translated into other languages, the worldwide nature of the electronically connected audience changes the dynamic on language considerably. If, as Matt Cohen stated, Whitman is read by more people outside the United States than in the United States and if more people read Whitman in languages other than English than they do in English, how does that affect your creative direction and its significance to the audience? The archive chose a graduate student from a literature program to create an e-edition of a Spanish translation of Whitman's poems from 1912, but this is a small portion of the archive. One argument might be that, as an archive, the materials are valid in their original language, but ultimately, the Google model of being able to work with material in multiple languages will prevail. The scholarship, economic, and political implications of this are significant.

Assistive technology initiatives are another audience issue that affects creation. While capabilities in this regard are developing, creators are challenged when it comes to implementation. These initiatives take time, expertise, and money, but as assistive technology mandates are largely unfunded, this is a major challenge for all creative works and particularly for non-mainstream works with fewer resources.

An assumption is also made that the audience has access to the technology needed to view these new creations and that, in turn, raises the "have" and "have not" issue that carries its own world of politics and moral responsibilities. Some vendors genuinely question whether e-books are an appropriate delivery mechanism for K–12, as was raised in my interview with Miriam Gilbert of Rosen Publishing Group.[35] Part of it is the practical cost of creation coupled with the ability to sell these materials in sufficient numbers. Capstone Press, for example, offers Interactive Books,[36] but how well they are selling is unclear. In addition to customer demands for which customers can't pay, the schools that might want these materials may have no technology on which to view them. Until that gap is addressed, commercial publishers will continue to have an uphill battle. Even if the gap is addressed, publishers haven't found the key yet, that certain something that will make e-books "go."

Technology

In addition to content issues, creators must now wrestle with server hosting, network, and backup; design issues, coding, and content preservation; and questions of upgrading, re-coding, and adapting to ever-changing technological developments. The working groups on these projects need representation from both content and technology providers. Politics and economics can easily drive decisions in these technological areas and jeopardize projects. The working groups formed for these various projects are keys to their survival and ongoing viability.

Audience access is also bound by technological limitations. Will separate e-readers be needed or will multi-function devices facilitate access to these new creations? Who will help with technology problems? Right now, help comes formally, if you are affiliated with an institution of some sort, informally, if you have a friend or contact with knowledge and willingness to help, or through payment to a service, if you have neither of these connections.

The Dynamics of Learning

We now live much more in a learning environment of "bites"—textual bites, sound bites, visual bites. What does this do to our learning? Many interviewees expressed a hope that textual reading and the print book would not disappear, but no one thought that it would continue to hold the same exclusive dominance as it has in the past. Moving into this new world offers access to a range of material, allows for a greater ability to create relationships among various pieces and forms of material, facilitates the user's interaction with the material, and generally creates a new dynamic for learning.

Wonderful as this is, there is a price to be paid and that price is not only sustained readability, but sustained reading. We listen to books, often with the accompaniment of revving car engines; we pick up pieces of related mini-books from a summary on the Web; and we watch a *YouTube* clip of an author or a review interview on the *Daily Show*, but do we read the book? The reason we like e-reference titles is that we can get snippets of information but experience those snippets holistically. Children see as normal an online encyclopedia with pictures of lions and tigers accompanied by appropriate roars and running motion. Perhaps there's even a little text underneath. The content world is permanently changed. Will our brains go with it? Will we be hard-wired differently? How are we

interrelating with information and how will we evolve as human beings as
the nature of information and the nature of that inter-relationship changes?

For Paolo Mangiafico, a Digital Project Consultant with Duke University
Libraries, "the interesting questions are around where filtering happens and
the discovery process."[37] In the era of print, the filtering process took place
before a book was published, when an editor or publisher decided whether
to invest in that work or not. Today, when the publishing conglomerates
have absorbed the independent publisher and independent booksellers are
an endangered species, this new world of experimentation is opening.
Today, when anyone can create anything and share it, the filtering takes
place after the publication. It happens through sites like del.icio.us[38] or
the LibraryThing[39] or Connotea;[40] it happens through blogs; it happens
through online social networks. The meaning comes through the digital
conversation or through the way the user engages with and manipulates
the content.

Will there still be a place and time for sustained reading with its accompanying extended thought? Is there still a place for the long, cohesive
argument? Or will the engagement simply be a continuous chain reaction
of "bites"?

THE WORLDS IN WHICH WE LIVE AND WORK

For academics, pursuing these new experiments is not without personal
risk at times of retention, tenure, and promotion. For the untenured in particular, there is significant risk that they will find themselves job hunting.
To hedge against this, a number are ensuring that they also secure publication in traditional environments. In tenure review, faculty still gives more
significance to publication in print than in e-form, although, ironically, as
users of information, they prefer to work with electronic information from
their homes or offices. At some point, preferably soon, this structure needs
an overhaul.

In mid-September 2007, ebrary facilitated an informal survey designed
by librarians to try to gain a better understanding of the faculty experience
with e-resources and print materials. As of this writing, the results are
not yet available [Ed. note: the survey appears elsewhere in this volume],
however, it is clear that something is still not quite connecting. Students love
print books in e-form, although I suspect they are not trying to read entire
volumes. It is too early to tell how they will respond to new experiments.
They certainly visit the Whitman archive and the Library of Congress

American Memory project, but are they merely a captive audience, sent there by their teachers? What proportion of them chooses these materials independently?

For those in the commercial world, the pressures are enormous. The demands for information in new formats with multiple capabilities are not balanced out by the non-corporate customer's ability to pay. Commercial providers also experience a good deal of frustration. They would like to move faster, keep up with customer demands, provide what is requested, but they must see a profit. There is fear that the profit won't be there, that the risk they take may be their last, after which they will either be sold to the highest bidder or put out of business. There are also lingering assumptions that may or may not still be true—the "need" for equipment to read them or issues with platforms they have known and not loved. Some vendors are thinking about partnerships and who might be willing to take a risk with them, thereby spreading and minimizing the economic danger to all.

The Role of the Librarian and the Library

We librarians have long seen ourselves as providers of information. That includes collecting it, organizing it, providing access, teaching information literacy, and a host of other activities centered on "things." This is rapidly becoming a "thing" of the past. As mentioned above, only librarians really care about whether a book is a book or a serial is a serial. The reason for that concern has been the embedded structures we have developed to organize the information. However, what does that mean if a project, like the Gates project, is created by multiple contributors, comes in multiple formats, and is finally housed in multiple places?

One fascinating thing about these new experiments is that their format and structure are emerging organically from the material itself. In poetry, this happened a long time ago. The pre-structured form—sonnet, villanelle, haiku—once provided a framework for ideas and content. When "free" forms emerged, the poem's intrinsic nature led the creator to the final form—number of lines per stanza, lined poem vs. prose poem, and so on. With these new experimental e-books, the same thing is happening. The material itself is driving the form and the future will likely bring forms we have yet to imagine. This has significant implication for organizing the information and the material, if librarians continue to see that as their role.

Information is scattering both physically and intellectually—to institutional repositories, to Web 2.0 (soon 3.0 and beyond), to new configurations, to multiple creations, to forms of text and sound and visual images—both still and moving. In addition, these materials are not "collectible." For years now, we've rented information rather than buying it. Now, we are unlikely even to rent it. Our role in preserving information is still strong, but collecting it is another issue. It is good to note that librarians are involved in the American Memory project and the Whitman archive. These librarians are collaborators on the creation teams with a positive role to play, brokering the information by participating in and facilitating the conversation among creators and users. This is a very different role than what they played in the past.

In terms of access, our role is also more social. As Web search engines continue to improve, many users find it easier to find what they want independently. For the foreseeable future, we will likely provide access to content by paying for commercial offerings—databases, media, some print material—but that role is predicated on a sufficiency of budget, on a budget that continues and expands along historical lines, and on continued use of our services by vendors. There have been attempts in the past to sell directly to the user and those could easily come back into play as the pay-per-view model gains momentum. Clearly, one can buy Rechy's e-book directly through the Web, but to provide general access, will a library have to "collect" it or will there be some other way to make it available? The material could potentially be accompanied by advertising, shifting the cost in that direction, as SpiralFrog is doing, although that particular title might not be considered popular enough or mainstream enough to warrant that effort.

As a result of these shifts, our role in information literacy is increasing and will continue to do so. If users can find what they want independently, our role is to help them interpret what they find. While we currently also teach them how to navigate our archaic world, that element is less prominent and the new reality is how to manage Web 2.0, both in terms of content and tools. We also need to help users understand what's out there. The example of IT IN place with its minimal comments illustrates the nature of this issue and the importance of librarians' role in this regard. Again, it is about facilitating the conversation rather than about providing the information. The information is provided directly by the creator; the post-publication filtering, as Mangiafico noted, is where the peer-review and selection takes place.

And what about the library itself? That, too, requires transformation. If everything is "e," what's the space for? Of course, retrospective print materials will be around a long time and still need to be provided, but the library is now a conversation place where technology and content merge (perhaps also with coffee!) in an atmosphere that, once again, facilitates the conversation. That conversation can be between the user and the information, among users and information, just among users about information, but it's a conversation that can be facilitated and brokered effectively in the library.

CONCLUSION

In 2002, when my mind was opened to the potential of e-books, I couldn't wait for them to emerge and integrate with other daily offerings of information. It has taken longer than I expected, and we are far from the finish line. There are also those who think the e-books' day will pass before they get fully off the ground, as we move on to other inventions. While commercial vendors must make e-books fiscally viable, those who are supported by their academic institutions or by foundations and non-profits can experiment. Yet, in spite of the challenges in getting e-books transformed and into the mainstream, I believe they will ultimately make it, offering continuous and current updating, incorporating images, audio, and video as a matter of course, and providing features that are still to be dreamed. On a practical level, think of a nursing textbook with a mouse-over demonstration of a technique. Think of a music text with audio examples. Think of mousing over a poem to hear it read by the author or seeing a flash poem that can never appear in print, all with complementary Web sites, blogs, and/or wikis for comment, discussion, and influence over the evolution of the e-book itself.

The e-book, or e-whatever, offers an amazingly complex future and one that promises great excitement, engagement, and proactive learning. And, I still hope, a good read in bed!

NOTES

1. GOODBYE PAPER. *Popular Science* 269, no. 6 (2006): 48. *Academic Search Premier*, EBSCO*host*. Retrieved September 16, 2007.
2. Sony Learning Center. *Product Overview*. [2005; cited September 16, 2007]. Available from <http://www.learningcenter.sony.us/assets/itpd/reader/>.
3. Ibid.
4. Levy, Steven. The future of reading. *Newsweek*, November 26, 2007; cited November 28, 2007. Available at <http://www.newsweek.com/id/70983>.
5. Ibid.
6. Institute for the Future of the Book. [undated; cited September 16, 2007]. Retrieved from <http://www.futureofthebook.org>.

7. Institute for the Future of the Book. *About Us.* [undated; cited September 16, 2007]. Retrieved from http://www.futureofthebook.org <http://www.futureofthebook.org/blog/about.html>.

8. Institute for the Future of the Book. *CommentPress.* Version 1.4. [undated; cited September 16, 2007]. Retrieved from <http://www.futureofthebook.org> <http://www.futureofthebook.org/commentpress/about/>.

9. Institute, op. cit. Retrieved from http://www.futureofthebook.org <http://www.futureofthebook.org/>.

10. Northmore, Sarah. "Tough crowds." *Print* 60, no. 6 (2006): 20. *Academic Search Premier*, EBSCO*host* (accessed September 16, 2007). For greater detail, see "Book 2.0." *Chronicle of Higher Education* 52, no. 47 (2006): A20-A24. *Academic Search Premier*, EBSCOhost. Retrieved September 16, 2007. <http://www.futureofthebook.org>.

11. Institute for the Future of the Book. *Gamer Theory.* [undated; cited October 29, 2007]. Retrieved from http://www.futureofthebook.org <http://www.futureofthebook.org/mckenziewark/gamertheory/>.

12. Ibid.

13. Harvard University Press. *Gamer Theory.* [undated; cited October 11, 2007]. Available at <http://www.hup.harvard.edu/catalog/WARGAM.html>.

14. Institute for the Future of the Book. *Sophie.* [undated; cited September 16, 2007]. Available at <http://www.sophieproject.org/>.

15. Institute, op. cit. Available at <http://www.futureofthebook.org/>.

16. Institute for the Future of the Book. *Operation Iraqi Quagmire.* [undated; cited September 16, 2007]. Available at <http://www.futureofthebook.org/iraq>.

17. Institute for the Future of the Book. *Media Commons.* [undated; cited September 16, 2007]. Available at <http://mediacommons.futureofthebook.org/about>.

18. Institute for the Future of the Book. *The Gates: an Experiment in Collective Memory.* [undated; cited September 16, 2007]. Available at <http://www.futureofthebook.org/gatesmemoryblog/>.

19. Ibid. In checking Flickr on October 27, 2007, there were 3,627 results for the "gatesmemory" project.

20. John Weber, "Re: Request for Interview of New Types of E-books," personal email (25 September, 2007).

21. Institute for the Future of the Book. *IT IN place.* [undated; cited September 16, 2007]. Available at <http://www.futureofthebook.org/itinplace/>.

22. Bring Your Brain.com. *Mysteries and Desire.* [undated; cited October 29, 2007]. Available at <http://wwww.bringyourbrain.com/product/index.php?pro=6>.

23. Ibid.

24. Library of Congress. *American Memory.* [updated 08 August, 2007; cited October 29, 2007]. Available at <http://memory.loc.gov/ammem/index.html>.

25. Folsom, Ed, and Kenneth M. Price, editors. *The Walt Whitman Archive.* [undated; cited October 29, 2007]. Available at <http://www.whitmanarchive.org/>.

26. Sullivan, Erin. Interview by Aline Soules, 5 September, 2007.

27. Lehman, Paula. "Free Downloads—After This Message." *Business Week* no. 4004 (2006): 95. *Academic Search Premier*, EBSCO*host* (accessed September 16, 2007).

28. Rice University Press. *About Rice University Press*. [2007; cited October 12, 2007]. Available at <http://ricepress.rice.edu/>. Note: readers need to scroll down to this section on the press' home page.

29. Harvard University Press. *Connexions is*. [undated; cited October 12, 2007]. Available at <http://cnx.rice.edu/>.

30. Craddock, Ashley. *Commoners: Rice University's Connexions*. [1 October, 2005; cited September 16, 2007. Available at <http://creativecommons. org/education/connexions>.

31. Goldberg, David. Interview by Aline Soules, 25 September, 2007.

32. Whitman Archive, op. cit. *Conditions of Use*. [undated; cited October 11, 2007]. Available at <http://www.whitmanarchive.org/fair_use/index.html>.

33. Cohen, Matt. Interview by Aline Soules, 5 October, 2007.

34. Whitman Archive, op. cit. *Audio Recording*. [undated; cited October 11, 2007]. Available at <http://www.whitmanarchive.org/audio/index.html>.

35. Gilbert, Miriam. Interview by Aline Soules, 27 September, 2007.

36. Capstone Press. *Capstone Press Interactive*. [2004; cited October 22, 2007]. Available at <http://www.capstonepress.com/interactive/>.

37. Mangiafico, Paolo. Interview by Aline Soules, 10 October, 2007.

38. del.icio.us. *Social Bookmarking*. [undated; cited October 22, 2007]. Available at <http://del.icio.us/>. This site allows you to put all your "bookmarks" in one place and check out what others are "bookmarking."

39. *LibraryThing*. [undated; cited October 22, 2007]. Available at <http://www. librarything.com>. This site allows you to catalog your own books and be part of the "world's largest book club."

40. *Connotea*. [2005-2007; cited October 22, 2007]. Available at <http://www. connotea.org/>. This site allows "free online reference management for all researchers, clinicians and scientists."

APPENDIX

Interview Questions

1. What new types of e-books are you currently creating? NOTE: By new, I mean types of e-books that are not simply e-formats of print books, but books that can only appear in e-format.
   a) What are the challenges?
   b) What are the benefits?
   c) What other considerations should we discuss?
2. What experience or knowledge do you have with user interactions with these new e-books? How do you envision users interacting with these new types of e-books as the users gain greater familiarity with this new type of information source?

3. Why do you think e-books have taken so long to "take off"? What difference will new types of e-books make to that adoption curve?
4. With what new types of e-books are you currently experimenting?
   a) What are the challenges?
   b) What are the benefits?
   c) What other considerations should we discuss?
5. How do you envision user interactions changing with these new experimentations?
6. What is your long-term vision for new types of e-books, both in terms of technology and in terms of use?
   a) What are the constraints to reaching this vision?
7. In the digital world of movies, YouTube, streaming audio/video, and other types of multimedia,
   a) What role do e-books have?
   b) Why will users choose e-books over other forms of information sources?
8. After our discussion to this point, how do you define the term "e-book"? What characteristics distinguish it as a unique type of information source?
9. Do you have any other points, ideas, or issues to share? What questions have I omitted to ask?

Integration of Electronic Books into Library Catalogs: The UIC Library Experience

Kavita Mundle

PRELIMINARY OBSERVATIONS

Ever-mushrooming electronic resources, advances in technology, and changing user expectations are posing new challenges to libraries in providing appropriate and timely information about their collections. Libraries are subscribing to a variety of electronic resources ranging through electronic journals, online databases, and electronic books (e-books) from different aggregators, vendors, and publishers. As libraries are investing more of their collection development funds into buying electronic resources, librarians are not only grappling with the issues of their acquisition and licensing but are dealing with their multiple formats, their seamless integration into the library catalog, and maintaining their holdings in the library catalog. Although the debate still continues over whether users prefer electronic or print, e-books are getting slow but steady acceptance among library users. Remote access, convenience of use, saving of physical space, full-text searching capabilities, and citation linking are some of the advantages e-books offer over print publications, although lack of marketing and inadequate promotion of e-books in libraries create barriers to their use and acceptance (Connaway, 2003; Bennett and Landoni, 2005).

Most commonly, libraries are providing access to electronic books through library Web sites and through their Online Public Access Catalogs (OPACs). Integrating Machine-Readable Cataloging Records (MARC) for e-books into a library's catalog enhances access to its collection and allows users to view a library's print and electronic holdings at the same time. As many vendors and publishers of e-books now offer MARC records for e-books, libraries have the option of either batch-loading those vendor-supplied records to their OPAC or cataloging their e-books locally. The sheer volume of most e-book collections, shrinking budgets, and the constantly evolving cataloging standards make it very difficult to catalog these resources locally in a short time. Hence, adding ready-made catalog records supplied by vendors has become the trend in libraries. However, as not all e-book vendors and e-book publishers offer MARC records for titles in their collections, libraries do have to take on the responsibility of cataloging some of the e-book collections to provide unified access to all e-book holdings through their catalogs.

The University of Illinois at Chicago Library (UIC Library) started subscribing to e-books in 2000, but the real impetus and growth in adding e-books peaked in 2004 and, by 2006, the library had already subscribed to more than 55,000 e-books. When vendors started offering MARC records for the titles in their collections, the UIC Library decided to offer greater visibility and access to its electronic resources by adding vendor-supplied MARC records of e-books into its local catalog, UICCAT. The case study below describes our experiences in integrating vendor-cataloged electronic books into the local catalog, examines unique cataloging problems presented by this electronic format, and attempts to offer guidelines for accepting outsourced catalog records into the OPAC. Additionally, it describes our efforts in cataloging some of the e-book collections for which vendor-supplied catalog records were not available.

LITERATURE REVIEW

In recent years, literature on e-books has shown a steady growth in covering topics ranging through the acceptance of e-books in libraries, collection development, licensing, bibliographic control, and studies on their use.

Despite advances in telecommunications technology, print book publishing still dominates the publishing industry. There appears to be a slow uptake of e-books by libraries and users. Thomas reviews several underlying issues with e-books such as the lack of standardized product with a sustainable business model, limited selection of titles, subscription based access, and not knowing enough about reading in a digital environment, and states that these are some of the factors that make the use of e-books more complex (Thomas, 2007). In general, e-books have become the preferred format primarily for reference or research purposes and are frequently used by distance education students (Littman and Connway, 2004; Gunter, 2005, p. 521).

Moreover, some subjects such as computer science, technology, engineering, economics, medicine, literature, and business seem to be more popular among students (Gibbs, 2001; Gibbons, 2001). Despite such preferences for e-books for some uses and subjects, research indicates that (a) e-books are not as heavily used as print books, (b) users prefer print to e-books to read longer passages, (c) users usually read e-books only if print is unavailable, and (d) users do not read e-books for sustained periods of time (Levine-Clark, 2007, p. 13; Christianson and Aucoin, 2005). Poor screen resolution on a computer monitor, difficulty in reading and browsing, the need to use special equipment to read, and restrictions on printing are some of the factors that influence users' continued preference for learning with print (Liu, 2005; Gunter, 2005; Chu, 2003).

Libraries have been experimenting with e-books by adding them into their collections and providing access to them through homepages and/or library catalogs. Studies on humanists' information-seeking behavior highlight that humanists use the library catalog as a primary resource for browsing and finding information and are thus more familiar with e-books than their colleagues across campus (Levine-Clark, 2007, p. 8). Undergraduates and postgraduate students, on the other hand, show low usage and awareness and prefer to search the library's homepage to select library resources. They do not want to read the book entirely and do not use e-books if they are not listed in the drop-down menus or suggested by their faculty (Hernon, et al., 2006). Those who find e-books through library catalogs seem to have greater awareness of them than others who do not use the catalog to find e-books. As libraries are investing more money into buying these resources, promoting, marketing, and making them available via library catalogs is essential for their potential to be exploited fully.

Accessing E-books through Library Web Sites and Library Catalogs

Predominantly, libraries are providing access to e-books through their Web sites and/or OPACs. A study by Dinkelman and Bates investigated how academic libraries in the Association of Research Libraries (ARL) are providing access to e-books through their library Web sites (Dinkelman and Stacy-Bates, 2007). This study also highlighted the merits of various approaches used to access e-books through library catalogs. The study reported that 56% of the library Web sites had separate pages devoted to e-books, with 85% of these pages residing two clicks away from the library's home page. In regard to accessing e-books from the library catalog, multiple limit search options in the OPAC created confusion and a barrier to access, and only 30% of library catalogs allowed limiting the search to e-books in a single step. The study suggested that library Web sites should avoid ambiguity in the terminology used to describe electronic resources, group e-books by subject and alert patrons to check locations other than library Web sites (e.g., check the catalog to search for e-books). In regard to e-book searching through a catalog, the study recommended improving the search functionality by having a search limit option for "e-books" on the basic or keyword search screen.

McCall assessed how health science libraries were providing access to electronic books through their Web sites. He reported that 19 libraries out of 21 provided title-level access through their Web sites and stated that out of 21 libraries, 20 created catalog records for their online medical books and one library provided analytical access to e-books at the chapter level (McCall, 2006).

Several studies have confirmed that the inclusion of records for e-books in the catalog increases usage (Gibbons, 2001; Langston, 2003). A study at Texas A&M on NetLibrary e-books reported a 230% increase in usage of e-books owing to the addition of MARC records to the catalog and their promotion and advertising on the campus and in the consortium (Ramirez and Gyeszly, 2001). Dillon at the University of Texas also reported a dramatic increase in usage of e-books with the addition of e-book records into the catalog. Within three months of adding records, the number of times users accessed e-books increased by 100% (Dillon, 2001).

Adding Vendor-Supplied MARC Records into Library Catalogs

Despite evidence that adding records for e-books to catalogs increases use, the literature offers little guidance on how best to add them. Bothmann's article published in 2004 offers detailed guidance to catalogers on how to actually catalog e-books locally (Bothmann, 2004), but most of the literature calls for using vendor- or publisher-created records. Martin stated that librarians had been slow and reluctant to catalog e-books as standards are underdeveloped, e-books are available only via subscription, and electronic resources are still viewed as supplementary rather than a core part of the library's collections. She also emphasized that the cataloging workflow should be incorporated into the e-book acquisition process (Martin, 2007). Gravett at the University of Surrey asserted that importing batches of vendor-cataloged records is a suitable option for libraries because it saves time. Gravett called on vendors to provide reliable and standardized records to the libraries (Gravett, 2006).

In 2006, the Program for Cooperative Cataloging (PCC) developed a guide for vendors and publishers called "MARC record guide for Monograph Aggregator Vendors." This guide offers standards and recommendations to vendors and publishers in creating MARC records for electronic books in MARC 21. This guide assists vendors in creating accurate bibliographic descriptions of electronic books in order to produce MARC record sets for libraries to be loaded into their catalogs.[1]

A study by Nelson described some of the practical issues surrounding the integration of e-books, in particular Net Library e-books at Victoria University Library. The study indicated that although an evaluation of a sample load of records showed them to be of high quality, problems occurred. Loading the profile of catalog records generated print orders, the load program crashed and subject headings did not load (Nelson, 2001). Gedeon and Meyer reported that vendor-created records lack quality and authority control and these deficiencies made librarians reluctant to load those records to the catalog. Gedeon and Meyer also found that manipulation and revision of records added to costs and created significant delays in loading the records (Gedeon and Meyer, 2005). To date, only the study by Sanchez, et al. actually described in detail how a library cleaned up NetLibrary records before batch-loading them into its catalog. The article discusses problems identified in the records and their ramifications. It describes how the records were corrected and upgraded to suit local cataloging practices and standards by using software such as MarcEdit, MS Word, and Excel (Sanchez, 2006).

As many e-book collections are subscription-based, titles are added or deleted from a library's subscription, and there is a time lag between vendors sending the updated files of records, causing a lack of access to users through the catalog. As a result, maintaining an up-to-date catalog becomes very challenging and a time consuming process for libraries (Blummer, 2006). Moreover, the entire process of batch-loading records not only involves editing and importing records but entails creating holdings records, maintaining OPAC displays, and also not loading duplicate records for identical titles that might be offered through different collections. All in all, managing e-book collections and their bibliographic control remain challenging areas for librarians, who have to be creative in finding the right ways of incorporating outsourced catalog records into the library catalogs.

Integrating Vendor-Supplied MARC Records of E-books at the UIC Library

The text below describes how the UIC Library evaluates, improves, and utilizes vendor-supplied catalog records for electronic books. It also describes the library's efforts in cataloging e-books when vendor-supplied catalog records are unavailable.

The University of Illinois at Chicago is an urban land-grant university with a population of more than 25,000 students. The UIC Library has three locations on the Chicago campus: Richard J. Daley Library (Main), a science library, and a major health sciences library and its health sciences site libraries in Rockford, Peoria, and Urbana. The library has more than 2.2 million volumes and subscribes to more than 26,000 serial titles (including more than 10,000 electronic journals). The library is a part of a consortium of Illinois libraries, CARLI, and uses Voyager as the local Integrated Library System (ILS).

Given the increasing availability of electronic resources and users' preferences for them, the UIC library has expanded access to them. The library has been subscribing to e-book collections since the year 2000, and by 2006 had licensed more than 55,000 e-books. Until 2006, access to e-books was provided only at the collection level on a Web page that listed electronic resources alphabetically. Additionally, for health sciences e-books, a separate Web page, "LHS Electronic Gateway," listed e-books arranged alphabetically by the name of the collection and by subject. As the library expanded its e-book holdings and e-book vendors started offering MARC records for their collections, the library decided to experiment with adding those records to its library catalog. The large number of e-books argued against local cataloging and made batch-loading vendor-supplied MARC records a preferable option to consider and experiment with. For e-books from vendors and publishers that were not offering MARC records, the catalog department decided to catalog them locally.

When the library negotiated access to ebrary e-books in 2004, the contractual agreements offered MARC records for all titles in the collection. Later on, vendors such as Credo Reference, ACLS History e-book project, Empire Online, and Oxford Online followed suit. Previous experiences of adding vendor-supplied records for electronic journals influenced our decision to review and analyze the file of ready-made MARC records for e-books to assess their accuracy and quality before adding them to the online catalog. To lead that assessment, an "E-book Evaluation Team" composed of three catalogers and a Library Technical Services Systems Specialist was set up. The charge of the "E-books Evaluation team" is to find ways to facilitate access to e-books through the catalog. The team also tries whenever possible to find ways to make corrections needed on a batch of vendor-supplied records before they are loaded into the catalog.

Initially, each team member separately evaluated about 20 records from the files purchased from ebrary and Credo Reference, and later from Oxford Reference Online and Empire Online, to ascertain their accuracy and quality. We found that reviewing these records could give us an indication of what types of problems could be found throughout the entire file of records. This initial evaluation was carried out in three steps: (a) The Library Technical Services Systems Specialist converted vendor-supplied MARC records into a readable tagged text file by using MarcEdit software;[2] created individual folders for team members, and added a discrete set of records in each folder to be reviewed; (b) the individual team member then carefully assessed the records in the file to identify possible problems; and (c) the team then reviewed and compiled all the identified problems.

From our initial evaluation of discrete records from four different vendors, it was clear that a set of mandatory criteria were needed for accepting vendor-supplied bibliographic data for electronic books. The criteria we set were as follows:

1. All vendor-catalog records should be created in MARC21 format;
2. The records should conform to current national cataloging standards for full-level cataloging; and

3. All records should have subject headings established according to LCSH and/or MeSH.

Our further intensive qualitative evaluation of records from multiple vendors revealed that the quality of vendor catalog records varied from vendor to vendor. The problems found in records created barriers to consistent user access and made some items irretrievable by users. Therefore, the team developed a set of guidelines that could be applied to vendor-supplied records before they could be loaded in the catalog. These guidelines are, in effect, the UIC standards and are highlighted in the Appendix. Tables 1 and 2 in the Appendix list those guidelines. Our E-book Evaluation Team applies those guidelines to each batch of vendor records received to assess their quality and accuracy.

With our evaluation of multiple vendor records, we identified a number of problems and those problems are highlighted in Table 3.

The problems documented in Table 3 affect users searching the collection and make at least some part of the collection irretrievable. For example, the absence of some of the most valuable access points such as MeSH would reduce retrievals by topic. Also, absence of corporate name headings would not allow users to retrieve all relevant titles under the name that was being searched. The absence of MARC fields 006 and 007 would not allow users to limit searches by the format and the lack of "general material designation, [GMD]" as [electronic resource] would lose the distinction between a print and an electronic resource. Furthermore, inconsistencies in series treatment prevent collocation, which leads to problems in searching because all untraced series titles do not get indexed and hence are hidden in the collection. Thus, these problems would make at least some part of the e-book collections disappear from many user searches.

So far, most of the vendor records have met all of the mandatory criteria (for batch-loading of e-books records) as outlined in the Appendix. However, as said earlier, these records vary in how well they conform with respect to the use of "the Primary" and "the Secondary fields" highlighted in Tables 1 and 2. The catalog department accepts a batch of vendor-supplied records only after their careful and thorough assessment. The records are corrected and edited before they are loaded into the catalog and made available to users. The team makes every effort to identify and correct as many problems as possible with MarcEdit software, but not all problems can be corrected mechanically. For example, cataloging inconsistencies found in tracing and not tracing series cannot be corrected using any mechanical tool. Therefore, only in case of systemic failure on the

55555555555555

part of a vendor to follow national guidelines that would seriously affect the integrity of our catalog does the team recommend rejecting the records outright.

For example, in one of the vendor record sets, the records did not conform completely to full-level national cataloging standards, which is one of our mandatory criteria for accepting any vendor-supplied bibliographic data into the catalog. The team observed that the records simply did not have any fields to indicate that they were e-books, except for the addition of an 856 field and that, too, without a proxy URL added on all records. The vendor had basically provided records for print books. The records were missing a general material designation [GMD], [electronic resource], no 006 and 007 fields were added, series treatment was very inconsistent (some series were traced and some were not), a note (MARC field 533) that shows that the item is an electronic reproduction of a print version was missing, and no genre/form heading for electronic books was added to these records. The integration of such records into the catalog would have matched print records we already had in the catalog and hence the E-book Evaluation Team rejected the set, and the records were not loaded into the catalog.

Correction of Vendor-Supplied Records

The Online Public Access Catalog is a gateway to any library's collection. Errors introduced in the catalog lead to underuse of the collection and users' frustration. Any incorrect bibliographic data that have invalid MARC fields, subfields, or indicators prevent records from getting batch-loaded into the catalog and creates confusing OPAC displays. Moreover, typographical errors or poorly constructed access points make items difficult to locate and retrieve through the catalog. It is, therefore, very crucial that the data that are added to the catalog are accurate, searchable, and retrievable by users.

The correction of vendor-supplied records involves editing and importing records along with identifying duplicate titles from all e-book collections that may get added into the catalog. As the library owns various e-book collections, some of the titles in one collection may overlap with some of the titles in another collection; thus, in order to avoid duplicate records getting loaded into the catalog, the catalog department is also looking into developing procedure/s to identify duplicate titles in the catalog.

With any e-book collection, our E-book Evaluation Team evaluates many, but not all, records from the collection. We identify and list problems found in the records and compare them with our set of library cataloging standards. Once the collective decision is made to load the records into our OPAC, the records are edited and imported, and their holdings are created in Voyager. The following discussion summarizes actions that we undertake to complete the batch loading of records for an e-book collection.

Editing Records

The Library Technical Services Systems Specialist scans the entire file of records to assess the extent of problems identified by the team. Then, by using the editor in MarcEdit software, the edits are made. The editor helps in editing various fields, subfields and indicators and finding and replacing text in a file of records. The corrected copy is generated and saved back in the MARC format. The MarcEdit software includes a tool that can break MARC records into a readable tagged file and another tool that can reinstate or fix broken MARC records back into MARC format. Depending on the vendor and the peculiarities of the catalog records, various fields are edited. For example, we deleted the 773 field from one set of vendor records, as it was coded incorrectly and was duplicating the information from MARC field 710. We also make sure that as a part of the 856 field, our proxy URL information gets added to that field so that our off campus users are able to access e-books. Table 4 describes MARC fields that we edit before records are loaded into Voyager.

Importing Records

Once edited, all records are batch-loaded into Voyager. The Consortium of Academic and Research Libraries in Illinois (CARLI) loads our data in Voyager after we give them the corrected file of e-book records. CARLI uses our bulk import rule and loads our data overnight. Our bulk import rule involves setting the rule to load all bibliographic records and creating holdings information.

Creating Local Holdings Data

When our holdings records are created, we use "NET" as the location code to represent all our electronic resources. Thus, for all e-books, holdings records are created by adding location code "NET" with a call number added in subfield "h" if available in a bibliographic record. We do not retain any phrases or words such as "Internet" or "Online" or "Eb" that are used as a part of the call number.

OPAC Display

The location code "NET" displays as "Electronic Collections" in UIC-CAT. An 856 field in a bibliographic record provides a URL link to the actual resource with a proxy URL added before the actual link with a public note in subfield z with the text "Available only to UIC users." UICCAT does not display the actual URL for the resource but displays a textual link, "Available only to UIC users" in full view or brief view. The actual URL can be viewed in the "Staff (MARC) view."

Quality Assurance and Maintenance

E-book collections constantly get updated with new titles added or deleted, and thus batch-loading records for them every few months becomes an on-going part of managing these collections. Vendors very often choose to send all deleted records in one file and new records in another file. For all "delete records," based on the vendor control number defined in the MARC 035 field in a bibliographic record, we write Voyager access reports to get the bibliographic identification number (Bib ID#) and holdings or mfhd numbers. Then using Voyager delete software by Paul Asay,[3] the bibliographic Id numbers and mfhd numbers are deleted from the catalog. Also, when the updates of new or active records are received, records for new books need to be added, and changed records need to be overlaid with the active records. Updates are also evaluated and corrected in the ways described earlier. So, downloading, customizing and bulk loading of files turns out to be time consuming and an ongoing maintenance concern.

Finding Duplicate Vendor Supplied E-book Records

As we tend to buy collections rather than individual e-books, there is a possibility that titles may be included in more than one collection. So far, with our vendor batch loads, we have not encountered any duplicate titles. However, to avoid that problem in the future, the catalog department is investigating writing a duplicate title detecting bulk import profile that can identify duplicate titles before the records get loaded into the catalog. We hope that the bulk import profile set to match on the MARC field 245 with subfield a, b, and h will be able to identify duplicate titles and help in not adding those records to the catalog. We would want the system to load only one record per title into the catalog and so, in the case of a title that is being offered by two different vendors, we will have to manually add multiple holdings to a single record to indicate the availability of the same title from different vendors.

Cataloging of E-books by the UIC Library

Not all e-book vendors and e-book publishers are offering MARC records for their collections. The UIC Library subscribes to a number of health sciences e-books from vendors such as AccessMedicine, Access-Surgery, Books@OVID, MD Consult, and Merck Manuals, which do not offer MARC records for the titles in their collections. As ready-made catalog records are not available, the catalog department decided to catalog these collections of e-books locally. An assessment of titles in these collections revealed that (a) these collections not only had monographs but also a few integrating resources and serials; (b) the existing library collection has equivalent print counterparts for some of the titles, so some of the titles would duplicate the existing collection; (c) a few of the titles provided access only to the "latest edition" for which the library had an entire run of previous editions in print that were cataloged as "serial" titles; (d) some of the titles received frequent updates on publishers' Web sites that were incorporated into the same online edition; and (e) a few of the titles had numerical designations or edition statements, but were not receiving any updates.

Taking into consideration these characteristics, the library first decided to catalog these titles on separate records, similar to our decision of loading vendor-supplied data on separate records. Second, to catalog titles that were accessible only in the "latest edition," Bothmann's article on how to catalog e-books, *Anglo American Cataloging Rules* (Second edition, Ch. 9 and 12) (AACR2, 2002), and Library of Congress Rule Interpretation, (LCRI) 1.0 were consulted.[4] The library decided to catalog these titles as "electronic serials" with the addition of a text, "Latest edition available only to UIC users" added to an 856 field in a bibliographic record. The MARC field 856 was also added to a holdings record as per CARLI customization guidelines. Third, notes were added to indicate restrictions on access (MARC field 506), to which collection the title belongs (MARC field 500), and if the resource received any updates on the publisher's Web site (MARC field 500). Subsequently, separate online serial records were created in OCLC for each title and our holdings were updated in OCLC.

Titles that did have a numerical edition and year (that were only in their 1st or 2nd edition) and were not getting updated on their Web sites were cataloged as monographs. Frequently updating resources bearing no numerical designation such as year or edition information or which were online databases were cataloged as integrating resources. Our holdings in OCLC were updated for all new records that we created and also for the already cataloged titles that we used to represent our e-book holdings.

Searching E-books in UICCAT

The evidence suggests that adding catalog records for e-books increases their use, and it is hoped that adding vendor-supplied records for e-books when available and adding locally cataloged records of some of the e-book collections would increase the use of e-books. Just as many catalogs do not offer ways to limit a search to online resources (Tennant, 2004), our local OPAC does not offer a limit-search option either to "electronic resources" or to "e-books" on either the basic or advanced search screen. Keyword searching and/or Boolean searching on the phrase "electronic books" coupled with a subject or an author is the only option that users have to use to search for e-books. The keyword search usually results in a large retrieval pool. Hence, providing an option to limit searches to "electronic resources" or more specifically to "e-books" in our OPAC would improve the efficiency and usefulness of the local catalog.

Proposed Guidelines for the Integration of E-books in Library Catalogs

The OPAC is an important discovery tool that facilitates the identification and retrieval of library resources. Keeping libraries' holdings up-to-date with e-books has been challenging owing to the evolving nature of standards in cataloging e-books and variations seen in vendor-supplied records for e-books. Further, in today's shrinking technical services departments, taking on the additional responsibility of cataloging infinitely growing electronic collections of e-books locally does not seem to be the cost-effective option for libraries. Vendor-supplied catalog records are often available but often require human intervention to raise the quality of the records up to existing national and/or local cataloging standards. What we did at the library was an experiment to see how best we can add outsourced bibliographic records of e-books into the catalog and how best we ourselves can catalog e-books to suit our local user needs.

Working closely and collaboratively with one of the vendors to fix some of the errors we found did help in improving the quality of the records received from that vendor. On the basis of our experiences of working with vendor-supplied catalog data, we think that the following guidelines would help other libraries in adding outsourced catalog records to their local library catalogs. The guidelines we would like to propose are that (1) all vendor-supplied records must be carefully checked to ascertain their accuracy and quality, (2) all vendor-cataloged records should be created in MARC 21 format, (3) all records should have name and subject headings in accordance with the National Authority File, (4) the records should conform with current national cataloging standards for full-level cataloging, (5) librarians should encourage vendors to follow the PCC's guidelines for producing MARC record sets and readily customize records to meet local cataloging standards, (6) librarians should lobby with vendors and/or publishers in creating standardized bibliographic data to be integrated into library catalogs to better serve our user communities, and (7) a clause should be included in the subscription contract whereby the vendor will satisfy the institution's optimal requirements for the creation of MARC records for e-books.

CONCLUSIONS

Research suggests that adding catalog records of e-books leads to significant increase in their usage. Integrating records for e-books into library catalogs is a challenging and time-consuming process for today's libraries. Cleaning up vendor record loads requires human intervention, which costs money and time. For successful implementation of e-books in the catalog, all stakeholders in the e-book industry—librarians, publishers, and vendors—must work together. Librarians should encourage vendors to follow PCC's MARC Record Guide for Monograph Aggregator Vendors <http://www.loc.gov/catdir/pcc/vendorguiderevised.pdf> for producing MARC record sets for e-books. More important, a clause should be made a part of the subscription contract whereby the vendor will satisfy the institution's requirements for the creation of MARC records for e-books. If the library catalog continues to be a gateway or "one-stop" for finding all resources that the library provides access to, then adding e-books into the catalog is essential. It still remains to be seen how far the users will be satisfied by finding them through the catalog. In-depth studies of how users search the catalog for e-books and how and to what extent e-books are being used will help determine future efforts to catalog e-books.

NOTES

1. Program for Cooperative Cataloging. (2006). MARC Record Guide for Monograph Aggregator Vendors. Retrieved November 7, 2007, from <http://www.loc.gov/catdir/pcc/sca/FinalVendorGuide.pdf>.
2. MarcEdit Homepage: Your complete free MARC Editing Utility. Retrieved November 7, 2007, from <http://oregonstate.edu/<reeset/marcedit/html/index.php>.
3. Voyager Record Delete Download at Indiana State University Libraries. Retrieved November 6, 2007, from <http://paulasay.indstate.edu/voyagerdelete/>.
4. Library of Congress Rule Interpretation 1.0. Retrieved October 12, 2007, from <http://www.loc.gov/catdir/cpso/1-0rev3.pdf>.

REFERENCES

Bennett, L., & Landoni, M. (2005). E-books in academic libraries. *The Electronic Library*, *23*(1), 9–16.

Bothmann, R. (2004). Cataloging electronic books. *Library Resources & Technical Services* *48*(1), 12–19.

Blummer, B. (2006). E-Books revisited: The adoption of electronic books by special, academic, and public libraries. *Internet Reference Services Quarterly*, *11*(2), 1–13.

Canadian Library Association. (2002). *Anglo American Cataloging Rules*, 2nd ed. Ottawa: Author.

Carlson, S. (2005). Online textbooks fail to make the grade. Retrieved November 4, 2007, from <http://chronicle.com/weekly/v51/i23/23a03501.htm>.

Christianson, M., & Aucoin, M. (2005). Electronic or print books: Which are used? *Library Collections Acquisitions & Technical Services*, *29*(1), 71–81.

Chu, H. (2003). Electronic books: Viewpoints from users and potential users. *Library Hi Tech*, *21*(3), 340–346.

Connaway, L. S. (2003). Electronic books (ebooks): Current trends and future directions. *DESIDOC Bulletin of Information Technology*, *23*(1), 13–18.

Dillon, D. (2001). E-Books: the University of Texas experience: Part 2. *Library Hi-Tech*, *19*(4), 350–362.

Dinkelman, A., & Stacy-Bates, K. (2007). Accessing E-books through academic library Web sites. *College & Research Libraries*, *68*(1), 45–58.

Gedeon, R., & Meyer, B. (2005). eBooks at Western Michigan University: a case study. *Against the Grain*, *17*(1), 52–54.

Gibbs, N. J. (2001, 2002). Ebooks two years later: the North Carolina State University perspective. *Against the Grain 13*(6), 22–26.

Gibbons, S. (2001). netLibrary eBook usage at the University of Rochester Libraries. Version 2. Retrieved November 6, 2007, from <http://www.lib.rochester.edu/main/ebooks/analysis.pdf>.

Gravett, K. (2006). The cataloguing of e-books at the University of Surrey. *Serials*, *19*(3), 202–207.

Gunter, B. (2005). Electronic books: A survey of users in the UK. *Aslib Proceedings: New Information Perspectives*, *57*(6), 513–522.

Hernon, P., et al. (2006). E-book use by students: Undergraduates in economics, literature, and nursing. *Journal of Academic Librarianship, 33*(1), 3–13.

Langston, M. (2003). The California State University e-book pilot project: Implications for cooperative collection development. *Library Collections, Acquisitions, and Technical Services, 27*(1), 19–32.

Levine-Clark, M. (2007). Electronic books and the humanities: A survey at the University of Denver. *Collection Building, 26*(1), 7–14.

Littman, J., & Connaway, L. S. (2004). A circulation analysis of print books and e-books in an academic research library. *Library Resources & Technical Services, 48*(4), 256–262.

Liu, Z. (2005). Reading behavior in the digital environment, changes in reading behavior over the past ten years. *Journal of Documentation, 61*(6), 700–712.

MacCall, S. L. (2006). Online medical books: Their availability and an assessment of how health sciences libraries provide access on their public Websites. *Journal of the Medical Library Association, 94*(1), 75–80.

Martin, K. E. (2007). ATG special report—cataloging eBooks: an overview of issues and challenges. *Against the Grain, 19*(1), 45–47.

Nelson, L., & O'Neil, F. (2001). Electronic monographs in the academic library: An implementation story. *LASIE, 32*(2/3), 13–20.

Ramirez, D., & Gyeszly, S. D. (2001). netLibrary: A new direction in collection development. *Collection Building, 20*(4), 154–164.

Sanchez, E., Fatout, L., & Howser, A. (2006). Cleanup of netlibrary cataloging records: A methodical front-end process. *Technical Services Quarterly, 23*(4), 51–71.

Tennant, R. (2004). The trouble with online. *Library Journal, 129*(15), 26.

Thomas, S. E. (2007). Another side of the e-book puzzle. *Indiana Libraries, 26*(1), 39–45.

APPENDIX

Evaluating vendor-supplied records for electronic books (e-books)

On the basis of analysis of vendor-supplied records for electronic books from different vendors, the Catalog Department proposed the following criteria and guidelines to evaluate the vendor-supplied records to ensure their timely and successful integration into our catalog.

Primarily, all vendor supplied-records must initially meet the following three mandatory criteria to be considered for their further in-depth evaluation.

1. All vendor catalog records should be created in MARC 21 format.
2. The catalog records should conform with current national cataloging standards for full-level cataloging.
3. The records should have subject headings established according to LCSH and /or MeSH.

If the above criteria are met, the records should be considered for their further evaluation and inclusion into the library catalog.

Procedures for evaluation:

- A representative sample of records should be requested from the vendor.
- The E-book Evaluation Team should carefully evaluate the sample records to ascertain their accuracy and quality.
- The E-book Evaluation Team should use the guidelines as outlined in Table 1 (**the Primary fields**) and Table 2 (**the Secondary fields**) to evaluate a batch of records and find ways to make corrections needed whenever possible.
- A significant number of problems discovered in the records that would create problems in retrieval and access of e-books with respect to the "**Primary fields**" and/or the "**Secondary fields**" may result in rejection of the records.

TABLE 1. The Primary Fields to be Evaluated on a Batch of Vendor-Supplied Records

MARC Fields	Problems Observed	UIC Cataloging Standards
1XX and 7XX (Author fields)	Absence or failure to follow the authorized form	All name authority headings should follow AACR2 guidelines
4XX and 8XX (Series Fields)	Absence or failure to follow the authorized form	All name authority headings should follow AACR2 guidelines
6XX (Subject Fields)	Absence or failure to follow the authorized form, absence of MeSH headings in appropriate subject categories (e.g.: medicine, pure sciences, or any health related subjects)	All subject headings should conform to LCSH or MeSH to facilitate the uniform access and retrieval of the items in the collection
856 (Electronic access and location field of the resource)	No URL or a broken or wrong link to the URL	The URL for the resource should be for the actual resource itself with a proxy server URL added to allow off-campus access to remote users

TABLE 2. The Secondary Fields to be Evaluated on a Batch of Vendor-Supplied Records

MARC Fields	Problems	UIC Standards
006 field (additional material characteristics)	Absence of the field and wrong coding values used	The right coding values to be used according to current AACR2 guidelines
007 (physical description of the resource)	Absence of the field and wrong coding values used	The right coding values to be used according to current AACR2 guidelines
008 (date of publication, language of the item)	Absence or wrong coding of the values	The right coding values to be used according to current AACR2 guidelines
Leader (type of record and bibliographic level)	Absence or failure to code appropriate values	The values should be coded according the current AACR2 guidelines. (Type of record-"a"; Bibliographic level-"m")

TABLE 3. Problems Identified with Vendor Record Sets

Problems Identified	Consequences
Name or Subject Access problems	
Stripped of 710s (corporate body names) –Stripped of MeSH headings (subject)	The ability to retrieve relevant titles under the name or subject being searched is lost.
Records lacking 655 genre term for e-books	Identification of a resource by its physical format is lost
Cataloging & Classification problems	
Records lacking general material designation [GMD] as [electronic resource]	Distinction between a print and an electronic resource is lost and that makes an item unavailable in a search limited by format
Records lacking 006	Identification of a resource by its physical format is lost
Inconsistencies in the use of series (series traced and/or not traced)	Excludes those titles from the retrieval pool and makes that part of the collection difficult to find.
050 or 090 MARC field with lacking $b	Incomplete or incorrectly formatted call numbers are unavailable for browsing

(*Continued on next page*)

TABLE 3. Problems Identified with Vendor Record Sets (*Continued*)

Problems Identified	Consequences
URLs-related problems	
No proxy URL added to an electronic link in MARC field 856	Off campus users will be denied of access if no proxy server information is added.
Typographical errors/MARC tagging problems/Typos/other errors	These errors make various access points index inaccurately, causing
Misspelling and typographical errors in various MARC fields of a bibliographic record	inconsistent OPAC display making the collection unreachable.
Inappropriate coding of 1st and 2nd indicator values in MARC field 856	
Missing ISBNs for e-books (other)	Incomplete catalog records affects
Missing 043s (geographic headings)	the quality of the catalog

TABLE 4. Editing MARC Fields on Vendor-Supplied Records

MARC Field	Action
006	Add if missing or coded improperly
050 or 090	Delete $b (Internet/Eb/Online). Any word or phrase used as call number in the call number field is deleted
655	Add second indicator as "0" & add $a Electronic books
710	If not already present, it is added to represent the name of the aggregator/vendor
773	Delete if coded incorrectly and used improperly
856	Add our proxy URL to the link to the actual resource & change $z from a generic access note to a note specific to our users as "Available only to UIC users"

Managing Users' Expectations of E-books

Elizabeth Kline
Barbara Williams

INTRODUCTION

Publishers are beginning to market e-books to libraries because digital resources are a main focus of collection development. The vendors who provide access to e-books tend to have differing technical requirements and dissimilar procedures for accessing their content, which leads to user expectations that currently cannot be met. Partly because of these user frustrations, increasing the use of e-books on our campus is a formidable undertaking. We hope that in the not-so-distant future, e-book platforms will resemble one another in technical requirements and modes of accessibility. Such similarity across vendor platforms will allow customers to easily traverse the myriad e-book options in a seamless unmediated environment. However, until the e-book industry becomes more streamlined in its technical requirements and modes of accessibility, librarians must find ways to minimize users' frustrations with the status quo.

THE STATUS QUO

Librarians are keenly aware of the advantages of digital resources, including space savings and lack of geographical constraints. Yet despite the anytime, anywhere convenience afforded by the digital format, e-books still lag in adoption by customers. The 2007 ebrary survey (see elsewhere in this issue) revealed that faculty preferences for e-books lagged noticeably behind e-journals, online reference databases, and educational, governmental, and professional Web sites. This lack of acceptance may be a manifestation of the confusion library users experience when confronted by the variety of accessibility modes, vendor platforms, and variant technical characteristics of e-books.

Customers who experience barriers when interfacing with e-books are quick to point out their disapproval and frustrations. In fact, customers frequently submit complaints about e-books via feedback forms on our library Web site, and we suspect they quickly become overwhelmed and uncomfortable when using these resources. Librarians equally voice their disappointment with these resources, but while librarians are well versed in the issues users experience and can facilitate customers' interaction with e-books, the challenges could be greatly reduced by changes in our own acquisition and access processes. Many different library staff, including those in cataloguing, licensing, and technology, are involved in the acquisition and access processes, and not all know what is essential for resources to function well in the public sphere when released to the user.

Information seekers are accustomed to clicking links in a networked environment and with such action they expect to access full-text content that is related to their topic of interest. This is not an unreasonable expectation, and it is not surprising to librarians that users are unaware that the information they are accessing has been made available by their libraries. Information seekers are busy trying to get the information they need, and they are not concerned with where the content comes from. Their main concern is to find what they are seeking in a timely manner. Streamlined access, therefore, is an essential characteristic for all digital products. So it is desirable for libraries to obtain MARC records for all available resources in a timely manner. Cataloguing departments can quickly process good records in one quick swoop by batch processing, thereby allowing users to search and connect to the needed resources from the online catalog. However, e-book vendors do not always provide MARC records in a timely manner, and different vendors require different procedures to access the content. This procedural access continuum ranges from easy, just a click, to complex, such as the necessity of entering one's institutional identification number.

MARC records are not always readily available for individual titles, and vendor-supplied MARC records are not always usable or distinguishable from records for the printed book. For this reason, searching and finding information beyond the online catalog is difficult for a user because library systems are not the first sources users consult at the start of their search for information. The recent agreement between OCLC and Google to exchange data and link to electronic content is a major development for libraries because library resources will gain more visibility, which leads to increased use. When items are not easily discoverable, not only do resources remain underutilized but collections are impacted because of duplication, and library users cannot conduct their work in an optimal setting.

If users are lucky enough to be able to maneuver around the current array of access barriers to e-books, they still must cope with the assortment of platforms available and each vendor's idiosyncrasies. Much like databases, e-book interfaces vary by publisher. Some platforms mimic their print counterparts with turn-the-page technology while others have chapters sectioned into portable document formats (PDFs). Some platforms restrict the number of pages that can be printed while others do not exert limits. Users get particularly troubled when they discover that in some instances checking-out an e-book makes it unavailable to others. It is counter-productive that an electronic resource is not available simultaneously to all users. This is extremely problematic for faculty who assign a reading to a class because it means that the item is unavailable to the majority of students in the class. Unless the librarian is aware of this assignment and provisions are made to place the item on reserve, this has serious ramifications for faculty as adjustments have to be made to curriculum schedules.

Librarians not only contend with the multitude of problems associated with managing large e-book collections from multiple vendors but they must also contend with the management of stand-alone e-books, too. In some instances, the process involved in troubleshooting stand-alone e-books can potentially be more costly than the resource itself. Calculating the amount of time individuals at various hourly rates spend troubleshooting a problem can be a motivating incentive for advocating for uniformity in e-book access and licensing.

For example, a customer recently contacted a librarian with concerns about accessing an e-book. We expended an immense amount of time documenting, understanding, troubleshooting, and solving the problem. In the end, we discovered that users had to create an account to access the resource, and in working with the representative, we were able to change the access so that titles are accessible by IP range, which is our default access preference. In this situation, we recognized that our processes operate independently and not in synchrony. The best solution for this type of issue is to make all work processes transparent so that all library staff can easily understand the purchase agreements and troubleshoot any issue in the least amount of time. In this documented incident, the combined amount of staff time required of our library and vendor to troubleshoot a problem with one resource was disconcerting and more so when the user's time is factored in. Had this customer not contacted us, we would not have known that a problem existed. It is even more disturbing if similar problems occur with the multitude of resources libraries make available because resources will not be used and the money spent on them will be wasted.

Acquiring and installing e-book collections seem to require a lot of cooks in the kitchen in order to coordinate the considerations and accommodations of both the users and the librarians. When it comes to accessing and navigating e-books, the kinks are still being worked out, and undoubtedly vendors will continue to improve their products if they are to remain competitive. The discussion that follows identifies strategies to minimize users' frustrations when their reasonable expectations cannot be met.

MANAGING USERS' EXPECTATIONS OF E-BOOKS

It seems perfectly reasonable to expect to be able to access an e-book with one click and to expect that any plug-ins or devices necessary to access an electronic resource would be imbedded in the technology. Often the speed at which information can be found in a print resource is contrasted with how quickly information can be retrieved from its e-book counterpart, and it seems reasonable to expect that retrieving information from an e-book would be quicker. However, some very reasonable expectations users have of e-books currently cannot be accommodated. When it comes to managing users' expectations of e-books, the best defense seems to be a good offense.

Sixty percent of those who responded to the 2007 ebrary survey indicated that their use of electronic resources was impeded by technical difficulties. While we suspect that more than a few of our users would concur with the above assessment, we do not have the data to substantiate our suspicions. Our supposition is that in order to minimize users' frustrations caused by technical difficulties and manage their expectations of e-books, a preemptive marketing strategy disclosing the known strengths and weaknesses of the resource should be widely shared with the user community. The concept of a preemptive marketing strategy emphasizing a resource's strengths and weaknesses with an emphasis on its weaknesses was suggested by a frustrated mechanical engineering student who had tried for 30 minutes to use one of our e-book platforms to no avail.

According to the student, fully disclosing the technical difficulties one is likely to encounter when trying to access the library's electronic resources can be used as a preemptive strike to lower a user's expectations of a particular product while the kinks are being worked out. Why would we purchase a resource that we promote by highlighting the product's flaws? The short answer is that to give a new technology or resource the chance it needs to work out its kinks requires constructive and useful feedback from the user population—and lots of patience.

Casting the user in the role of critical evaluator makes users a part of the solution of bringing forth a product that meets their expectations. One is more likely to be tolerant toward a new product if one is asked to critique the product and provide feedback to the vendor. It has been noted in several engineering disciplines that when new electronic resources are simply publicized without any disclaimers of potential problems, they tend to generate more complaints. On the other hand, when new electronic resources are promoted as a resource of the future still in its developmental stage, the feedback received is more constructive, and the users do not appear to be as frustrated.

Managing product expectations typically requires being proactive in the dissemination of information that can be used to preempt or negate negative associations with a product whose technology has not been sufficiently developed to accommodate the reasonable expectations of its users. While being proactive in managing expectations of a product will not lessen the desire for specific functionalities, it may buy some time for the technology to catch up with the expectations.

In other instances, we fail to factor in how the campuses' changing technological environment and policies will impact our electronic resources. Recently a number of the staff computers on campus were configured to prevent staff from installing and updating software and plug-ins. Although the staff had been informed that their "computer administrative privileges" were being restricted, the full implications of this change were not readily understood by all. Immediately after the release of a new e-book platform, we received a stream of technically related inquiries complaining that the resource was not working. The problem was that a plug-in had to be installed and the user did not have permission to install the plug-in. The inability to download software plug-ins necessary to access certain electronic collections was frustrating to some. This served as a reminder that librarians can be proactive and contact the campus IT departments and make sure that the plug-ins necessary to access a given resource are already installed on public and staff computers.

Other problems have arisen as users try to take advantage of e-books. For instance, reference books are organized so that information can be looked up quickly once you understand the organizational structure of the resource. Yet, to some engineers, the problem with the types of e-books used in their disciplines is the e-books' inability to mimic their print counterparts in the quick retrieval of data—or so they think. Once users consider the enhancements that allow them to manipulate data and use other interactive tools as well as the capacity to create new data sets, it is no longer as important that the electronic version mimic its print equivalent.

COMPUTATIONAL CAPABILITIES OF E-BOOKS

Several instructors were surprised to discover the advanced functionality and interactive tables now included in some reference e-books. The instructors wrongly assumed that a particular electronic reference handbook was the exact equivalent of its print counterpart. Therefore, when instructors were encouraged to use the library's e-books for their course reserves, most did so without thought. Shortly thereafter, one instructor complained that he was blindsided by the additional capabilities of a particular e-book. Apparently, the instructor regularly issued a certain type of problem for extra credit only to discover that an e-book, which he listed on his syllabus, could calculate the problem for the students. To the instructor's dismay, no one alerted him that all students had to do to earn their extra credit was to plug in a series of numbers and the system would calculate their problem.

Now, because instructors cannot ensure that students are not using the e-book to calculate their homework problems, other methodologies for measuring one's ability to do manual calculations have to be devised. This is a legitimate concern for educators trying to build rudimentary skills. As e-book tables become more interactive and pervasive, routine homework assignments designed to build a particular skill must be reconstituted so that the development of the skill is not lost. When this concern was brought to one of our engineering librarians' attention, the frustration expressed was the instructor's inability to stay on top of the growing functionality of e-books with all their other responsibilities. There seemed to be an expectation on the part of some that those responsible for the purchase of these e-resources should keep abreast of how future software enhancements could impact the way course material is taught. However, as e-books gain more enhancements and functionality, it becomes increasingly difficult for librarians to maintain the skill level to teach students how to use these interactive enhancements.

Finally, the dependence of e-books on technology provided by the Web or university network makes it vulnerable to accusations of dysfunctionality when in fact problems may have nothing to do with the resource itself. When the user tries to access an electronic resource and it does not work, the user assumes the resource to be at fault and never digs deeply enough to resolve the problems and give the resource another chance to prove its wealth.

CONCLUSION

The list of things that need to be negotiated, anticipated, maneuvered around, and tested continues to grow proportionally with the increasing functionality of e-books. First impressions are hard to dispel when formulated by reasonable expectations that fail to materialize, and trying to erase a negative first impression is like trying to get the genie back into the bottle. When it comes to unveiling new e-books, it is extremely important to explain to customers what they can expect. To err in determining the correct technical requirements necessary to operate a particular product may be human, but trying to convince users to give that same product another look typically requires a Herculean effort. Informing users up front of technical difficulties that may impede their use of e-books is just a good marketing strategy.

Consortia and E-books: Expanding Access and Defining Business Models

Timothy Cherubini
Sandra Nyberg

Libraries are a significant force in the e-book market, as primary purchasers and providers to the public. According to the National Center for Education Statistics, U.S. academic libraries held nearly 32.8 million e-books, and public libraries held 7.6 million e-books in 2004.[1] Sales of e-books have been growing, up 24% from 2005 to 2006 according to the Association of American Publishers (although e-books still represent less than 1% of net sales for the year).[2] Library consortia have played important roles in promoting e-books and providing access to e-book collections, roles that will continue in the future. As libraries expand their e-book (and other electronic resource) offerings in the future, consortia are in a unique position to take on new roles in regard to e-books in such areas as improving business and distribution models, implementing standards to support interoperability, promoting improved functionality both from the user and library management perspectives, and addressing library concerns for long-term access.

THE "PLAYERS"

Consortia are but one of many players in the e-book arena; others include publishers, aggregators, distributors, software and hardware developers, libraries, and library patrons. The interests and concerns of the many players are different and sometimes in conflict. The landscape is complicated by ongoing changes in the publishing, library, and technology communities, such as the growth of mass digitization projects, intensified scrutiny of digital rights management, and improvements in portable e-book readers. E-books have not been around for very long, and the business and distribution models that currently support them are not as stable or well defined as those that support printed books.

From the perspective of a library consortium, the players list in the e-book world begins with the individual library that acquires or wants to acquire e-books. A library will go one step further in identifying the beginning point as the needs of its users: students, faculty, researchers, community residents, and businesses. The needs of those users will determine the content of the e-books the library acquires and even whether an e-book format is the best choice to meet the users' expectations. Library e-book decisions are strongly influenced by cost, a factor that is further influenced by whether the library wants or needs to provide short-term or long-term access to the e-book. Other factors affecting the purchase/subscribe decision include potential duplication of print holdings, the availability of MARC records for e-books, functionality of the access platform, software needed at the library to store and/or access e-books, and the ability to provide access to remote users. In the end, although each library's needs are different, they want e-books that are easy for patrons to find and use, are integrated into existing collections and resources, provide functionality beyond printed books for patrons and the library, and meet the content needs of the community at an affordable price.

At the other end of the "player" spectrum are the publishers, the producers of the content that is packaged into an e-book. Publishers want and need to get a fair price for their content; it is the revenue that runs their business and enables them to invest in the development of more and new content. Publishers set the fee for the content in a pricing model similar to that used for print materials, often working through multiple distribution channels to sell as many copies as possible. As with print materials, the publishers' primary interest is in providing the content, not in providing access to the content. However, e-books provide options for access that do not exist for print books, such as multiple and simultaneous users of one book, easy duplication, and print-on-demand. The conflict between the publisher and librarian points of view in regard to access is very apparent with e-books: Publishers prefer to sell a copy of each e-book to each user; librarians prefer to buy one copy and let all users access it at the same time and as often as they want. Since e-books can be more easily shared than print, publishers are more interested in controlling access and reproduction capabilities for e-books, to protect their intellectual property (the asset upon which their publishing business depends). This has resulted in a more complex pricing and distribution model for e-books. Though many e-books are protected by copyright, increasingly noncopyrighted or public domain books are being made available electronically through large-scale book digitization projects (such as Project Gutenberg, National Academies Press, California Digital Library, University of Virginia Electronic Text Library, the Open Content Alliance, and Google Book Search). Some of these projects provide free access to their e-books through open access platforms. While not the original publishers of the print content that is digitized, these projects and services are nonetheless the publishers of the electronic content and have similar interests in pricing and distribution models.

Between the library and the publisher are multiple distributors. Though some publishers do distribute e-books directly (such as Elsevier and Wiley), many distribute their e-books through aggregators (such as NetLibrary, ebrary, Books24x7, Knovel, and Credo Reference). Some publishers distribute only directly, others distribute directly and through one or more aggregators, and yet other publishers distribute only through aggregators, often as many aggregators as possible. Aggregators select and purchase or lease the content from the publisher, then sell access to it to libraries. Access is provided through the aggregator's (or publisher's) own software platform, each of which has its own features and functionalities. Libraries pay to acquire the content and to purchase access to it (these fees may be integrated in a subscription pricing model or distinct in a model that provides "perpetual" access, in which the library acquires the content and can maintain it on local systems or pay an annual fee to maintain access on the aggregator's platform). The aggregators' revenues come through selling access; this motivates them to provide good platforms that libraries will buy but also to keep those platforms proprietary, to protect their business's primary asset. Proprietary platforms do not often integrate with one another, which causes problems for libraries providing access to e-books from multiple aggregators. Although some publishers distribute their work through only one channel (for example, Safari is the sole provider of e-books from O'Reilly Media), there is significant content overlap among many aggregators, as most publishers seek to distribute their e-books through as many channels as possible. These aggregators compete with each other for library business based on the functionality of their platforms; the breadth, scope, focus, and organization of content; and pricing.

Library consortia come into the e-book market between aggregators/publishers and individual libraries. As organizations set up and managed by their member libraries, consortia represent shared interests of libraries in acquiring e-books, organizing e-book collections, providing e-books to users, and strengthening combined collection resources. The primary roles of consortia in regard to e-books have been to educate members about e-books and acquire e-books for members on terms and pricing negotiated to meet the needs of the group. The value for aggregators and publishers is that they deal with one entity instead of many individual libraries for contracting and billing. The value for individual libraries is that they can access e-books at reduced rates and with less administration, on terms that address their needs, focused on those e-books that provide resources of most use to the collective membership. While this is a positive perspective for libraries, consortial involvement has probably contributed to the confusion about e-book business models, as each consortium may have different terms, conditions, and pricing.

In the early days of e-books, consortia were crucial players in introducing the new format into libraries. Many consortia engaged in cooperative or "shared" collections with one of the earliest and most influential e-book aggregators, NetLibrary. One ongoing example is the group of NetLibrary

Shared Collections developed by the Southeastern Library Network for its members. The nine NetLibrary Shared Collections not only pool the financial resources of participants to acquire e-books but allow participants to select titles for inclusion in collections. Participants pay a fee to "buy into" the collection, for which they have access to all titles in the collection, including those selected by other participants. The content of the shared collection is built as participants join; it is not pre-selected. This approach extends the role of consortia from negotiating prices to active collection development and produces a collection that can truly be shared among all participants, in a way that print collections cannot. It also leverages the fees the participating libraries pay to enable individual libraries to acquire much more through the shared collection than they could acquire on their own.

In spite of the success of consortial purchasing and shared e-book collections in expanding library acquisition and patron use of e-books, the shared collection model has been a factor in the current trend of diminishing ability for sharing content across libraries. It can be argued that the early adopter approach aggregators took with early shared collections led to unrealistic expectations among participating libraries with regard to the cost of e-book content and its delivery. The largest cooperative efforts brought forth large amounts of revenue for publishers but at the same time raised concerns within that group about the probability of lost revenue owing to the shared nature of some content, leading to an increasing reluctance among publishers to participate in shared collections. At the same time among libraries, early challenges around how to make e-books accessible to patrons (MARC records in catalogs has emerged as the preferred method) and ongoing challenges with regard to how to measure use of e-books, platform functionality and support, and duplicate purchase of content in print and electronic formats have led some libraries away from not only cooperative purchasing but also addition of any e-books to their collections. A "wait-and-see" attitude was adopted by many and persists for some today.

Consortia have played a central role in connecting libraries to e-books in the past and will continue to do so in the future. However, as the e-book landscape continues to evolve and as libraries continue to seek new and better ways of providing e-books to users, the role of consortia also will change, with new opportunities for consortia to address some of the current issues and influence future development of e-books. Three areas of issue for libraries currently are pricing and distribution models, platform functionality and management, and preservation.

Pricing and Distribution Models

The earliest concern of libraries in assessing e-books was cost, which continues to be and will always be a concern. The e-book business is often criticized for its confusing array of pricing and distribution models. In a recent survey by ebrary (see elsewhere in this volume), 80% of respondents found e-book models somewhat or very confusing.[3] Each publisher and aggregator uses different models, and some have multiple models in place. It is not always clear to libraries what options exist, what ongoing costs to expect, and which approach best suits the needs of users and the collection. Excluding open access e-books (which are free and freely distributed but may nonetheless have restrictions on copying and redistribution), the variables in the current e-book pricing and distribution models include the following:

- Purchase or subscribe to the content: Purchasing content (selecting individual e-book titles) is similar to the print model in pricing, with a single fee for purchase; subscription to collections of e-books is similar to buying access to a database or journal, with annual fees for continued access and new content;
- Single or simultaneous use: Some e-books can be used by only one person at a time; others can be used by multiple users at the same time; and
- Perpetual or term access: The library can own the e-book content acquired through the purchase or subscription (i.e., "perpetual access") or it can lease access to content for a defined period of time. If the content is owned, the library may be able to store and provide access to the content directly (without the added functionality provided by the publisher/aggregator platform), or it may pay an annual service fee to the publisher/aggregator for providing access through their system.

The two most common models are the print model (one book, one user at a time, for a fixed price, with the potential for ongoing access fees if "perpetual access" rights are part of the purchase and ongoing access is to be provided on the publisher/aggregator platform) and the subscription model (licensed access to a full or partial collection for a fixed period of time with simultaneous, multi-user access to the licensed collection, usually without "perpetual access" provisions). These models are obviously similar to traditional library acquisition models for monographs and serials. The lines are blurring, though, as options unique to the e-book world emerge, such as applying subscription terms for short-term access by multiple users to purchased e-books (for example, to support reserves). In addition, although not widely adopted, other models exist, including pay-per-use and lease-to-own.

Consortia are in a unique position to influence pricing and distribution models. They already work with publishers and aggregators to negotiate prices on behalf of members. Consortia can also be an effective intermediary between libraries and publishers/aggregators to define pricing strategies that will work both to meet library service and access needs and publisher/aggregator revenue and rights management needs. Though many publishers/aggregators use pricing models based on print materials, e-books bring new variables into the model, such as number of users and the cost of providing ongoing access through software platforms. Consortia can play a role in helping publishers and libraries develop meaningful price models that relate costs (of producing and providing access to e-books) to how e-books are actually used in libraries.

In addition, consortia can work with their members and publishers/ aggregators to develop and implement effective distribution models for e-books. E-books are not used in the same way as print books; many users access them for reference purposes or to pull relevant information from subsections (chapters). E-books have the potential to allow for simultaneous use, use by multiple libraries in shared collections, use by patrons not physically at the library site, and use that readily incorporates other forms of electronic information (such as links to other electronic resources outside of the e-book collection or data manipulation in tables and charts). Distribution models based on print (one book, one user) do not allow full use of the e-book potential, although they may be best at protecting the publishers' intellectual property. Consortia can be a resource for developing and exploring new distribution models that take full advantage of the added functionality possible with e-books.

Pricing and distribution models that are based on the way e-books are actually used may be more effective at providing both broad access through libraries and adequate revenue for publishers and aggregators to support increased growth in content creation, functionality, and delivery. As an intermediary between libraries and e-book sources and as major purchasers of and subscribers to e-books on behalf of their members, consortia can work with both to develop pricing and distribution models that are straightforward, easily understood, fair, and equitable.

Platform Functionality and Management

Aggregators provide e-books through their own proprietary platforms. Publishers manage e-books through their own platforms also, and many make their e-books available through one or more aggregators' platforms. Different platforms do not work with one another, so a library user has to move from platform to platform to view and use e-books provided by different aggregators and/or publishers. As each platform looks and works differently, this can be both confusing and frustrating to users. Lack of platform interoperability extends to the hardware for viewing and using e-books (i.e., workstations, PDAs, cell phones, MP3 players, and dedicated reading devices). Users want to be able to access e-books on multiple devices, with consistent views and functionality, in platforms that make it easy to find and use the content. Functionality often restricted by platforms includes download capability, copying and printing capability, support for multiple file formats, personalization features, integration with courseware systems, citation formatting and capture, note taking, and tools that allow users to manipulate data and content.

In addition to the users' perspective on how existing platforms promote and/or inhibit access, libraries want e-book platforms that support a variety of management functions, such as usage and other operational reporting, e-reserve capability, bibliographic records to integrate into library catalogs, integrated authentication modules, ability to provide remote access, and tools to provide user support. As with user functionality, management functionality varies with each platform. This challenges libraries not only with the need to support multiple platforms, but also with the inability to provide a uniform set of services and obtain a uniform set of assessment data for e-book collections as a group, much less integrated services and assessment with other collections (book, audio/video, etc.).

Consortia can be a source for platform management on behalf of their members. They can establish platforms on behalf of all members, provide support for libraries and library users, and centralize management functions on behalf of individual platforms or a group of platforms (such as usage reporting or MARC record integration). As a further step for libraries interested in long-term ownership of e-books, consortia could download content to a shared (potentially open-source) platform that is developed and supported by the consortia, designed to accommodate the needs of its members.

In addition to actual platform management, consortia can serve as a source for evaluating and assessing proprietary platforms and providing input to aggregators and publishers on design and functionality. Consortia also play a valuable role in the development and promotion of standards for e-book file formats and platforms. Standards can support eventual integration of e-books into other collection resources, an integration that both libraries and their users want. Standards also can provide the base for more uniform functionality among platforms in regard to management features, such as gathering meaningful usage statistics. Finally, standards are the base upon which preservation of e-books can be successfully built and managed.

Preservation

> Publishers and e-book hardware and software manufacturers need to be concerned with the bottom line. Libraries, by design, are concerned with the preservation of information and its continued dissemination long after the need to sell a particular book has passed. . . .[4]

Preservation of e-books includes not only preserving the e-content but preserving access to it (in e-book parlance, "perpetual access"). Some who purchase e-books with perpetual access rights download them to local systems for long-term storage. This, however, will result in the loss of functionality in the e-book that is tied to the publisher's/aggregator's platform. Storing many e-books long term can also strain the system capacity and infrastructure of some libraries. On the other hand, providing for long-term access of the e-book through the publisher's/aggregator's platform means that the library pays an annual access fee. In addition, access is possible only as long as the publisher's or aggregator's platform is viable (i.e., they're still in business and still supporting the platform).

Consortia can provide a valuable service to their members in preserving purchased e-books. They can provide not only shared storage capacity but the infrastructure to maintain the digital content and migrate it as needed for long-term preservation. They also can develop and provide a shared platform for accessing the preserved e-books, as noted above. The costs of long-term preservation can more easily be shared among many libraries than absorbed by one, especially in regard to e-books. Finally, consortia can ensure that preservation needs of e-book collections are addressed through contracts with publishers and aggregators.

MOVING THE CONSORTIA E-BOOK AGENDA FORWARD

Consortia will continue to play an important role in the adoption of e-books within the library community. E-books are still a young format, and as publication, pricing, distribution, and collection models evolve, consortia will remain involved in their traditional role of acquiring e-books for their members. As noted throughout this article, however, there are emerging roles for consortia in such areas as promoting e-books, improving their functionality, expanding use and adoption, assessing and evaluating content and use, and preservation.

A first important role for consortia in regard to e-books in the future is providing ongoing education directed at their members. The library community is large, and though most librarians have heard of e-books and quite a few have had first-hand interaction with them, the big picture of how they fit into library services remains a challenge, as does navigating the many choices available in the market today. Collection development librarians can use assistance in tracking the various platforms, access models, and pricing options. Public service librarians can use assistance to understand how e-books are used. Publishers and aggregators have been the primary researchers in this area, but librarians should be conducting their own research. Strong beliefs that some librarians hold about e-books, especially their usefulness, are not based on research and data but rather on impressions and anecdotes. Having more objective and verifiable data can educate librarians about the true costs and benefits of e-books in their collections. Education also should be a factor in the various emerging digitization efforts (e.g., Google, the Open Content Alliance, and Microsoft) that increasingly have the ability to put more and more e-book content in front of the same people who are library patrons but in different and sometimes perhaps more useful ways. The availability of large collections of e-books through these mass digitization efforts will no doubt lead to increased demand for current e-book titles from commercial providers (publishers and aggregators). And while consortia educate their members about e-books, they also can assist their members in educating library users about e-books.

A second important role for consortia in the future is to lead and foster research and experimentation in regard to e-books. Besides providing content, how else can e-books serve the library community? An emerging notion among some e-book providers that has yet to gain strength with librarians is that e-books can save space by supplanting print books already in collections. Pushback from librarians on this question usually comes in the form of not wanting to pay for content multiple times. Publishers, on the other hand, are not yet consistently releasing electronic and print versions simultaneously and have concerns about the impact of such releases on revenue. A consortial approach to this question could minimize risk for all parties involved, perhaps through shared collections.

In addition to the potential for saving physical space, e-books have the potential to serve the library community better than print books in disasters. Some libraries that lost collections during Hurricanes Katrina and Rita are replacing them with electronic resources. They see that e-books can be stored or backed-up on remote servers, so that the books are accessible after a disaster even if the actual library building is not open. In addition, e-book collections can be provided to patrons who have been evacuated from the area. In these ways, e-books and other electronic resources enable a library to begin providing service sooner after a disaster.

A third role for consortia is expanding use of e-book platforms. Vendors new and old put significant energy and resources into platforms, and many of these platforms can be used to host content beyond commercially published books. Platforms may be the true "gold" in the e-book world today, leading the way to transforming e-books from just being replicas of print books to becoming a fully functional format in their own right. In addition, platforms can provide the means for libraries to create and provide access to their own e-content. The many library-based digitization projects blur the lines between publishers and libraries. Many libraries, particularly medium-to-small ones, often do not have the staff or wherewithal to create and support their own platforms for access to digitized library collections. Consortia are well positioned to direct energy to thinking of expanded applications of e-book platforms and addressing some of the more practical matters, such as repetitive distribution of content and standard interface issues. The presence of tools embedded in platforms that enable and allow users to manipulate data is becoming an expectation in some fields, yet it is an expectation that library-created platforms cannot meet to the extent that commercial platforms can. Consortia and librarians could pair with users to advise and drive platform development.

A fourth valuable role for consortia is to begin gathering data, performing analysis, and publishing results to address some of the questions that appear repeatedly during discussion of e-books and may be holding up adoption of e-books. For example, obtaining and interpreting usage data is an ongoing challenge, yet important to understanding the benefits and barriers to e-books. The Code of Practice put out by COUNTER (Counting Online Usage of Networked Electronic Resources), an initiative to standardize online usage statistics, is relatively new. Librarians continue to need education about it, and case studies of its use would be a valuable asset to the library community. As with other aspects of COUNTER, the code related to e-books will continue to develop. Consortia that are heavily involved with e-books on their members' behalf should be part of that discussion. Consortia may also be in a position to help publishers tackle questions, to answer and, hopefully, allay concerns over the impact of shared e-book collections on revenue. This is an area where assumptions run rampant, but data are lacking. Finally, a common criticism of e-books is that because user behavior is unknown, the players are simply replicating the print world. Consortia again, with their "view from the middle" and cooperative skills, can be major players assessing user behavior and e-book functionality in the library context. Consortia can bring not only the shared expertise of their members but the ability to focus resources on a common issue or need among members and to research these issues or needs from the library perspective (not the publisher's or aggregator's).

A fifth consortial role, and one critical for libraries, is to address the preservation problem. Preservation of resources for future users is core to the mission of all libraries, one of the bases for providing access, as access is impossible if the content no longer exists. Some assume that preservation is not a concern with e-books, as they are widely available and many copies exist in many libraries. However, only a few libraries make the conscious and public decision to preserve e-books, along with addressing all of the attendant concerns related to preservation of digital resources (such as migration, format standards, and preservation of hardware and software). Preservation is a commitment and long-term responsibility. One organization cannot do it all, but likewise, other organizations should not just assume someone else is taking care of it. Preservation is a shared, distributed responsibility, and consortia are often the perfect resources for ensuring preservation of both print and electronic content through shared, potentially distributed solutions.

Many consortia are involved in moving the e-book agenda forward. However, success depends on active engagement of all of the players in the e-book environment—publishers, aggregators, digitization initiatives, standards organizations and, most important, libraries themselves. Libraries create consortia to further their joint interests, and consortia can do so in the arena of e-books with ongoing and active support from their members. The path of e-book evolution will continue to wind, with many potential directions and unforeseen forces that can impact development. Consortia will, nonetheless, continue as important organizations in moving e-books down the path so that they eventually are no longer considered new but rather are fully integrated and fully functional parts of all library collections.

NOTES

1. Academic library data from B. Holton, K. Vaden, & P. O'Shea, *Academic Libraries: 2004,* NCES 2007-301 (Washington, DC: National Center for Education Statistics, 2006), p. 7. Retrieved November 6, 2007, from <http://nces.ed.gov/pubs2007/2007301.pdf>. Public library data from Access version of the Public Library (Public Use) Data File for Fiscal Year 2004. Retrieved November 6, 2007, from <http://harvester.census.gov/imls/data/pls/index.asp>.

2. American Association of Publishers 2006 S1 Report. Retrieved November 6, 2007, from <http://www.publishers.org/main/IndustryStats/indStats_02.htm>.

3. ebrary, ebrary's Global eBook Survey. Retrieved December 10, 2007, from <http://www.surveymonkey.com/s.aspx?sm=kqxPd1nXerb91RVf9ZWjQQ%3d%3d>.

4. James E. Gall, (2005, March). Dispelling five myths about E-books, *Information Technology and Libraries*, *24*, 27.

From Print to "e": An Industry Perspective

James Gray

E-books are not new, but when they are discussed or their evolution is analyzed, they are frequently still described as an experiment in the making. Yet products called e-books have existed for at least half a century; Project Gutenberg was founded in 1971,[1] and NetLibrary set up the first commercially oriented aggregated e-books platform in 1997 and was then acquired by OCLC, a company with a much older tradition in exploring the possibilities offered by electronic content.[2] Nevertheless, particularly in academic circles, e-books are often regarded as something novel if not alien, whereas electronic journals have been relatively rapidly absorbed into scholarly life. Why is this?

Writing in 1997, Edward J. Valauskas provided at least some of the answers:

> Electronic scholarly journals differentiate themselves from printed scholarly journals by accelerated peer review, combined with mercurial production schemes ... the sheer interactive nature of digital journals—providing ample opportunities for peers to critically analyze articles—and the ability to access the complete archives of a given title on a server make that sort of publishing a significant departure from the long established traditions of print.[3]

The first e-books, in fairly basic PDF format with limited or no searching capability, did not offer similar benefits over print, and in fact, a key criticism, leveled at them on many occasions was that they provided a reading experience in every respect inferior to hard copy. There can be no doubt about the fact that replacing print books with electronic ones can stir emotion in users in the way that replacing print journals with electronic ones doesn't, and some academics have felt that their autonomy in choice of resources, the size of their workload, and even the nature of their teaching and the learning experience offered by their institution have been threatened by the advent of electronic learning materials.[4] Others have dismissed such scruples briskly by making the point that electronic books, like other types of academic resources, are simply a means to an end for people doing a job.[5]

Of course, librarians and academics, while sharing most of the same goals, often adopt different approaches toward achieving them. There is incontrovertible evidence that electronic resources are a boon to librarians challenged both by standstill budgets and diminishing shelf space and that this has been a major reason for adopting e-books in the United Kingdom and elsewhere in Europe, with librarians in the United States now also voicing the need to find solutions to similar constraints. Today, many universities, even "wealthy" ones, operate a "digital-preferred" policy. A librarian recently explained[6] that this helps to "manage student expectations." Students know exactly which resources the library will be able to provide and how accessible those resources will be and can therefore better plan which of the items on their reading lists they need to buy for themselves, and in what format. The many concerns that librarians originally felt about e-books when the first collections became available had reduced sharply by the time that one international librarian advisory group revisited its views on e-books in 2006, when the members said that the main attributes that they looked for were as follows:

- That a sufficient percentage of the content must be relevant to the study programs and research interests of the students belonging to the institution;
- That the interfaces must be attractive and user-friendly and the platform easy to navigate; and
- That regardless of whether the product was purchased via license or outright sale, it must be affordable.[7]

As they have committed more resources to e-books, so librarians have also become increasingly concerned about their visibility, or findability. Not assisted particularly well by the main bibliographic agencies, who were slow to catalogue the e-book format, they have had to rise to the dual challenge of making academics aware of what is available for the library to purchase electronically and then making sure that students, academics, and researchers can find the material that they have bought.[8] Concerns have therefore switched from doubts about the congeniality of the medium to questions of how to find specific e-books, how to select, acquire and develop collections, how the library should best facilitate access, and how to address the complexities of licensing, DRM, and pricing.

So far, this article has listed several of the key pros and cons of purchasing and using e-books that academic acquisitions librarians have had to address, some of a practical, some of a more or less philosophical nature. None of these issues is the primary concern of the biggest group of end-users: the students. This study will now go on to consider the needs of students in one institution in particular—the University of Toronto—where the rapid commitment to a massive e-book pilot initiative was driven by a single, fairly dramatic, empirical discovery: that many of its students no longer wished to visit the library. More than that, often they couldn't visit the library. As Warren Holder, Electronic Resources Coordinator of University of Toronto Libraries, stated in a presentation given to the United Kingdom Serials Group in London in November 2005, "50% of our students take classes more than 30 kilometers from the main campus. Medical students take classes in 'academies' in teaching hospitals."[9] Even when the students did take classes on the campus, research carried out by the library demonstrated unequivocally that they preferred working remotely to working in the library—"I find pretty much all that I need online" was a typical and recurring comment. As Warren Holder observed, "Today's students have grown up with the Internet; expect immediacy; are adept at multitasking; learn asynchronously; think they know everything; prefer image to text; and prefer electronic to print."[10] If the library was to maintain its position as the university's main provider of learning, teaching, and research resources, it needed to act decisively and quickly.

Toronto already held some e-books. Now it took the decision to embark upon a very large scale e-book pilot project, to take place over a three-year period, with stringent monitoring and evaluation throughout. It decided that it would conduct the project with one carefully chosen e-book provider, and for this it selected MyiLibrary. Here were its reasons: MyiLibrary offered the "right" cost model; it offered the "right" use model; it operated through standard (PDF and HTML) readers; it offered a wide range of content (which has since increased very significantly); it could support dealer selection plans; and it was publisher-neutral. Aside from all of these attributes, MyiLibrary was genuinely interested in working with Toronto as a partner and contributing to the project in such a way that both organizations could learn as they collaborated. Finally, Toronto knew that MyiLibrary was highly regarded by publishers as well as librarians: "I think that the publishers trust them," said Holder, "especially when it comes to digital rights management."

In December 2006, MyiLibrary became part of the Ingram Digital Group (IDG). The Toronto project continued, with significant extra benefits now available from the broader IDG suite of services.

Since the Toronto pilot project began, the academic e-book world of which it is part has become significantly more complex but also more e-book-friendly. Predicting the future of academic publishing, Lynne Brindley, Chief Executive of the British Library, commented recently that "by the year 2020, 40% of UK research monographs will be available in electronic format only, while a further 50% will be produced in both print and digital. A mere 10% of new titles will be available in print alone by 2020."

Meanwhile, the challenges facing the libraries have increased. Budgets are even more squeezed than they have been in the past. Moving investment from print to electronic products is widely regarded as one effective way of dealing with this. The ARL statistics for 2005 demonstrate that though library budgets mostly remained static in 2004–2005, the proportion of expenditure on electronic materials, including e-books, continued to increase—a trend that has not been bucked for many years.[11] Meanwhile, end-user requirements are changing. Lecturers can now see new applications for online materials, such as delivery through virtual learning environments, repurposing and personalization of content, and "chunking." Students, in particular, appreciate the advantages of being able to buy micro-content or bespoke e-books created "on the fly" that take chapters or smaller amounts of content from several different volumes.

The choices facing librarians as they consider which e-content systems to purchase have increased in complexity. Integration has become a key buzz-word—integration of metadata with A & I databases; integration of content platforms with library acquisition processes; detailed usage reporting across the library's full e-content corpus; and, above all, to support their users properly, the need for a clear search interface that is intuitive to use and incorporates easy-to-use links that don't "break." As noted at the beginning of this chapter, a user-friendly interface has always been a crucial requirement, as has the need for broad-based but relevant content within e-collections.

This raises the question of whether it is best for libraries to invest in publisher-specific or aggregated e-book collections. Some publishers believe that the answer to this is not clear-cut—that the best approach to take is a "horses for courses" one. It is why some of the academic publishers most committed to the e-book format (e.g., Taylor & Francis and Oxford University Press) place their e-books with several aggregators as well as hosting them on their own platforms.

An unpublished survey carried out with academic librarians in the United Kingdom in January 2007 on behalf of a well-known publisher[12] attracted 42 responses, of which only nine were hostile to publisher-specific collections. However, more detailed examination of all the responses indicates that aggregated platforms may in fact often be more appropriate for the librarians' needs, whatever their expressed opinions:

- "When we first started with e-books, we preferred to buy large collections to give us a critical mass of material to test the format. However, we find that we are now purchasing copies of single texts on the core reading lists, targeted to particular modules. We have recently been purchasing these via [a well-known supplier]."
- "By offering our researchers access to the vast and diverse MyiLibrary collection, we have responded to their demands for mass aggregation of content, thus enabling timely information discovery. We encourage Publishers of scholarly content worldwide to meet the needs of researchers such as ours by choosing to host their electronic content on the MyiLibrary platform."

- "The e-books we have purchased were on a book-by-book (annual) licence (not outright purchase) via MyiLibrary. We haven't gone for any collections."
- "Generally we prefer to buy on a book-by-book basis, but if the pricing model were attractive, we would be happy to consider licensing a collection. It would depend on cost: if the cost of the collection was similar to (but not necessarily less than) the sum of the titles that we were really interested in, then we would certainly consider the collection."

The last of these comments raises another thorny issue: that of pricing models. There are only two basic pricing models—outright sale and licensing—but within these, perhaps in response to the unpopularity of the price-plus one-book, one-user model with which commercial e-book deals began, both publishers and aggregators have created an array of options and incentives. The University of Amsterdam, for example, currently holds more than 200 different online collections, paid for in a burgeoning variety of ways.

Despite this confusing array of delivery methods, librarians often find either that they can't get the content that they want or can't get it on the platform that they want. Writing in the April 2007 issue of *Against the Grain*, Michael Levine-Clark, Collections Librarian at the University of Denver, said, "A final barrier to full integration of eBooks into approval plans is the multiplicity of eBook vendors and the seeming reluctance of some publishers to make their content available to all."[13] In the same article, he points out that "in order for eBooks to be successfully and meaningfully integrated into the approvals process, approval vendors need to have a significant amount of frontlist eBooks available to them at the time of publication."

I concur with the view that lack of availability of frontlist titles is one of the last big barriers in the transition from "p" to "e" for academic libraries, but I view the progress being made with optimism:

Currently eBooks make up quite a small proportion of overall book sales, but it is growing rapidly. The driver for that growth is how fast publishers can make available their front-list content. ...Today's most forward-thinking publishers—Taylor & Francis, Elsevier and Oxford University Press are examples—are publishing simultaneously in 'p' and 'e' to allow libraries the choice of formats to suit their needs.[14]

Even if the library can just about manage fragmented content offers, different access restrictions,[15] different pricing models, diverse training requirements, and lack of available content in some areas, librarians are finding that their users cannot cope with a plethora of interfaces, and a single perfect interface might almost be described as the librarian's holy grail.

To return to the case study of the University of Toronto: As already mentioned, for the purposes of the pilot it decided to address all of these issues by making MyiLibrary/IDG its principal supplier. As well as answering all of the points raised above by providing a single, simple, comprehensive solution—with a user-friendly interface—MyiLibrary devised a package of other advantages to help address Toronto's specific challenges in its move from "p" to "e." Here are some of the most significant ones:

- The availability of bulk purchases of backlist at significant discounts;
- The development of a bespoke frontlist selection plan for librarians in order to control purchases;
- Local loading of content owned by the institution (i.e., a repository facility) and branding on behalf of the university; and
- Simultaneous multi-user access.

The bulk order proposals were impressive and included 11,300 Taylor & Francis titles, 4,500 Oxford University Press titles, 4,500 titles from Wiley, 12,000 titles from Springer, and 5,500 from IGOs—the WHO, World Bank, and the like—as well as thousands of others from a wide range of publishers.

What next for Toronto? Essentially, it wants more of the same.

More than two years after the start of the pilot, Warren Holder makes the following reflections on the impact of MyiLibrary on his users and on the success of the library in addressing their changing needs through the electronic delivery of resource materials:

> As we have added new content to the collection, we have been very pleasantly surprised by the increase in take-up. The more content that becomes available, the more variety and depth we are able to offer. The usage statistics are steadily rising, and not just in the STM subjects—also in other areas such as Humanities and Social Sciences. The list of top ten titles borrowed constantly varies. We have now embarked on a study on how users read and engage with e-books.[16]

Speaking at a seminar that took place in June 2007 and asked what advice he would give to librarians setting out on the same odyssey that Toronto began in 2005, he offered the following:

> First of all, develop a strategy—understand the how, what and why of what you propose to do. Start to develop specific strategies for the acquisition and management of e-resources and e-books; then strategically align and integrate your choices with work flows and work processes. Secondly, support aggregation—streamline the situation as much as possible by using a single aggregator, so that you get easily accessible, cross-searchable content from all publishers on one platform via one interface.[17]

NOTES

1. See <http://promo.net/pg/history.html#beginning>. Retrieved October 15, 2007.

2. See <http://www.oclc.org/about/history/default.htm>. Retrieved October 15, 2007.

3. Valauskas, Edward. (1997, December). Waiting for Thomas Kuhn: First Monday and the evolution of electronic journals. *First Monday*, 2(12). See <http://www.firstmonday.org/issues/issue2_12/valauskas/>. Journals also enjoy a spurious kind of superiority because of the great lengths taken by academics to assess and tabulate their worth. There are, for example, five types of journals citation listings methods now in use. It is ironic that while librarians can't always get hold of the books they would like in e-format, the choice of journals is now bewildering: "There are now so many journals available that it is difficult for academics, university managers, librarians and institutional auditors to determine the currency and relative value of publications in different sub-fields." See Morris, Huw, et al. The case for journal ranking lists and the case of the Association of Business Schools' Journal Quality Guide. (Article to be published by Emerald, Autumn 2007.)

4. David Noble adopts a neo-Marxian perspective in his critical assessment of the use of Internet-based education in the United States: see Noble, David. "Digital Diploma Mills: The Automation of Higher Education," New York University Press, New York, 2002. Rhona Newman and Fred Johnston use Foucauldian analysis to speculate about the possible impact of Web-based instruction on universities in the future: see Newman, Rhona and Fred Johnston. (1999). Sites of Power and Knowledge? Towards a critique of the Virtual University. *British Journal of Sociology of Education*, 20(1), 79–88.

5. Bruce Ingraham, for example, debunks the "armchair reader syndrome" approach to academic reading by pointing out that academics are usually sitting at a desk working rather than reading for pleasure and that therefore the most efficient way of accessing material is going to have more appeal than the most aesthetically pleasing

method. See the chapter entitled "Academic print in digital formats" in "Exploring the frontiers of e-learning: borders, outposts and migration." Research Proceedings of the ALT-C Conference 2005, pp. 32–42. Association of Learning Technology, 2005.

6. At a librarian focus group meeting that took place at the (UK) Copyright Licensing Agency on September 10, 2007.

7. Cited by Linda Bennett in "E-Book Platforms and Aggregators: an evaluation of available options for publishers," *Research Report*. The Association of Learned and Professional Society Publishers. London, 2006, p.8.

8. For a discussion of this, see Linda Bennett and Monica Landoni. (2005). E-books in academic libraries. *The Electronic Library*, *23*(1).

9. See <http://www.uksg.org/sites/uksg.org/files/imported/presentations5/holder.ppt#318,4,Goals>. Retrieved October 16, 2007.

10. See <http://www.uksg.org/sites/uksg.org/files/imported/presentations5/holder.ppt#290,32,Today's students>. Retrieved October 16, 2007.

11. See Martha Kyrillidou and Mark Young. ARL Statistics 2005: A Compilation of Statistics from the One Hundred and Twenty-Three Members of the Association of Research Libraries. Washington, DC: 2006.

12. I am indebted to Gold Leaf for this information.

13. See Michael Levine-Clark. (2007, April). Electronic books and the approval plan: Can they work together? *Against the Grain*, *19*(2), 20–24.

14. See Katina Stauch. (2007, September). ATG Interviews James R. Gray. *Against the Grain*, *19*(4), 41–42.

15. It was a further finding of the librarian focus group meeting that took place at the (UK) Copyright Licensing Agency on September 10, 2007, that some libraries cope with different access restrictions by simply applying across the board the ones stipulated by the most stringent supplier, in order to save time and prevent user confusion. QED, many publishers and aggregators are expending their resources and ingenuity for little or no result!

16. Interview with the author, September 22, 2007.

17. James Gray and Warren Holder, "It's what the users want. E-Content aggregation to suit library needs and end-user demands." Presentation at the O'Reilly *Tools for Change* seminar that took place in June 2007.

INDEX